P Halpin sc.

Mme DE PARABERE.

New York

PHILOSOPHERS

AND

ACTRESSES.

BY

ARSENE HOUSSAYE,
AUTHOR OF "MEN AND WOMEN OF THE EIGHTEENTH CENTURY," ETC.

IN TWO VOLUMES.

Volume Second.

REDFIELD,
110 AND 112 NASSAU STREET, NEW YORK.
[Second Edition.] 1853.

STEREOTYPED BY C. C. SAVAGE,
13 Chambers Street, N. Y.

CONTENTS OF VOL. II.

PHILOSOPHERS AND ACTRESSES.

CHAMFORT.

> To accustom one's self to live, is to accustom one's self to the wrongs of time, and to the injustice of men.—CHAMFORT.

WIT—I do not now speak of that which we find in the streets—is occasionally in literature the flash of genius, the touch of the master, the immortal expression which the sculptor or the painter dashes on to the marble or the canvass. Rulhières used to say, astonished that he should be considered wicked: "I have committed but one piece of wickedness in my life."—"When will he be through with that one?" asked Chamfort. This profound and unexpected remark will survive all Chamfort's works, as Voltaire's tales have outlasted his tragedies—as the thoroughly Flemish little pictures of Breughel will survive his large ones modelled on the Italians. There are men of wit who have left but a single joke as their entire legacy—no slight bequest, either.

Posterity is constitutionally lazy; she likes those best who reach her without heavy baggage for her library, who do not number their thousand volumes. She has opened the door to Chamfort, solely on the condition that he should leave his books at the threshold. Fontenelle—who, although almost a century old, did not let a day pass without going into society—said to his neighbors: "I am here, but do not count upon my having my wits about me; conversation is a volume of which I have but little knowledge left; give me, now and then, the title of the chapter." Posterity is like old Fontenelle, she contents herself with knowing the title of the chapter.

Chamfort—born in Auvergne in 1741, died in Paris in 1794—has, so to speak, traversed the entire eighteenth century—that eighteenth century of abbés, marchionesses, queens of the Parc-aux-Cerfs and the Trianon, of the Encyclopedists and the revolutionists. He knew Voltaire and madame du Barry, Diderot and Marie Antoinette, Saint Just and Charlotte Corday. He was always the man of his times, except in 1793, when he dared to be still a man of intellect. "The fraternity of those wretches is like that of Cain and Abel, or Eteocles and Polynices. Let them inscribe on all their monuments: 'Be my brother, or I will kill you." Although he had commenced the revolution with Mirabeau, he was taken to the Madelonnettes, which was then the high road to the guillotine.

Chamfort's mother was "companion to a lady." When it was perceived, in the house, that she was on the point of adding a new-comer to the company, they turned her out of the house. Chamfort consoled her by furnishing her something to love. He came into the world with no other patrimony than the name of Nicholas. Paris is the sacred ark, which saves from shipwreck all the wretched of the provinces if they are crowned by a ray of intelligence. The mother and child came to Paris. Nicholas, it is not known on what recommendation, was admitted to the college of the Grassins in the capacity of bursar. He studied much, and at a later day repented of it. "What I have learned I no longer know: the little which I do know, I have found out for myself." In rhetoric he took all the prizes at the great competition, except that for Latin poetry. His masters told him, on the renewal of the contest, that to gain four prizes out of five was only a partial victory; they plainly hinted to him, that if he did not choose, during the coming year, to redouble his efforts in order to obtain all the prizes, he must lose his bursarship, his sole resource. He resigned himself to this at the thought of his mother. At the second trial he carried off the five prizes. "Last year," he said, "I failed of the prize for Latin verse because I imitated Virgil; I have taken it this year because I imitated Buchanan." In reality, there was in his composition a description of the cannon and cannonade which gained the suffrages of everybody except Chamfort.

After this second conquest, Chamfort was a citizen of the republic of letters. A descendant of Malherbe, and Letourneur who translated Ossian, were at the college. Chamfort was their master and corrected their verses. The desire of travelling took possession of their adventurous spirits: they fled one night from the college, determined to make the tour of the world. They went as far as Cherbourg; but, as they were on the point of embarking, Chamfort said to his friends, as more than one philosopher has said to his disciples: "Before we make the tour of the world, should we not make the tour of our own selves?" How many there are who go to Timbuctoo to study its costumes, and return to die at home, without ever having had the curiosity to travel into the unknown land of their hearts! How many sentiments and ideas do we have within us without our ever examining them, like the virgin forests to so many of the populations of the new world!

The three re-entered the college like so many prodigal sons of science. Chamfort became an abbé. "It is a dress, and not a profession." The principal of the Grassins promised him an abbey. "No," said he to him, "I shall never be a priest, for three reasons: I love honor and not honors, philosophy and not hair-cloth, women and not money."

He had so far borne the name of Nicholas only.

He baptized himself with that of Chamfort, and threw himself, for better or worse, into the chances of literary life. He was repulsed by the gazettes and the booksellers. His mother had no bread, and naught but her tears, to give him. He met a young preacher, one of his friends, who was going to court. —"Well, Nicholas, what are you about?"—"I am composing a sermon to my evil star."—"So you understand sermon-making too?"—"Yes, listen to me;" and Chamfort forthwith poured forth a fluent apostrophe to his bad fortune.—"Ah, you are a happy fellow!" exclaimed the preacher; "for my part, I can never find anything to say when I mount the pulpit! If you choose to write my sermons, I will deliver them, for I have a good memory."—"Agreed; a louis a sermon."

The preacher shook hands with Chamfort on the bargain. He wanted a sermon a week. Chamfort lived in this way for nearly a year.

He found some pages to write in the gazettes, but he was more solicitous to write in the book of human life, that attractive volume which is partially opened at twenty, and in which one writes with a pen of fire. The gay and charming passions, the open-armed sirens, seized him and enticed him into perils manifold. He came again to the shore, but wearied and worn out, having at the outset exhausted his strength and torn out of his heart the whole spring-time of his life. Like Duclos, he had built his card-house of love among courtesans, and he had not even found among them a Magdalen to weep with him over the profanation of the altar. A mournful preface to the life of a poet is that youth in which flourishes naught which is pure! Such was the youth of Piron; and as is the youth, such is the poet. The muse is a maiden of good memory.

While following in the dust the arrogant chariot of the courtesans, Chamfort had not once encountered the wheel of Fortune. He was poorer than ever. He lived alone, with no other hostess than misery. It was then the usage for every poetical new-comer to compete for the prize of the academy. It was, so to speak, dancing attendance upon poetry. Chamfort competed, he was not above mediocrity, and obtained the prize. Owing to this triumph, of which he was not proud, he was in request in society, where, thanks to his figure, he became the rage. All the marchionesses had great regard for a man of whom madame the princess of Cra—— said: "You fancy he is only an Adonis, but he is a Hercules." The eighteenth century was then in its second crop; the last of love's harvests were mowed down with full sweep of the scythe.

It seems that Hercules-Chamfort was submitted to too rude labors, like his predecessor; for, at the expiration of certain years, we find him again, for his sins, at the waters of Spa, at those of Barèges, everywhere where Cupid was put under regimen, and set to drinking the waters. He returned to Paris, resolved on penitence, and actually competed a second time for an academic prize. He did not even obtain a notice. He consoled himself by his comedy of *La Jeune Indienne*, which made some noise on its representation. The name of Chamfort was already celebrated; but he rarely had money in his pocket, and lived by chance on the condition of dining out. He brought his wit as ready money, saying, like Piron: "They lend me on pawn;" or, like Rivarol: "I can not say a stupid thing without people crying out, 'Stop thief!'"

Madame Helvetius, who had a literary hospital at Sèvres, lodged Chamfort there for some seasons. He would have remained there a longer time had it not been for the friendship of Chabanon: Chabanon had a pension of twelve hundred livres from the *Mercure;* he liked Chamfort, and forced him to accept these twelve hundred livres. The republic of letters may, therefore, write the word *fraternity* on more than one of its monuments. Chamfort wished to decline, but Chabanon assumed the indignant, and talked of fighting a duel rather than put up with this insult from a friend. About the same time, Chamfort obtained two new prizes at the academic competition for the eulogy of Molière and that of La Fontaine. La Harpe had vanquished him in poetry; Chamfort valiantly took his revenge in prose.

His health returned at intervals; but, as soon as he recovered his strength, he gave the rein to his ardent passions. "One must choose either to love women, or to know them; there is no middle course." Although he knew women, he persisted in loving them. Duclos took up with the first who came to hand. "For my part," said Chamfort, "I seek especially for those who live out of marriage and of celibacy. Such are sometimes the most honest." Although the romantic element was wanting in his heart, he had some gleams of poetry in his loves.

He, better than any other maker of paradoxes, could have written the history of love. He had studied woman and women. He knew the thousand and one points of attack, against the strongholds of virtue. He often commenced the siege at the *petit lever*. In the eighteenth century, the marquises went to see the rising of the women, as the philosophers the rising of the sun. The sun and the women are still of this world, but they no longer rise in public. Chamfort found that noon has a sort of severity fatal to lovers. At three o'clock one could open the romance, on condition of breaking off at the first page; at six it was needful to be in the jocose rather than the tender mood; at nine, to tell some moving story; at midnight to follow one's inspirations, and once in the field, never retreat, even if the house was on fire. According to Chamfort, women are so illogical that they are never taken by reasoning. One must understand how to be in the same moment a man of wit and a fool, a master and a slave, a sage, and a madman. "Do you know," said Chamfort to Mirabeau, "why I succeeded with madame de——? It was because I was the first to discover that since she had changed the blue furniture of her room into crimson, it was necessary to change with her the tone of the conversation."

The women of society, consulted Chamfort as a confessor of the profane order. "My son is about to enter into the world," said madame de Montmorin to him one day, "how am I to save him in his first voyage?"—"Advise him with earnestness to fall in love with all women."

He always had something to say, but never anything to write. There were already in his time, too many books, he did not want to give the royal censor the pleasure of approving one folly the more. "What book is to be written? They are executing at the opera the *qu'il mourût* of Pierre Corneille. Men of letters have but one resource for originality; it is to make Noverre dance the *Maxims* of La Rochefoucault, or the *Pensées* of Pascal."

He contented himself with scattering his wit like small change, as Rivarol, Rulhières, and some others. He went and talked in the celebrated saloons in the middle of a circle of pretty women. It was the way at that time, of making up a feuilleton, and this feuilleton when signed Chamfort, was not forgotten the day after.

Chamfort gained a hearing at court, through the duchess of Grammont, who had met him at the waters of Barèges, and taken him to Chanteloup. His tragedy of Mustapha, was played at Fontainebleau, before all the royal personages, those by the grace of God, those by birth, those by beauty. The king bestowed a pension upon him of twelve hundred livres; the prince of Condé offered him the post of secretary. Chamfort accepted, but he was born with a taste for freedom; scarce was he established in the Palais-Bourbon, when he was possessed of a single idea, that of getting away, without however offending the prince of Condé. He passed six months in writing epistles in prose and verse, that his resignation might be accepted. He was then forty; he became a misanthrope; he was gay, but at times moody. He had seen all forms of human vanity in motion about him, upon every stage. He had seen a great deal of the world, but had not yet discovered a man. He had studied himself, without being very well contented with the living book entitled Chamfort.

It was at this period that he retired to Auteuil, like the aged Boileau, to the house of the satirist, saying to his few friends: "*It is not with the living that we should live, but with the dead*" (that is to say with books). However, scarcely had he entered his retreat, scarcely disturbed the dust of that sepulchre, styled a library, when he fell in love. The misanthropes who make their calculations on the absence of love, must reckon twice. Chamfort had met at Boulogne, I do not know where, a lady of the court of the duchess of Maine, that is to say, a beauty, who had counted full forty-eight summers. It is the story of Piron over again. This lady had wit, had seen a great deal, had a great deal to relate. Chamfort married her, as he would have purchased a curious book. The lady herself was a misanthrope. They found that at Auteuil, they were too near the world; they took refuge at Vaudouleur, not far from Etampes, without letting their friends know of the move. They lived there six months, as Calypso and Ulysses might have done; but the honey-moon then assumed a funereal aspect. The lady fell sick and died. Chamfort inconsolable, sought relief in travel. He resided in Holland with the count de Narbonne. On his return to Paris, he married the academy, widowed by Saint-Palaye. His epithalamium was lukewarm, without color or movement. He returned to the world and the court. He said at that time: "My life is a tissue of apparent contrasts with my principles: I do not love princes, and I am attached to a prince: I am known to possess republican principles, and I live with men of the court. I love poverty, and I have friends only among the rich. I fly from men, and men have come to me. Literature is my only consolation, and I see no literary men. I was desirous of belonging to the academy, and I never go there. I believe that illusions are the necessary luxury of life, and I live without them. I believe that the passions are more useful to us, than the reason, and I have destroyed my passions."

Queen Marie-Antoinette said one day to Chamfort: "Do you know, monsieur de Chamfort, that you have pleased everybody at Versailles, I will not say on account of your talent, but in spite of it." "The reason is very simple," said Chamfort in his plain way; "at Versailles I resign myself to learning many things which I know, from men who are ignorant of them.'

It has been said that Chamfort ceased frequenting the court, after having failed there in a love adventure. We have no other traces of this adventure, or rather of this romance, than the following letter which has the air of Cyrano de Bergerac: "It is now some eight days that it has been impossible for me to free myself from a poetical fancy. By day, by night, even in sleep, I am full of it. I did not suppose that I was so young. Nothing has been able to mitigate this sudden passion. It is like being bitten by a mad dog. The dog was not a large one, but a wolf-dog, or rather a canine lion, a mixture of the horrible, the charming, and the ridiculous, of reason and folly. I will go some morning to your *lever*, my formidable lap-dog; I hope that it will amuse you, and bite to your heart, with its sharp teeth."

The count de Vaudreuil lodged him in his mansion, which soon became a second academy, for Chamfort if he wrote without warmth and individuality, spoke always in a picturesque manner. He was a living journal of the literary and political world. He then counted his three descriptions of friends, those who loved him, those who loved him not, and those who cared nothing at all about him. Among the first figured Mirabeau. The lion sought the cat for her malicious cunning and delicate gracefulness, or rather Mirabeau and Chamfort were both hot-headed and sarcastic. Nature had been liberal to them; but they wanted in everything faith, faith which they replaced by rage at solemn moments. What will appear strange is, that, in this friendly alliance, Chamfort was not the disciple but the master. The following letter of Mirabeau's is very curious: "I have quitted my cradle and my swaddling-clothes at too late a period. Human conventionalities choked me too long, and when the bands were a little relaxed (for broken they never were) I found myself still laced over by the livery of opinion. I was besides too passionate; I had given too many pledges to fortune, to become a man of nature. It is not in the midst of dangers that one can pursue a determined route. Ah! had I known you ten years ago, how many ravines and precipices should I have avoided! There is not a day, and above all, not a circumstance a little serious, in which I do not surprise myself saying:

'Chamfort would frown, let us not do, let us not write that;' or else, 'Chamfort would be content with this, for Chamfort is of the temper of my soul and my mind.' "Every man has thus an internal conscience in a friend, who always stands sentinel over his actions." Happy is the friend who watches over Mirabeau!

Mirabeau was to read at the national assembly in 1791, a report on the academies. This curious fragment, found among his papers at his death, was the work of Chamfort, who more than once worked at the speeches of his illustrious friend.

Chamfort, who had entered the academy in 1781, scarcely ever spoke like an academician. "Helvetius, Rousseau, Diderot, Mably, Raynal, and all free spirits, have openly shown their contempt for this body, which has not made great those who grace its list, but which has received them great, and sometimes made them small." Farther on he maintains that this school of servility, has never produced either a man or an idea. He is indignant at the prizes for virtue. "Render to Virtue the homage of believing that the poor man also can be paid by her; that he has, like the rich man, an opulent and solvent conscience; and in fine, that he can like his rich neighbor, place a good deed between heaven and himself." After some pages of declamation, he arrives at this eloquent conclusion: "You have enfranchized everything, enfranchized talent. Let there be nothing between it and the nation. 'Stand out of my light,' said Diogenes to Alexander, and Alexander did so. Since the academies will not stand out of our light, we must annihilate them. A corporation for genius and the arts! It is a thing which the English have never conceived of, and the English are our masters in common sense. Corneille, criticised by the French academy, exclaimed: '*I imitate one of my three Horatii! I appeal to the people.*' Trust Corneille, like him, appeal to the people?"

Meanwhile, the revolution broke out. Chamfort followed Mirabeau into the tempest. He forgot his ancient friends, saying, that those who have passed the river of revolution, have passed the river of oblivion. He frequented the clubs and was a street orator. He was one of the first to enter the Bastille. The revolution had swept away everything he possessed, but he was forgetful of himself. He entered one day the house of Marmontel, who was weeping for the loss of his pensions. "You weep, Brutus-Marmontel?"—"I weep for my children, who will die of hunger." Chamfort took a child on his knees, "Come, my little friend, you will be superior to us: some day you will weep over your father, on learning that he had the weakness to weep for you, from the idea that you would be less rich than himself." After the first excitement was over, he resumed his pen, and prepared the literary portion of the *Mercure*. This journal was royalist, but while the political editor kissed royalty on one cheek, the literary editor smote it on the other. He was for sometime secretary of the Jacobin club, but when he saw that republican France was submitting to the yoke of King Robespierre and King Marat, he withdrew to the club of the *émigrés* of '89. He was at the termination of his political enthusiasm. The most of those who were carried away by the current, or suffered themselves to be carried away by it, went on in darkness, governed by the events of the day, without seeing the shore where the dove had already flown to pluck the sacred leaf. The political life of Chamfort terminated with the fall of the Girondins. Although recognised by a certain number of men of the Mountain, on account of his ideas and his sarcasms, he never crossed the Rubicon, and this ruined him. He was perhaps arrested by a feeling of gratitude, rather than by the conviction that the Mountain was going too far.

Roland had divided the national library into two departments; he had given one to Carra and the other to Chamfort. These were two acts of justice which made two Girondins the more. Chamfort moreover, must needs have been lost in the revolution, by following the wave, for, born for criticism and not for enthusiasm, he spared no popular royalty, that of Citizen Marat, no more than that of Citizen Robespierre. He did not even spare the convention. In order to celebrate the anniversary of the second of January, the convention had solemnly visited the Place de la Revolution, where an expedition of the guillotine was presented to them. "It is," said Chamfort, "the gratuitous exhibition for the convention." (Gratuitous theatrical representations were given to the people then, as in 1848.) Chamfort's sarcasms, good or bad, were transcribed and denounced. It is related that, in some of the saloons which were yet open, he amused himself by sketching, with much gayety, the portraits of the chiefs of the convention. "Take care," some one said to him one day, "you have more than one claim to the hatred of that infuriated party, who have no liking for either penetrating minds, philosophers, or elevated and firm souls, because it is not of such materials that slaves are formed."—"I have no fear," he replied; "have I not always marched in the first rank of the republican phalanx? Have I not loudly proclaimed my hatred against kings, nobles, priests, in a word, all the enemies of reason and liberty? Was it not I who gave as a motto to our soldiers, on entering a hostile country: 'War to the castles, peace to the cottages.'" However, on the denunciation of a miserable wretch, Tobiesen Duby, a subaltern of the national library, Chamfort was committed to prison.

Politicians will study Chamfort as a philosopher in open revolution. He has his hours of anger and folly, but he almost always maintains the control of his sovereign reason. Every man of sincerity, if he listens to the passionate beatings of his heart, will have known, said Rivarol, "his nocturnal days," in political agitations. It is there, on that ever-agitated sea, that the point of view every instant varies. In politics, a man is always in the right, but he usually comes too soon or too late. How few arrive at the right time! He who passes for a fool to-day, will be studied fifty years hence, perhaps to-morrow, as a profound legislator! How many eloquent examples of this, since the encyclopedists!

Chamfort had not foreseen the revolution. He was not one of those glowing apostles who come into the world, to recall to our minds the Divine Revolutionist who was born at Bethlehem. A man of wit, rather than of thought, he had the laugh of Rabelais, or of Sterne, and not the savage tear of Jean-Jacques Rousseau; in a word, Democritus was his master, and Heraclitus his fool. This great epoch of 1789, had however retempered all hearts in the living spring of passion. The most indifferent threw themselves with enthusiasm, into the regenerating flood, in which human liberty had just been steeped, like Achilles in the Styx. Chamfort had thrown himself desperately into the movement, happy to find himself again young in the presence of liberty, that ideal mistress whom we have all adored, in the glow of youth. Chamfort had by a sterile philosophy, bridled all his passions, fearing their generous impulses; he gave full sway to his revolutionary inclinations. Passionately fond of the unknown, he needed not the golden spurs of his friend Mirabeau; he took part in all the assemblies, in the streets and the clubs, elbowing Robespierre and Barnave, the reds and the whites, with Mirabeau at Versailles, with Camille Desmoulins at the Palais-Royal. Changing as the sky of Paris, he spoke in turn for everybody and against everybody. "History," he exclaimed at the Jacobins, "is but a series of horrors. If tyrants detest it during their lives, it seems that their successors suffer the crimes of their predecessors to be transmitted to posterity, to divert men from the horror which they themselves inspire." The day after, he spoke as follows: "Let us beware, we are only Frenchmen, and we would fain be Romans. The character of the French is a combination of that of the monkey, and the setter. Droll and playful as the monkey, he is mischievous like him; like the setter, caressing and licking the master who beats and chains him, he bounds with joy when he is set loose for the chase." Rivarol, who had talked with the enemies of the revolution, said one day to Chamfort: "You have lost your wit in your fury against royalty. One can not love at the same time the republic and the arts. A Louis XIV. was needed to produce Molières and Racines."—"Ay," replied Chamfort "you belong to the class who forgive the priests all the mischief they have done, because without the priests, we should not have had the comedy of Tartuffe." Rivarol reminded Chamfort that he was formerly one of those who pleaded for the nobility. "It was, you used to say, an intermedium between the king and the people."—"Yes," said Chamfort, "but I have finished the sentence; yes, an intermedium, as the hound is an intermedium between the hunter and the hares!" Chamfort was then considered violent and dangerous. In 1790 he had the revolutionary opinions of the democrats of 1792. As a contrast to himself, let us remark, that in 1792, seeing his ideas triumphant, he was the first to condemn them as wicked children, who have grown up far from the paternal heart. He had invoked the social revolution with all his powers: "We must recommence human society, as Bacon said human reason was to be recommenced." It was not therefore the unsightly branches which he wished to cut down, but the entire forest. "It seems that the greater part of the deputies of the national assembly, have demolished prejudices only to reassume them, like those people who tear down a building, merely to appropriate to themselves the fragments." Chamfort did not wish to see the clay of the ancient world used to model the new. "You preach disorder." "When God created the world," he replied, "the movement of chaos must have made chaos seem more disorderly, than when it reposed in a peaceful disorder." "Reform, but do not destroy," was again urged on him. "You want to have the Augean stable swept clean with a feather-brush!"

In the clubs, Chamfort demanded the floor *to say one word.* He hated speeches. The clock of revolutionary times moves too quickly for rhetoricians. One evening he mounted the tribune, and announced that he would speak on despotism and democracy. Here is his speech at full length: "*I, everything—the rest, nothing: that is despotism. I, another; another, I: that is democracy.*" He wished to descend, which was objected to. "La Rochefoucauld-Chamfort, speak to us longer," said a clubman.—"Tell us the truth," cried a woman to him.—"The truth? the truth is, that there are in France seven millions of men asking alms, and twelve millions not in a condition to bestow them. The truth is, that Paris is a city of fêtes and amusements, in which four fifths of the inhabitants die of mortification under slavery. Poor, sacrificed people! why have you not the pride of the elephant, who will not bring forth in servitude?"—"Citizen Chamfort does not know what he is talking about!" cried a woman (perhaps Théroigne de Méricourt). "Did not the infant smile on his mother, under Domitian as under Titus?" They knew their Roman history then, as the clubs of 1848 knew their history of 1792. God alone has made his own book; men never make theirs without the inspiration of previous books.

The men of the pen are always men of party, even when they have no political faith; indifference would save them in revolutions; but no one is indifferent who has experienced the joys and torments of the mind. In 1793, every one had the liberty of being the friend of power; but all the discontented were imprisoned in the name of liberty. Chamfort was taken to the Madelonnettes in company with the abbé Barthélemy, whose crown of white hairs they suspected. The prison to which some then accommodated themselves, to such an extent was the virtue of resignation possessed—the prison was odious to Chamfort. "It is not life, nor is it death; there is no medium—I must open my eyes on the heavens, or close them in the tomb." He became free again, but scarcely had he time to breathe in the open air, in company with a gend'arme, when the prison reopened to him. He swore to deliver himself: when they came to seize him, he fired a pistol at his forehead; the ball shattered his nose and put out an eye. Astonished at still being alive, he seized a razor and attempted to cut his throat. Death did not desire him. In vain did he gash his breast, open a vein, strike everywhere, distracted by grief. The blood flowed, he fell exhausted, but alive. To those who were conducting him to prison, he dictated with a firm voice: "I, Sebastien-Roch-Nicolas-Chamfort, declare, that I wished rather to die a freeman than to live a slave in a prison." He signed with a firm hand, with a flourish written in blood, this thoroughly Roman declaration.*

Will it be believed? Chamfort did not die at that time; but, what is more incredible, he did not obtain pardon. He was condemned to that strange slavery which consisted in paying a crown a-day to a gend'arme, in consideration of which a man was kept in sight for the security of the state. He survived all these tortures of body and soul. Did he not resemble humanity, which so many disasters have afflicted—which has scattered over every path

* This is an account written by a friend of Chamfort: "I arrived a little while afterward, and shall never forget the sight. His head and neck were enveloped in bloody bandages; his pillow and clothes were also spotted with blood. The little which was visible of his face was still covered with it. He spoke with less vehemence, and began to feel his feebleness. I remained mute beside him, overcome by emotion, admiration, and grief. 'My friend,' said he to me, holding out his hand, 'you see the manner in which one escapes from these fellows. They pretend that my aim failed, but I feel that the ball has remained in my head, and they shall not go in search of it.' All that he said had this character of energy and simplicity. After a moment's silence, he continued with an air of perfect calmness, and even with the ironical tone which was quite familiar to him, 'What would you have? See what it is to be clumsy-handed! One succeeds in nothing—not even in killing one's-self!' He then began to relate how he had *perforated* the eye and the lower part of the forehead, instead of penetrating the skull, then *hacked* his neck instead of cutting it, and *gashed* his breast without succeeding in piercing the heart. 'At last,' he added, 'I recollected Seneca, and in honor of him, I wanted to open my veins; but he was rich; he had everything he wanted—a good warm bath, in a word, everything convenient. I, for my part, am a poor devil, and have none of these things. I have injured myself horribly, and here I am still; but I have the ball in my head—that is the chief thing. A little sooner or a little later—that is all!'"

its blood and tears—which, riddled with wounds, marches ever onward, urged on by the invisible master? He succumbed, however, to so many miseries. "Ah! my friend," he exclaimed as he expired, "I am at last leaving this world, in which the heart must either break or turn to bronze."

Rivarol, who wrote in verse, as a summing up of his life—

> "For me—of Nature the abandoned child,
> Nursed by the hands of indolence and ease,
> Unnerved by pleasure—it must be my doom
> To find at once oblivion in the tomb,"—

Rivarol could call himself, to some little extent, the disciple of Chamfort: he has the same biting and merry wit, and the same relentless satire. They have both left scattered fragments of noble works; but it is not sufficient to be able to construct the pediment of a palace, when the palace itself is not built. Although they had been the contemporaries of Jean Jacques Rousseau and Bernardin de St. Pierre—although French genius was then enriched from two divine springs, revery and sentiment—Chamfort and Rivarol, men of the past, denied the hopes of the future. They did not see the sky beyond the stormy horizon. They believed that the human mind had long since made its last utterance in France as in Greece, in the age of courtesans. They believed, therefore, in death and oblivion. They lived only for the visible works of God, like

Horace and the pagans, who sheltered their philosophy under the locks of Venus, at her feet of snow, and beneath the trellises of the vines cherished by the sun. We, however, whom they denied, we believe in them; we are not yet barbarians; and we willingly confess that Anacreon, Horace, Voltaire, loved no more heartily than we do.

The whole life of Chamfort blazes forth in witty sallies. As soon as he takes up the pen, he is no longer Chamfort; he is some writer or other, writing with the same smile of incredulity a comedy or a tragedy. His four volumes are, therefore, turned over only by those who are witty in the smaller journals. Since Molière, it has been very much the custom for men to get their living where they could find it. On looking at these four volumes, one is tempted to exclaim that there are four volumes too much for Chamfort's works. Why has he not always said to himself: "A man writes for celebrity; now, celebrity is the advantage of being known by those who do not know you."

Written poetry, though from the golden pen of Homer, is never anything but a sepulchre in which phantoms are moving here and there. The true poets live for themselves and not for others. They content themselves with the book which destiny writes in their hearts in letters of flame.

Chamfort died discontented with everything; he had gained only colds and indigestions by frequenting the gay world. "Do you find it advantageous to have lived with ministers?"—"Not at all; they are players who have almost always shown me their cards—who have even, in my presence, looked into the talon—but who have not shared with me their winnings." In hatred to blazoned fools, he had thrown himself fully into the revolution; in hatred to the revolution, he had dug his own grave, as if the last cry of humanity had been this: "*Brothers, we must die.*" He had studied humanity at every step of the ladder, and had arrived at this aphorism, that the honest man is a variety of the human species as well as the man of talent. "Why," somebody asked, "have you not succeeded in something, amid so many fools?"—"Because I never thought the world as stupid as it is." Chamfort calumniated the world, for he had succeeded in it better than he ought to have done. He understood marvellously well, how to excite public curiosity by tricks like those of an actress, who wishes to play upon the public. "Why don't you write, Chamfort?"—"Because the public treat men of letters, as the recruiters of St. Michel's bridge treat those whom they enlist: drunk the first day, ten crowns and blows with a stick, the rest of their lives. People urge me to work, for the same reason as, when they sit by a window, they want to have monkeys, jugglers, or dancing-bears, come along. No, I will not write, because I would stop half-way in Jeannot's career of glory, because I fear to die without having lived, because in fine, the more my literary sign becomes effaced, the happier I am." All these reasons were excellent ones to offer, but they were only cunning disguises of the truth. The truth was, that he did not write because he had nothing in his heart—nothing in his belly as the artist said. He was a thinker of the family of La Rochefoucauld; he rested six days of the week, and took pen in hand on Sunday, the only day in which he did not go into society. He has said somewhere, that idle people who collect maxims, resemble those who eat oysters or cherries, first picking out the best, and ending by eating all. He made the mistake of not leaving some of the oysters and cherries in his platonic repast. I shall reproduce, after a diligent search, twenty thoughts by Chamfort:

I. Man appears to me to be more corrupted by his reason than by his passions. These have preserved in the social system the little nature which is still to be found there.

II. Society is not, as it is thought, the development of nature, but really its decomposition. Or rather, it is a second edifice, erected out of the ruins of the other. These fragments are recognised with a pleasure mingled with surprise, as we recognise a natural sentiment in civilization. It happens, even, that this sentiment is the more pleasing, if the person from whom it escapes is of an elevated rank, that is, farther removed from nature. It is a fragment of ancient Doric or Corinthian architecture, set in an ungainly structure of modern times.

III. Men of intellect never succeed, because they never believe the world as foolish as it is.

IV. I bequeath my indolence to the wicked, and my silence to the fool.

V. "Are you not ashamed of wishing to speak better than you

can?" said Seneca to one of his sons, who could not recal the exor dium of an harangue which he had commenced. One may also say to those who adopt principles stronger than their characters, "Are you not ashamed to wish to be more of a philosopher than you are?"

VI. There are well-dressed follies, as there are well-clothed fools.

VII. The moment when one loses his illusions is often one of regrets; but we sometimes follow the illusion which has deceived us. It is Armida, burning and destroying the palace in which she was enchanted.

VIII. Doctors see no more clearly than the common run of men into diseases and the interior of the human body. They are all blind; but the doctors are the patients of the hospital of the *quinze-vingts*, who are better acquainted with the streets.

IX. A fool who has a moment of intelligence astonishes and scandalizes us like hack-horses at a gallop.

X. Providence? the baptismal name of Chance. Chance? a nickname of Providence.

XI. There are men who have a passion for raising themselves above the rest, whatever may be the pedestal. All is alike to them, provided they are conspicuous: the mountebank's stage, the theatre, the throne, the scaffold—they will always be happy if they have the public gaze upon them.

XII. Men, to enter the world, become small by gathering together. They are Milton's devils, forced to make themselves pigmies, in order to enter Pandemonium.

XIII. Ambition seizes more quickly on little than on great souls as the fire seizes more easily on cottages than on palaces.

XIV. To live with one's self, virtue is needed; to live with others, only honor.

XV. We are so far removed from nature, that those who love and paint her are accused of being romantic.

XVI. Men are governed by the head; men do not play at chess with a good heart.

XVII. The philosopher who wishes to extinguish his passions is like the chemist who wishes to extinguish his fire.

XVIII. Instead of wishing to correct men for their irregularities, we should correct the weakness of those who suffer them.

XIX. You ask how to make a fortune: see what passes at the door of a playhouse on a day when there is a crowd—how some remain in the rear, how those in the front fall back, how those in the rear are pushed forward. This simile is so true, that the word which expresses it has passed into the language of the people. They call making a fortune, "*pushing one's self.*"

XX. The mind is often to the heart only what the library of a mansion is to the person of the master.

Chamfort had faith in nothing, not even in hope, that virgin of the ideal world, who opens heaven to us in the midst of every tempest. He had been deceived by hope, as by a charlatan at a country fair. He affirmed that he had not been happy, except from the day when he had lost her. Thus he said in dying—sad moral of the volume of his life—that if he went to Paradise, he should write on the portal, the verse which Dante has placed over the gate of hell :—

"Lasciate ogni speranza, voi ch'entrate."

THREE PAGES FROM THE LIFE OF MADAME DE PARABERE.

I.

THE VINTAGE.

The courtesans of pagan antiquity were accomplished, more accomplished than loving. The "gay science," of which Montaigne speaks, is the only science allowable for women's lips. It is of no use for Aspasia, to talk to me about the immortal soul, and the liberty of nations with the eloquence of her disciple, the divine Plato; I hear only with my eyes: if madame de Parabère was there, I should think her the wiser of the two.

The first intellectual qualification of a woman, is her face, the last is her heart. The women of the eighteenth century had learned nothing, but they knew how to love, and they were beautiful. Under the regency, the women were like a rich harvest favored by Heaven and the sun; or, to speak more truly, they were handsome under the regency, and under madame de Pompadour, and under Marie-Antoinette, because they determined to be so—some through gallantry, some through grace, others through passion, and the rest simply through beauty. The art which Coustou had revealed, played an important part in the manner of dressing and carrying the head. Nature was made up for by art, where the former was neither exuberant nor forcible enough to appear in its simplicity. One who could not be the Venus of Milo, became the Bacchante of Posilippo.

The strongest contrast that can be opposed to the faces of one century, is to be found in the faces of the century which has preceded, and of the century which follows. How great is the distance between la Vallière or la Montespan, and la Parabère or la Pompadour! Love changes its character every hundred years. It is still love, but no longer wears the same mask.

I wish to detach to-day, three pages from the amorous life of the eighteenth century, in order to afford relief to our eyes from the somewhat serious pictures of 1850. What, however, can be more serious than the passions and the revolutions of the heart?

Supper was just over, one autumn evening, in 1717, at the château de Sainte-Héraye, situated on the bank of the Oise, not far from Paris.

Monsieur de Parabère and his friend, monsieur de Gacé, had been out shooting in the forest of Carmel, for the sake of killing time and getting an appetite for supper. Madame de Parabère was present at the meal, but like an apparition only. She had not been out shooting, and was not hungry. She retired from the table, under the pretext that she had three or four letters to write (she was not very precise) to her mother, sister, and aunt, who were not expecting to hear from her. But let us listen first to this duo of drinkers in a quartetto of bottles.

"Drink!" exclaimed Parabère.

"Drink!" echoed Gacé.

Parabère wiped away a tear, Gacé burst out laughing.

"Do you drink tears, then?" asked Gacé of the captain.

"And do you drink songs?"

"Yes; as the marquis de Saint-Aulaire says:—

"'Tis wine causes jokes round the table to fly,
'Tis wine, when it's good makes us witty and—dry!
'Tis wine causes man all his thoughts to disclose—
In a word, 'tis from wine that all poetry flows."

"Well said. Drink!"

"Why do you weep?"

"I am thinking that eternity will be a fountain of sorrows, if there are no vintages in heaven."

"Then, meanwhile, let us crown ourselves with vine-branches and roses, like the pagans, and let our lips be only used for women and the bottle."

Parabère sighed.

"My wife is dull," said he.

"And my mistress gay," added his friend.

"You let her tear about the town as she likes."

"And you imprison your wife. Believe me: marriage has its fatalities. If you are to be a Géronte in China, you must needs take your wife to China. One hasn't made the woman he marries."

"I am not so philosophical," exclaimed Parabère. "I profess to be both the husband and lover of my wife!"

"You begin to see double, so you must have drunk too much; it is a bad cask which can hold but a pint!"

"Empty this bottle then. He who drinks last drinks best."

"To the day of judgment, if you like."

"But my wife, zounds!"

"Come! you'll soon be under the table."

This seemed to be the truth, for Parabère had all the trouble in the world to keep his seat.

"Amphitryon, my friend," said Gacé, "what will become of me, for you are no longer drinking? If we were at Paris, I should go and talk nonsense at the opera; but here, buried as I am in a wood — a regular cut-throat place, peopled with chilly Hamadryades — all that I can do is to smoke myself and sleep like a Laplander."

"Drink," said Parabère, falling under the table, and nearly asleep.

Gacé poured some mouthfuls of wine over him, as we throw cold water upon a person in a swoon.

"Drink, my friend."

"Ah!" murmured Parabère, weeping, "it is very cruel of me to have imprisoned my wife. But I am as jealous as a tiger. More drink, Gacé!"

"Wait a minute," said Gacé, "I will go and fetch a funnel, or perhaps, as we are luckily in vintage-time, I had better carry you to the vat which is foaming in the press-room."

Gacé rose, but soon perceived that he was not in a state to go very far. He, therefore, looked at Parabère and began to laugh, without knowing why, according to his custom.

"Dead drunk," said he, making the sign of the cross over his friend Parabère. "Suppose I go and console his widow?"

The idea fired Gacé.

"She is as beautiful as an angel, who might have been a demon. But stay! it seems she is of formidable virtue, defended by bastion and battlement, she reads Bossuet and talks about a convent. You hesitate, Gacé! are you afraid of virtue? Forward."

He crossed the door-sill of the dining-room, without being any too well-assured whether he had not better retrace his steps. He advanced, and tumbled against a valet-de-chambre, who was asleep in an antechamber.

"Hollo, L'Epine!"

"Nothing, monsieur the captain, we have only been drinking."

"You rascal, we were calling you just now, for we were thirsty."

"I know you were, but it was La Rose's turn to go down in the cellar. He has been trying to find his way there for an hour. I know the place, it is a perfect labyrinth."

"I will have you both hanged."

Gacé proceeded on his way.

"M. the captain mistakes the door."

"Not a word, or you are a dead man!"

"Recollect, that M. de Parabère is the only person who enters this door after sundown."

L'Epine approached M. de Gacé with an air of anxiety.

"And besides," he continued, "M. de Parabère does not come every night, when madame the marchioness is reading Bossuet, for example."

The emotion caused by the perils of the attempt, had somewhat sobered Gacé. He turned toward L'Epine, seized him by the throat, and commanded him, on pain of death, to go and watch by his master.

"After all," muttered L'Epine, "this does not concern me, I will pretend to be asleep."

M. de Gacé opened the door with a violent beating at his heart. "This is not the place," said he looking around.

He had entered the chamber of one of the marchioness's waiting-women. The girl was asleep in an arm-chair, with a key in her hand. The noise of opening and shutting the door partially awoke her, but she still remained under the influence of a dream.

"I have not got the key," she murmured.

"What does that mean?" Gacé asked himself.

"I swear to you, monsieur the marquis, that I have not got it."

Gacé smiled, and gently took the key. She did not wake.

"It seems that this rogue is a vestal, who guards the entrance of the temple against everybody, the husband as well as the others."

Gacé having approached another door recognised the voice of the marchioness.

"In fact, she is reading Bossuet; it is a bad preface to the romance I wish to compose with her."

Gacé hesitated in his boldness. He put his ear to the key-hole but all was still.

"She is asleep, I like that better; I will awake her so gently, that she will only be able to go to sleep again."

Gacé put the key in the lock. "Well, I am entering on a somewhat risky business. If I had only given the marchioness some little hint! But must she not have understood some of my idolatrous glances? Have I not told her twenty times, that she was the most beautiful of women. Telling a woman that she is beautiful, is making a declaration of love to her—for—if I think you beautiful, marchioness, it is because I see you by my heart, and because you have been made for my eyes. And besides, we must leave prefaces to women. In their idleness they make twenty, even for a book which will never be opened."

Thus reasoned M. de Gacé on the threshold of the door.

He opened it.

In 1715 the eighteenth century had just begun; for the eighteenth century does not count eighty years, beginning with the regency and finishing with the revolution. In 1715, terrestrial paradise was nearly the only paradise believed in; all grand ladies, from duchesses to financiers' wives, built themselves, with the graceful ingenuity of the birds of the air, an amorous retreat, adorned with the richest carpets, pictures, mirrors, and flowers. The walls, ceilings, and even the glasses, were covered with cupids and flowers. It was the age of chains of roses. The only painter of genius who then reigned was Antoine Watteau.

In these terrestrial paradises of the amorous beauties of the regency, angels were sometimes seen, deceived by the looks of these arch little cupids, who under their white wings were real *mousquetaires*. But the angels, out of their element, were not long in discovering that there was little of heaven in these profane paradises.

Monsieur de Gacé had opened the door. A little Chinese lantern—for while we were sending out missionaries to convert China to the catholic religion, China was converting us to its ornaments, grotesque figures, painted jars, and lanterns—a little Chinese lantern then, hanging from the ceiling, spread over the apartment of madame de Parabère a mysterious light, very favorable to amorous dreams.

Gacé did not amuse himself as another might have done, by admiring the freshness, spirit, and brilliancy of the paintings, the work of some Gillot, careless of glory, who thought one or two smiles and three or four crowns a sufficient remuneration for his talent. He went to the bed and fell upon his knees, although he was not accustomed, in his regiment, to repeat his paternoster.

The bed was almost in the shade; ample damask curtains, scarcely parted by cords of twisted gold, fell in waves from the canopy.

"Since I am on my knees," thought Gacé, "I will take an oath: I swear that madame de Parabère will not get out of bed to put me out of the door."

Gacé thus raised his sinking courage.

"To tell the truth," said he, seizing the curtain, "I would rather cross the Rhine with Louis XIV."

He raised the curtain and advanced on his knees as far as the bed. He sought to grasp a hand.

"Pshaw!" thought he, "this is the attack of a tyro."

He rose and threw himself desperately upon the

bed, with a palpitating heart—but madame de Parabère was not there.

"And yet," said Gacé, somewhat confused, "I recognised her voice just now."

He listened, and this is what he heard in the direction of the boudoir:—

THE MARCHIONESS. Martial, you are unreasonable; this is the twentieth time I have bid you adieu.

MARTIAL. Then you drive me from you?

THE MARCHIONESS. Reflect that it has just struck three.

MARTIAL. Three hours of unhoped-for joy, for I came at midnight.

THE MARCHIONESS. Adieu; return the day after to-morrow. Do not forget the key of the park. Come, Martial, you will wrench my hand off; hasten away, so that I may shut the window, for I shall take cold. Adieu, adieu; take care of the espaliers. I hear your horse neighing and pawing the ground. Poor boy! ten leagues to ride through the forest! Adieu.

MARTIAL. Adieu. To see you and kiss your hand, I would travel round the world.

The casement was closed.

"It seems," said Gacé, "that the romance I wanted to write is already printed."

He asked himself what he ought to do. There was more than one course to take; the wisest was to retire. Gacé, however, remained, confiding himself to the genius of adventure.

When madame de Parabère emerged from the inner apartment, she saw a man and uttered a shriek. Gacé burst out laughing.

"One gone and one come," said Gacé, with a dash of impertinence, twisting his mustache.

Madame de Parabére, half dead with fright, fell back on the sofa.

"Madame," said Gacé, taking her hand, "it is no wish of mine to trouble you. Command, and I obey. I love you, but I come too late. I took the field when the siege was over. A thousand compliments to Martial; his is a name of good augury. If he desires a second-lieutenancy in my regiment, speak—"

The marchioness raised her eyelids, and let fall on Gacé one of those terrible and fascinating looks, of which serpents know the secret.

"Monsieur de Gacé," said she, "the marquis de Parabère invited you to come and drink his wine, but not to come and take his wife by assault; you violate the rights of hospitality."

"I am a great criminal, but I am in love. If I were not in love, I should be curious."

"I owe no account of my actions to any one but my confessor."

"What matters the confession! you are guilty and impenitent."

"Have you come here to preach me a sermon? Don't you suppose that I am sleepy? Leave me, or I shall call my attendants."

"Would you ruin yourself?"

"Myself? 'Tis you whom I wish to ruin."

The marchioness, who but just now bent beneath her shame, reassumed an attitude of confidence.

"I do not understand you," said Gacé. "What! I, the witness of your gallant adventure . . . ."

"A gallant man," interrupted madame de Parabère, "is never a witness of an adventure in which a woman is concerned. I have, therefore, nothing to fear from you, while you have everything to fear from me. If I call, my husband will awake and hasten here. Before you have time to explain, he will seize you, cut your throat, or throw you out of the window."

"The window!" exclaimed Gacé, laughing, "it would be a very pleasant route, provided you said to me, as you did to Martial, 'Take care of the espaliers.'"

"Pray cease, we have had jesting enough. Since you were there when he left, you know that I love him. It is my crime, but it will be my only crime."

"Madame," said Gacé, bowing with a skeptical air, "I will return at next year's vintage."

"Never! My heart has lost me, but my heart will save me. The day when I no longer love Martial, I shall go and bury myself in a convent."

"You mean that Heaven will be your second love? The twentieth, possibly, but the second never! Heaven, madame, is the winter which gathers the yellow leaves when the vintage is over. Adieu, marchioness, I shall keep the key of your apartment. I will return in a year and a day."

"Impertinent fellow!" exclaimed the marchioness, in a rage.

But Gacé was gone. Madame de Parabère walked in great agitation up and down her room.

"Ah! Martial," said she with a sigh, "you have opened a golden door to me, but it is the door of hell." She raised the curtain of a window. "Poor boy! ten leagues to travel in a cold and rainy night of autumn! I seem to hear the gallop of his horse in my heart. Ah, if I were with him, how happy I should be amid all the perils of an abduction!"

Meanwhile Gacé had returned to the dining-room. Parabère was still asleep beneath the table. He called to him in a voice of thunder.

"Here I am," answered the marquis.

"You don't know how to drink," said Gacé; "While you have been under the table, I have tossed off one-and-twenty bumpers. Let us go to bed; if your wife should find us at daybreak in such a company of empty bottles, she would never forgive either you or me. Do you happen to know Martial?"

"Martial?" said Parabère, getting up. "What Martial?"

"Some Martial or other. I don't know. Try and think."

"Stay—I have a cousin in the light-cavalry of the

name of Martial de Montluzun; a mere boy, still in leading-strings. When the days were longer, he used to come up to the château sometimes; he has been at Compèigne since the campaign. But what of him?"

"Oh, nothing," said Gacé, in a careless manner. "I have merely heard him spoken of at court as a young fellow who would be sure to rise."

"Nonsense! he can't drink. And whoever can't toss off a bottle for a stirrup-cup won't go far."

"Those poor espaliers!" thought Gacé.

II.

UNDER THE REGENCY.

A YEAR and a day after the above adventure, Gacé still had in his possession the key of the apartment of the marchioness; but the marchioness was no longer at the château de Saint-Hóraye.

She had been a widow for eleven months—Monsieur de Parabère having, as report said, died of thirst.

"No doubt," thought Gacé, looking at the key, "she is mourning Parabère, in company with Martial in some amorous solitude."

He came to Paris during the carnival. Was there ever a Lent under the regency? Gacé went a great deal into company. He was presented at the palais-royal, one day, when there was to be a masked ball in the evening. The regent invited him to the ball and supper. Gacé gave himself up, body and soul, to the pleasures of the ball-room, seeking for an adventure among those beautiful women who only lived for love.

The regent walked about the chambers sparkling with light, beauty, and diamonds, like a sultan in his seraglio. How few of these women entered the palais-royal by the grand entrance without going out by the private staircase! Suddenly, a great commotion was observed in the ball-room—a great commotion followed by a deep silence.

"Ah! there is madame de Parabère."

This name ran from mouth to mouth. She entered like a queen, followed by a thousand adorers. Gacé, quite thunderstruck, was about to rush toward her; but he was anticipated by the duc d'Orleans, who gallantly kissed the hand of the marchioness, and begged her to dance the minuet of Louis XIV. with him.

"And Martial!" murmured Gacé, who thought he was dreaming. "Can that really be madame de Parabère?" asked he of monsieur de Riom, who was standing next to him.

"Have you never seen her, then?" asked Riom. "She is no every-day beauty; when one has merely caught a glimpse of her, he knows her by heart."

"You are speaking to a convert," said Gacé, still looking with surprise at madame de Parabére.

The marchioness was that night as beautiful as

Diana and Venus—as La Vallière and Montespan. She drew after her, with the grace of a queen, a flowered brocade dress, on which Audran himself had strewn a field of roses. She wore none but her own hair, which she had been bold enough not to powder; and her tresses shone on her snow-white temples, like the wings of a raven, flying on the hoar-frosted branches of an oak. She had on neither rouge nor patches, which was also contrary to decorum; but, she was so lovely, and smiled with teeth so white, and eyes so blue, that every one forgave her —even the women, for women love beauty as they love flowers and diamonds. In a word, it was fairy-like to see this woman look so superlatively beautiful, in the midst of the dazzling groups, by the sole power of her own beauty, unaided by ornaments or coquetry.

"Beautiful by both day and night," said Riom to Richelieu, who was passing.

"Do you know her history?" asked Richelieu, recognising Gacé.

"I have read a page of it," answered the captain.

"Let us hear it, then, for it is well known here whither the marchioness is going, but no one knows whence she comes."

Gacé related his duo with Parabère, and touched very delicately on the subject of the espaliers.

"It appears," said Riom, "that she was born in Brittany, toward the end of the century. She was married to that brute of a Parabère, before she was aware of it. Parabère was jealous, like all those who are predestined. By dying, he did his duty. And now she is in possession of all the joys of widowhood. Conjugating in all its moods the verb *to rule*. The regent rules her, she will rule the world.

"I put myself in the ranks," said Richelieu. "What a charming schoolmistress. She would teach Cupid Hebrew!"

"But how did the marchioness get here?" asked Gacé.

"Very naturally," said a pretty mask, who was passing, in a mysterious manner; "moths always come and burn themselves in the candle; or rather the pale flowers of the country come to blow beneath the sun of the court."

"We knew that, fair mask. You are making almanacs for past years."

"You will not let me finish," continued the mask. "I know all, the future by the past. Listen to the past. Madame de Parabère was at the drawing-room held by the duchess the day before yesterday. Her carriage made some stir at the door, for she drives English horses, and her escutcheon is painted by Watteau. The regent always attends the drawing room when there are to be any fine women there. The lady has wit, and, what is better, does not know it. When she was about to leave, the regent, contrary to his custom, rose to accompany her to her carriage. He took her hand on the step. She was enchanted and quite confused at so much attention. She abandoned him her hand for an instant, blushing with pleasure and embarrassment. It was all over with the virtue of madame the marchioness de Parabère. As she sank back in the carriage, the regent sprang in beside her, closed the door, and off they went—where? I don't know. The marchioness has however the *Embarkation for Cythera* on her fan."

Richelieu had recognised the voice of the speaker. "Madame de Sabran," he whispered to her, "if you will, we will embark too."

The countess mingled with the crowd, either because she was afraid of being recognised, or because she wished to be followed.

Gacé and Riom were lounging through the apartments, when the duchess de Berri, disguised as an odalisque, came up, and taking the arm of her lieutenant in the guards, walked away with him, and Gacé was left alone.

He went from group to group, listening to what was being said of the marchioness, for every one was talking of madame de Parabère. He heard nothing but what he knew already, and had entirely given himself up to the bustle of the ball-room, and the lively notes of the music, when his curiosity was again excited by the animated conversation of two young men, who were quarrelling about the marchioness in the recess of a window

"I tell you," exclaimed the most noisy, "that her conduct is scandalous. She is her own mistress, but not mistress of our name. Let her abandon herself to the regent, if she likes; but not under the name of Parabère, monsieur de Montluzun."

"Excellent!" said Gacé, "I find them all here: there is Martial!"

The young cavalry officer was as pale and melancholy as a lover dying of despair.

"You are very absurd about your name of Parabère," said he to the other, with the haughty air of a man seeking a quarrel. "Do you wish to see that distinguished name canonized?"

"No jesting, if you please," said Parabère's nephew.

"It makes me laugh," replied Martial. "Monsieur de Parabère, your virtuous uncle, who died drunk, after having been for many years dead-drunk, gave his name to his wife, which distinguished name she has the right to bear, even at court."

"Let her please herself, but I have still one resource left. To-morrow, I shall write to tell her, that if she persists in bearing my name, I shall take another—that of my lackey."

"I forbid you to do so," exclaimed Montluzun, raising his voice.

"If you go to-morrow," said Godefroy de Parabère, "to the *petit lever* of the marchioness, you will see if I have obeyed you."

" 'Twould be an act of cowardice," said the lover of madame de Parabère. " Godefroy you know me; and if you do so, I will cut your throat."

" Agreed," said Godefroy; "but after I have sent the letter."

" No; before you send it."

At this moment, madame de Parabère went straight up to Gacé, who was standing at a little distance from the two disputants. " Monsieur de Gacé," said she to him, with a smile more disdainful than ever, " I shall expect you to-morrow at my *lever*."

" Where?" asked Gacé, with a rather impertinent air.

"You know very well," said she. " I am passing a season at the palais-royal."

All at once, the marchioness turned extremely pale, and tottered on her pretty foot, enveloped in white roses; she had perceived monsieur de Montluzun.

" Martial!" murmured she; " I thought he was in Languedoc."

She disappeared, as by enchantment.

" Yet," thought she, shading her forehead with her hand, as if the light offended her, " my heart told me that he was not very far away. I must not let this poor boy see me; to-morrow, he shall receive a lieutenancy, for Brittany or Périgord."

But monsieur de Montluzun had followed madame de Parabère.

"Oh! madame! madame!" said he in a stifled voice, bending down before her, white as a statue.

"Martial, not another word. It was my wish to save you from a fatal passion."

"Madame, madame, profane not the religion of my heart; say that you no longer love me; I shall, at least, think that you once did so."

"The only eternity I believe in is in heaven. The earth turns, I have turned. You were not by my side, and I went on without you. Adieu, Martial. Let us forget! The future calls you."

"What calls me, madame, is the past. I, at least, shall not forget. Adieu, madame."

Monsieur de Montluzun bowed sadly, with the dignity of one who suffers at the heart.

Madame de Parabère, who tried to stifle recollections still alive, nearly fainted.

"Martial!" murmured she, in a voice he knew so well.

He caught at the sound, and advanced toward her; but, a second afterward, other feelings sprang up to baffle Martial. Madame de Parabère still believed in the joys of her triumph at court. Her beauty spoke more loudly than her heart; and monsieur de Montluzun, whom she still loved, was sacrificed to the duc d'Orleans, whom she loved not yet.

"Martial!" repeated she, but in a tone of voice unknown to him, "let us remember; but, adieu!"

Monsieur de Nocé happened to pass at that moment. She familiarly took his arm saying:

"Accompany me to the regent?"

"If I understand rightly," said monsieur de Nocé, "a favor was being asked of you. See what are the prerogatives of the throne, for you are queen to-day!"

"Yes," replied madame de Parabère, sighing; "it was a favor; and, as I am queen *to-day*, I hastened to grant it, for who knows whether I shall be queen *to-morrow?*"

"For ever!" exclaimed monsieur de Nocé.

At supper, every one was gay. The regent was a philosopher, who amused himself for the whole of France. Mesdames de Sabran and de Phalaris, his mistresses of the day before, gayly took their revenge, having too much sense to weep, at the same time still hoping to reconquer the throne. Madame de Parabère allowed herself to run full-sail before the wind, braving the tempests. She loved the unforeseen, though filled with pit-falls. At dessert, Richelieu sang some of La Fare's couplets. Fontenelle, who was present, drew a parallel between the ancients and moderns, in order to prove that the moderns are right in their notions of beauty, dances, and song.

Madame de Parabère did not give much time to her slumbers. The duke d'Orleans had prepared for her a suite of apartments at the palais-royal, in a style of frivolity; these rooms opened directly on the garden. All the knick-knacks of fashionable luxury, were strewn in heaps about her bed-chamber, her drawing-room, and her boudoir. The regent had not forgotten the oratory.

On awaking, madame de Parabère rang for her women, stepped into her Persian slippers, hardly large enough for the feet of a child, and went to see the hour by a timepiece, a perfect jewel from Saxony, on which were represented the Graces in the Coysevoxian style of the Graces of the regency.

It was twelve.

Two women entered, the one carrying the female monkey of the marchioness, and the other a dressing-gown, and combs. As soon as she had slipped on her dress, the marchioness, who knew how beautiful she looked in the morning—she was hardly four-and-twenty—ordered the door to be opened to monsieur de Gacé.

Gacé had been waiting for an hour; the marchioness had not doubted that he would be there.

"Well, monsieur de Gacé, what sort of weather is it to-day?"

"Madame the marchioness, I have not noticed the weather; I have seen but you, for I was looking into my mind."

"What pretty nonsense! Arabella, take care, you are tearing my hair out!"

Arabella softened the caresses of the comb.

"Monsieur de Gacé, sit down there on the sofa by the side of my monkey. Is she not very pretty?"

Monsieur de Gacé remained silent. He did not know how to act; his heart beat as he inhaled the air, impregnated with love, which floated in the room.

"*A propos*, monsieur de Gacé, you promised to return in a year and a day, like the promise in a fairy tale; but you forgot me."

"Your coquetry is cruel, madame. While you were Parabère's wife, I dared to feed my ambition, for I was superior to him; but now that you are a widow, my hopes are fallen."

"Very delicately said. Do you wish to marry?"

"More or less. Have you, perchance, any cousin content to put up with my goings-on?"

Madame de Parabère turned toward monsieur de Gacé, and said to him with an air of curiosity and raillery:—

"Have you kept the key?"

Gacé drew it out of his pocket.

"There it is, madame. You see, too, that it is not rusty."

The marchioness smiled.

"Another time," added Gacé, "when I have obtained admission anywhere, I shall take care to remain."

"You will do rightly, monsieur de Gacé; you must never give your enemy a year's truce."

At this moment, a lackey brought in two letters on a highly-chased silver salver, of Florentine workmanship. The marchioness looked long and steadfastly at the two seals, hesitating as to which letter she should read first. She recognised the crest of Martial, whose letter she kept for the last, and broke open the seal of the other:—

"Madame: You have dishonored our name. A man of heart can no longer wish to bear it; therefore, this is the last time that I sign myself

"GODEFROY DE PARABERE."

A cloud passed over the forehead of the marchioness: "Oh, were I a man!" murmured she, crushing the letter in her grasp.

"Madame," said Gacé, "you have a man at hand."

"Then," said she, her eyes flashing fire, "I will give you a sword, and point out the heart you have to strike."

She opened Martial's letter, and read:—

"Madame: When you receive this letter, you will have already been revenged. Godefroy de Parabère will be dead, or my heart will have ceased to beat. "MARTIAL DE MONTLUZUN."

Madame de Parabère dismissed her attendants. "Adieu, monsieur de Gacé; I require an hour's solitude."

"Adieu, madame; do not forget that I expect a wife from your hands."

"Yes, yes; in a year and a day," added the

marchioness, with a careless air, in order to hide the wound her heart had just received, "you can order the violins."

As soon as the marchioness was alone, she fell on her knees, and entreated Heaven to spare monsieur de Montluzun. "Alas!" said she, "'tis I who ought rather to be prayed for. I have a presentiment that he has been killed by that hot-head of a Godefroy. Happy—happy, are those who thus die for a noble action in all the faith of twenty!"

The duke d'Orleans was announced. Madame de Parabère dried her tears, and went to receive him with the smile of a sultana who has never listened to the beatings of her heart.

"Ah, marchioness, how lovely you look this morning!"

"Do I not?" said she, in her clearest tone of voice. "I look lovely because I was waiting for you. Oh, Martial, what is become of you?" added she to herself.

"You are as beautiful as the rising sun," continued the duke d'Orleans.

"Yes, the rising sun; but here the sun sets early."

The regent seized the hand of the marchioness.

"Poor Martial! I should wish to be buried with him."

"What are you murmuring there to yourself, marchioness? are you saying your prayers?"

"The prayers of love."

"You know that Santerre is coming presently to paint us as Adam and Eve."

"In Paradise lost?"

"Lost or recovered, it is still paradise—above all, when madame de Parabère is Eve."

"Yes, but Eve ate the apples: the tree is no longer anything but the tree of science."

"The science of love."

"The science of death."

"Are we going to preach the funeral sermon of our adventure? Marchioness, I will have you painted as Minerva also. I see very plainly that you will be both Mentor and Calypso at the palais-royal."

"Yes, wisdom and folly."

Santerre arrived; he sketched, on the same day, the two celebrated portraits of madame de Parabère, distinguished by that chastely voluptuous touch which animates all the productions of this charming painter, impregnated with antique grace. On beholding the Minerva who was about to reign so imperiously at the palais-royal, the regent said that he would have the Judgment of Paris quashed by the parliament, and would give an apple to Minerva and an apple to Venus.

"I have just made a discovery," said the marchioness de Parabère, who had read a little ancient history: "the apple of Venus is the apple of Eve."

III.

THE TWO LOVERS.

MANY days have passed by. How does the wind blow at court? The regent is as amorous as ever; but who is the queen of the day? Yesterday he supped with madame de Parabère, madame de Sabran, madame de Phalaris, and a few others; but he is to sup to-night with a new-comer—madame d'Averne—"a jade who makes money out of her beauty." The regent has given her husband a captaincy in the guards, and her husband has consequently come, with tears of thankfulness, to propose to the regent to guard his wife with his company: "so that no one but monseigneur will be able to approach her."

Madame de Parabère is at Saint-Cloud. She has not forgotten Martial; but Martial, after having killed Godefroy de Parabère in their duel, fled to the Indies. Monsieur de Gacé is married, but he is not the lover of his wife. The regent spends every Tuesday and Wednesday at the château of Saint-Cloud, in the company of the marchioness; but madame d'Averne, playing the infuriated Hermione, will no longer allow the duke d'Orleans to go "and revel in the orgies of la Parabère." The regent has sworn that he will go no more.

"Never was such a passion seen," said madame d'Averne. "For two whole years has this woman turned your head."

"It is true," said the regent, "but I have often turned it in another direction."

"If you see this woman again," exclaimed the new favorite in despair, "I shall return to my husband."

"Calm yourself; I do not wish to condemn you to such an extremity; I will banish madame de Parabère."

The next day, the four-horse carriage of the marchioness bore her, like the wind, from Saint-Cloud to the palais-royal. The duke refused to see her, but she forced her way to him.

"Monsieur the duke, you drive me forth like a courtesan."

"What would you have, marchioness? we have nothing more to say to one another. Recollect that we have adored each other for a couple of centuries."

"Oh! you can have never loved me."

"Theseus never loved Ariadne so ardently."

"I will not leave."

"I will have you carried off. I know more than one person who would undertake to do so, for it is not I who am surrounded by courtiers, but you. Do you wish to be carried off by Nocé or by Nangis?"

"I tell you that I will not leave. I will go and speak to the young king, who will be sure to take my part."

"True. You have fondled him in your arms. He has told me that it was there he learned to love."

The regent, who was most fantastic in his amours,

changed his manner, and seized the hand of the marchioness.

"And it was you that also taught me to love; for, till I met you, I never knew what love was."

"And you drive me from you?"

"I call you back."

Madame de Parabère showed the regent her letter of banishment. He took it from her and tore it up.

"Forget this, marchioness; I will sacrifice that minx."

"Alas!" said madame de Parabère with an air of doubt, "this is the hundredth time you have made me a like sacrifice. Last year I reigned for a day together; now I have not an hour a-day."

"Return to Saint-Cloud and expect me at supper; you shall see whether I do not love you still. Wait till this evening. I am going to the council; we have twenty *lettres de cachet* to prepare for the banishment of those who intend renewing their appeal at the approaching council. We will not act any longer together in politics, marchioness; you made me sign a decree against the company of the Indies, which will cause me to pass more than one sleepless night. Then, this evening, we will have a *tête-à-tête*, if you promise to be in a good humor."

Madame de Parabère left with an air of triumph, and was handed to her carriage by Monsieur de Nocé.

"Where do you intend going?" he asked, when she was seated.

"I know not," answered she.

"But yet . . . . ?"

The marchioness remained thoughtful.

"Listen, Monsieur de Nocé," said she at last, "and let what I am about to tell you be kept a profound secret. Write to madame d'Averne, and tell her that I shall expect her this evening at Saint-Cloud, to bid her adieu and give her my will."

"What farce is this?"

"Not a word! To-morrow you will know everything."

That evening the regent and madame d'Averne met at the door of the château.

"So I have caught you," exclaimed madame d'Averne angrily.

"Madame," said the regent, whose former love for madame de Parabère had returned, "I did not come here to answer your questions. If you wish to speak to the marchioness, enter, and return to Paris as quickly as possible."

Madame d'Averne saw that she must not reply. They both entered.

"Where is the marchioness?" asked the regent.

"She is not yet returned from Paris," answered one of her women.

"Let an outrider be sent to meet her," added the regent, evidently uneasy.

"What are you come for?" continued he, turning to madame d'Averne.

"I am come because Monsieur de Nocé told me that the marchioness was waiting for me, to bid me adieu and to give me her will."

"Her will!"

The regent felt his heart beat. He called aloud, and ran up the steps to see if madame de Parabère was coming.

"Madame," said he to madame d'Averne, "take care; for if she does not return shortly, I shall be likely enough to kill you, seeing that it was that fatal letter of banishment, extorted by you from me, which took her this day to Paris."

Madame d'Averne hung down her head without daring to reply. Dismay spread over the whole château. All adored madame de Parabère, and every one evinced the utmost anxiety since the arrival of the regent. Suddenly, the tramping of a horse's feet was heard. The regent ran rapidly down the steps, to the great scandal of madame d'Averne. A messenger arrived with a letter.

"Adieu, madame," said the regent, showing madame d'Averne the letter; "this does not concern you."

"Who knows? You have not read it. Since I have been summoned here, there must be some reason for it. See."

The duke d'Orleans passed his hand over his forehead, and, in a tremulous voice, read as follows:—

"PRINCE: Now that I am free to remain, I leave. It is no longer you who banish me, but I myself. We must not, as the proverb says, drink together out of the same cup to the last drop; for, after such intoxicating draughts, the last drop is a tear of blood. It would have, indeed, been delightful for me to sup with you at the château, and fall asleep again with dreams of you; but I should have awoke. I wish now to awake for Heaven alone. You have banished me too often from your heart, for me not to banish myself from the world you live in. All that I required from you this morning was a reparation. I dreaded your contempt, but I have reconquered your heart—that heart which belongs to all, but to myself more than to any other. You told me to go and wait for you. Yes, I will wait, but doubtless in death alone. While staying for this last rendezvous, I will pour forth to Heaven, both for you and myself, all the tears and all the prayers of my heart. Adieu! I send you madame d'Averne, who, this evening, will cause you to forget

"MARIE DE LA NIEUFVILLE PARABERE."

"This evening!—never!" said the regent to madame d'Averne. "Leave me, madame; return to Paris: as for me, I remain here."

Madame d'Averne understood, stupid as she was, that she was vanquished in this struggle with madame de Parabère, whose heart was so embodied in her eloquent adieu. She bowed to the regent, and left with dignity. Could she have met the marchioness, she would have flown at her like a tigress, to tear her to pieces.

As soon as the regent was alone, he gave way to his grief with all his habitual warmth of character.

"Oh! she will return," said he, pacing up and down the room, "for it is she alone I love. She has borne my life away with her."

In the amorous reflux of his love toward the marchioness, the regent determined to honor her memory by passing the night in tears at the château.

"Let supper be served," said he to the attendants of the marchioness. "I shall sup alone, and will see no one. By supping alone," thought he, "I shall think she is still present."

As night advanced, his melancholy became more and more profound: he wept like a child. When he sat down to table, he had not the heart to eat. He looked around him, exclaiming, iu a harrowing tone of voice:—

"Ah! marchioness! marchioness!"

He still wept; but he was not the man to dig his own grave to the cry of the trappist. He never said: "Brother, we must die!" So far did he think himself still from eternity. He ate nothing, but he drained goblet after goblet of Constance wine, till, taking a sudden resolution, he exclaimed:—

"I shall never console myself here; drive to La Phalaris."

* * * * * * * *

Meanwhile, madame de Parabère returned to the château de Saint-Héraye. Though she fled the world, she still preserved in her heart, all her recollections of it. She already looked upon Heaven as her refuge, but she thought not yet of Heaven. This was the first time she had been at the château since monsieur de Parabère's death: she arrived there, accompanied only by a coachman and a footman. The gardener's wife came to light the fire and undress her; it seemed to her as if she were entering a tomb. It was night, and the lamp seemed like the lamp of a sepulchre. The whole of the furniture in her chamber was covered with crape, to protect it from the damp and dust. They seemed to her like shrouds.

"Yet, it was here *he* came!"

Thus at the time the regent was still weeping, madame de Parabère had already forgotten the regent. She asked the gardener's wife for some brown bread and fruit: she took this frugal repast, while warming her feet before the fire, at the moment that the regent was pouring himself out at her table, bumpers of Constance wine.

"Is he still at Saint-Cloud?" asked she of herself.

She smiled with the air of a conqueror.

"It was I who left him: D'Averne is my witness.

I know the regent: he is likely enough to drive her from his presence; it is true he will recall her to-morrow."

Madame de Parabère allowed herself to be carried away by the swelling flow of her recollections of former times. Her chamber was eloquent, and spoke to her of Martial. It was there—before that chimney—that he had, one evening, fallen a suppliant at her feet. That withered bouquet, which a breath of air would reduce to powder, had been left there by Martial. It was Martial who had read, with his impassioned and sonorous voice, out of that book which there lay open at that fervid page. Martial was everywhere. The marchioness went and opened, with still greater emotion, the door of the boudoir and advanced, with an unsteady step, toward the window looking out on the espaliers.

"Ah!" said she, drawing the curtains aside, "why did I not die the last time he came!'"

She looked out into the park.

"Yes, all is the same: the autumn, the leaves whistling in the wind, and cracking beneath the feet, and the moon, too — the moon, that always returns."

She leaned her head against the window.

"It was through that dark walk he used to come; and I used to hear, when the wind blew from that quarter, the galloping of his horse over the hills, and see sparks flash beneath its feet. The horse itself seemed to be in love; it flew along so rapidly."

Carried away more and more by the charm of her recollections, she opened the window.

"Great Heaven!" exclaimed she, covering her heart with her hand.

She had heard the violent galloping of a horse across the hill.

"What madness!" said she; "I thought it was he. Poor boy! If he be not dead, he must have suffered a thousand deaths. Those who leave for the Indies, when they are in love, never return to France."

The marchioness leaned over the balustrade of the window, and let fall a tear for Martial. Without knowing it, she remained with her eyes riveted on the dark linden walk. All at once, she uttered a shriek and fell down in a fainting fit.

"Madame—madame—be not terrified—it is I!"

Monsieur de Montluzun was in the boudoir as soon as his words.

"Marie—Marie—look up, so that I may die at your feet."

Martial carried the marchioness into her chamber, before the fire, and clasped her sobbing with joy, to his heart. She opened her fine eyes.

"Martial, tell me that I am neither mad nor in a dream. It is impossible. It is not you!"

"It is not I! Ah! you are not aware that for the last two years, since I was condemned to the Bastille for that duel—you are not aware, I say, that, since that time, I have seen you nearly every day!

But you are at last come back to the château, where I was waiting for you, madame."

"Yes," said she sorrowfully, "it is here that I passed my life, and it is here that I wish to die. Martial, when I am dead, will you forgive me?"

"Madame, you doubtless speak of death because you see me here again."

"No, Martial, it is because I feel that death is in my heart. I am twenty-four years old, and it was at twenty-four that my mother died."

Here madame de Parabère again fainted. But this time monsieur de Montluzun could not bring her to herself again. He turned giddy, and rang the bell; but, as no one came, he called aloud with all his might. At last the gardener's wife, still half-asleep, entered. On seeing Martial, she uttered a cry of fright.

"A doctor!" said he.

The marchioness raised her eyelids.

"No," said she, "not a doctor, but a priest. All will soon be over."

She pressed Martial's hand, disengaged herself from his hold, and fell upon the sofa.

"What! madame, am I then come to see you die?"

"Yes, Martial, yes; I am about to die; but do not let us complain. A broken chain of roses can never be joined again, when all their leaves are withered. Let us content ourselves with the remembrance of bygone times."

"But you were not ill," said Martial, without listening to her.

"Not ill! Had I the time to be so? By dint of smiling at court, I ended by believing in my smiles, my joy and gayety. Fêtes and suppers have half-killed me, and my heart has achieved the rest; for—why should I not tell you, Martial?—I always loved you."

Monsieur de Montluzun wept in silence.

"Now that I have made my confession, Martial, you must leave me. I wish to be left alone with death, for I want to have time for repentance."

"No, madame, I will not leave you. If you die, I will pray for you; if you live, I will live for you. Reflect that I have waited two years for you; I have counted the days and the nights, with the hours of the day and the seconds of the night. Oh! what a hell it was! but in the distance I saw paradise."

"Poor boy! But how did you happen to come here to-night?"

"Your lackey cost me a hundred louis a-year. You must recollect how he used to stop, under a thousand pretexts, on the road; he did this to send me word where you were going. A hundred times was I on the point of throwing myself at your feet at Saint-Cloud; but, by doing so, I should have lost everything."

The physician of Saint-Heraye arrived at this moment. He sorrowfully shook his head on seeing the lips and eyes of the marchioness.

"I asked for a priest," said she, "for I feel that to-morrow, if I still breathe, I shall no longer be conscious of what I say. This last shock has finished me. Delirium is taking hold of my brain."

The sight of Martial beneath the window of the boudoir had proved a mortal blow for madame de Parabère. She was placed in her bed, but she slept not; she prayed. Martial, who bent over her and staggered under his grief, did not dare speak to her of his love, which was his religion. From time to time, she appeared to comprehend the suffering of monsieur de Montluzun; she took his hand and pressed it to her heart, which was beating violently.

I will not relate all the incidents of the agony, which commenced that night and continued for five weeks.

Martial never quitted the marchioness; but she was nearly always occupied in prayer, even in her hours of delirium. Three days before her death, the doctor, speaking in a whisper to Martial, informed him that the regent had just died.

"I hear," said madame de Parabère.

She had a terrible crisis, after which she fell into a disturbed and painful silence. It was in vain that Martial spoke to her by both look and word; she would not answer. At last, on the day of her death, after having passed several hours in a state of delirium, she called Martial to her, and said to him, through her sobs:—

"Martial, you will never forgive me when I shall have told you the whole truth."

"Speak, madame: I am resigned to everything."

The marchioness raised herself upon her elbow, feeling that what she was about to say would stifle her.

It was twilight, and the winter sun cast its pale rays across the chamber; the ravens were heard croaking on the snow.

"Martial," said madame de Parabère, who was already as white as the shroud which was soon to envelop her—"Martial, I loved you; but I loved the regent. I love you still; but I feel that if he calls me on high, I shall go to him. . . . . ."

After having said these words, madame de Parabère hid her face, and no longer dared to look on Martial.

He remained for an hour deprived of speech, and motionless—changed by grief into a marble statue.

"Madame," said he at last, in a voice choked with sobs, "I loved you—I love you still—and I shall love you ever."

But madame de Parabère no longer heard the voices of earth—not even the voice of Martial!

ABELARD AND HELOISE.

Our age has this excellence, that the horizon expands indefinitely around it. It is at once the age of history, of philosophy, of criticism. It sees, it understands, it judges. In proportion as the horizon expands, the point of view is elevated. Poetry, which is often spoken of as an exile, is more than ever domesticated with us. She gives the historian his lively colors, the philosopher his elevation, the critic his perspective. Therefore, let us not doubt, the nineteenth century will leave behind it imposing and durable monuments. In the middle ages, cathedrals were built, which have come down to us; certain books of our time will in like manner traverse future ages. After the book of stone written for the eyes, comes the book written for the soul.

There are two ways of writing history.

Ardent imaginations have not the patience to light the lamp of tombs and monuments; they read the epitaph, decipher the inscription on the pediment, and pass by, more interested by a tuft of full-blown wall flowers on the top of the monument, than by the monument itself. They scarce open the old manuscript, resplendent with illuminations. Tradition is their touchstone; a name recalls to them an epoch—a portrait, a picture. They throw their hearts into the past, and contemplate the passions of former ages through the passions of the present—Abelard through Jean-Jacques or Werther, and Charlemagne through Bonaparte.

Studious minds who like the smell of the lamp, go direct to history, without revery or passion; for them the man disappears in the historian; they would willingly give an eloquent phrase for a useful note. In a ruined monument, they are more struck by its characteristics of its period, than its picturesque aspect. The expression of the head strikes them, and not the outline—the sense of the inscription, and not the letter. They breathe with a melancholy pleasure, the atmosphere of half-open tombs. Truth is their muse; they seek and follow it everywhere. They do not close the long-conned book, before having, so to say, translated it word for word. They avoid the poets, or know how to discover truth through fiction.

"Abelard is less known than celebrated, and his fame is romantic rather than historical," says his historian, Charles de Rémusat. And, in truth, the form of Abelard presents itself to us with that tender and passionate attraction which Tasso, Goethe, and Châteaubriand have imparted to their creations. Are not Tancred, Werther, or Réné, the poetical brethren of Abelard? Are they less real? Do we love them less? Imagination, whatever may be said to the contrary, will always hold a place in history, as truth does in romance. Has not romance been penned with history in view?

It is true, that, in the very life of Abelard himself, we find history and romance combined; there are two men enwrapped in one—the philosopher and the lover of Heloise—the head and the heart. We are acquainted with the heart; but, till now, no one has studied the grand character of the theologian's head.

Poetry is a maiden who lives on memory. Whether she be called Calliope or Erato, whether she sing of heroes or lovers, whether she listen to the world, or to her heart, it is ever to the past that she turns. God too takes pleasure in composing romances: these are immortal; those which we make are usually but the poor paraphrase of the romances of the great master. Is the Heloise of Rousseau, an Abelard of another age, equal to the Heloise created by God himself?

Is not this the proper place to introduce the following fine passage from the historian?

"The letters of Abelard and Heloise form a unique monument in literature; they have sufficed to immortalize their names. Less than a hundred years after the tomb had closed over them, Jean de Meung translated these letters into the vulgar idiom; and his translation is still extant, an irrefragable proof of the deep interest with which they soon inspired our poets. As the language of the passions, which are eternal, is, however, changeable, and follows the vicissitudes of taste and the fashions of the mind, the primitive expressions of the ardent and profound love contained in these letters have been retranslated more than once in order to be modified, altered, or embellished. If the author of the poem of *The Rose* imparted to them, in his Gallic idiom of the thirteenth century, an humble *naïveté* disdained by Abelard and unknown to Heloise, Bussy-Rabutin, in finished French of the seventeenth century, lent them a tone of elegant gallantry, another sort of falsehood. Thus an historical episode, supported by authentic documents, has become one of those literary themes which are preserved and altered by tradition, and are renewed according to the genius of the various epochs and the various writers. Perhaps, too, there were periods when no one knew that the original letters still existed, and with many the names of Abelard and Heloise have often been on the point of being confounded with those of the heroes of romance. On several occasions, their adventures have been appropriated as subjects for tales or imaginary correspondence. Authors have not confined themselves to retouching or paraphrasing their letters; they have invented new ones, and reality has given way to fiction. Poetry has also come to play, in its turn, a part; it has lent these lovers of another age the finesse of sentiment, the struggles and remorse which belong to the dramatic morality of modern times. It has distorted their real love, thinking to render it more interesting; and such is the power of certain literary conventionalities, that these distortions sometimes appear more natural than the truth itself. The Heloise of Pope became, for a time, the Heloise of history to such an extent, that the author of the *Génie du Christianisme*, when sketching the Christian lover, could think of no better description of her than that found in the verse of Colardeau!* The feeling for the real, has however, begun to show itself among us; and it is in their authentic correspondence that we now look for Abelard and Heloise. What has just been said, seems to me sufficient to make it known. We can not think of comparing these letters to any others but the *Lettres Portugaises*, unless the latter are the work of imagination. In the first, the hidden recesses of two suffering souls appear to us under forms agreeing with the spirit of the times; love and grief borrow the language of erudition without discernment, of art without beauty, and of philosophy without depth; but, in spite of this

* In the "Genius of Christianity," part ii., verse cv., are to be found these words: "Wife of Abelard, she [Heloise] lives, and she lives for God." I like better the opinion expressed by D'Alembert, in answer to Rousseau: "When you say that women *do never know how to describe, or even feel love*, it must be because you have not read the 'Letters of Heloise;' or read them only in the version of some poet who has spoiled them."

pedantic language, it is still the heart that speaks, and the heart is in some measure eloquent of itself. Though taste may not have embellished the temple, yet the fire which burns on the altar, is a divine fire. Happier than thought, passion can more easily dispense with perfection in form, and, in whatever garment unskilful art may have clothed it, like the goddess in Virgil, it is known by its step: *Incessu patuit dea.*"

The historian has divided his book into three parts: the life of Abelard, his philosophy, and his theology. The first part forms in itself an entire book, showing us, as it does, the life and passions of the noblest character of the twelfth century. Never before had the beautiful face and beautiful soul of Heloise been shown, surrounded by a like glory of grace, love, and grandeur; never before had so pious a hand woven that thorny crown of human passions, beneath which still lurks the perfume of its withered roses. Monsieur de Rémusat has well understood "the first of women," that illustrious character, whom Pierre le Vénérable compared to Deborah the prophetess, and to Penthesilea the queen of the Amazons, that sublime creature who retained her love beneath the sackcloth of the nun, at the altar's foot, until the hour of death — that philosopher with a woman's heart, who maintained the sacred liberty of thought, in the austere cell of the Paraclete.

Till now, poetasters and pedants, have misrepresented the character of this adorable woman; Monsieur de Rémusat has sketched her with pious respect, enthusiastic love, and fervent adoration for beauty embellished by genius. The historian seems to know and understand Heloise better than Abelard himself did. Abelard was only a learned philosopher like Aristotle. Thus, if he relates how he came to love Heloise, he affirms, after saying that with his name, youth, and person, it was not possible for him to fear a refusal, that the love of science created between her and himself a community of ideas and sentiments; and that, in consequence, he resolved to love Heloise. "He was mistaken," says his historian, "a noble and hidden instinct told him that he ought to love her who had no equal."

It is not known how Abelard first met with Heloise. He was desirous of teaching her the sciences and love at the same time. He called on Fulbert, the canon, who consented to intrust him with the literary and theological education of his niece. With Fulbert's consent and recommendation, he could "give her lessons night or day, and correct her as a master, if the pupil were disobedient."—"What more shall I say?" exclaims Abelard in his confessions; "we had but one house, and soon we had but one heart." Words truly eloquent in their simplicity. "Abelard, impatient and enchanted, used that genius which threw all the schools of the world into commotion, to seduce a poor, inexperienced, and confiding girl. The pleasures of science, the joys of thought, the emotions of eloquence, everything, in fact, was employed to charm, trouble, and plunge into intoxicating and unknown frenzy, that tender and noble heart which never had but one love, and but one grief—that heart which Heaven itself was not able to dispute with its lover. But what lessons did Abelard give Heloise? Did he teach her the secrets of language and the learned arts of antiquity? Did he lead her penetrating and inquiring mind along the rugged paths of dialectics? Did he reveal to her the obscure mysteries of faith in the luminous language of philosophical reason? Or did he read to her those poets which he quotes in his most austere works? and did the professor of theology recite to his pupil, in his acknowledged and talented style of diction, the impure verses of the 'Art of Love'? What, in short, what, I ask, was the book which served, as in the narration of Dante, to seduce this woman, the historical model of the poetical Francesça de Rimini? No one can answer this, and yet it is well known that Abelard's whole talent was the accomplice of his love. Triumphant passion at last hurried the lovers on to the limits of its empire. Everything was sacrificed to their unalloyed and boundless happiness, and all the gradations of love were traversed by them. Even the duties of instruction, even the master's punishment, became (it is Abelard's avowal) impassioned sports, *whose pleas-*

ure surpassed the sweetness of all perfumes. All that love can dream of, all that the imagination of two powerful minds can add to its transports, was realized in the intoxication and novelty of an unknown happiness."

The romance continued to grow more and more poetical and adventurous, until the day when Heloise, the erudite and impassioned girl, pronounced in a voice stifled by her sobs, that lament which Lucan makes Cornelia utter, when she first sees Pompey after the battle of Pharsalia:—

"Nunc accipe pœnas,
Sed quas sponte luam."

The sacrifice was great, unbounded, worthy of herself: she abandoned her lover, and all the joys of love, of the world, and of liberty, to enchain herself, without faith or hope, to the divine spouse, who was henceforth to occupy all her thoughts, without descending into her heart.* Abelard tries in vain to prove to her, that she is working for Heaven, and that she is agreeable to the Almighty.† "Beware

* "Heaven knows that, in every position in life, I am more fearful of offending thee than of offending Heaven; it is thou more than Heaven that I desire to please; it was thy order, and not divine love, that made me assume this dress. Behold, then, what a wretched and deplorable life I lead, enduring here so many useless ills, and having no reward in a future life."—*Letter of Heloise.*

† "Thou hast already given him a troop of spiritual daughters. What a deplorable misfortune it would be, if now, abandoning thyself to the defilements of earthly pleasures, you should unhappily give birth to children of earth, in place of that numerous family you have joyfully bestowed on Heaven!"

of being no more than a woman, you who have surpassed man, and who have changed the malediction of Eve into the benediction of Mary." But Heloise is proud of, and frightened at, still feeling the heart of a woman beat within her breast: she is as much a daughter of Eve as a daughter of Mary. It is Abelard who has ceased to be a man, in both heart and mind; each word that he pronounces before the abbess of the Paraclete is stamped with the glacial accent of the words of the Trappist: "Brother, we must die! Yes, brother, we must die!" Such are the words which his heart, dead, but still jealous, continually whispers to the heart of his mistress. I am acquainted with no poem more solemn or more painful than this slow death of the heart of Heloise. It is in vain that she presses against it the Book of Prayer; in vain, that she crowns her thoughts with the bleeding thorns of the Redeemer, her new master; it is in vain that Abelard digs the grave deeper and deeper every day: the heart will not die; it burns beneath the chilling years of age; it beats beneath the shroud, and makes their bleached bones rattle from century to century. Ought we to be astonished that the legend says: "When her corpse was brought to the tomb they had just opened, her husband, who had breathed his last many days before her, raised his arms to receive her, and closed them embraced around her." If Heaven ever permitted a miracle, may we not be allowed to believe in this one? What other woman in the world was so worthy, after so long a widowhood, of being embraced in the tomb by him who was waiting for her in that dark and final rendezvous.

If Abelard, the courageous controvertist, prepared us for the exercise of the liberty of thought—did not Heloise, who, it can be said, courted the sciences merely to give more bounds to her love—did not Heloise, daughter of Eve rather than of Mary—proclaim, by her passion and struggles, the liberty of the heart?

Abelard did not always give proof of a noble mind, and never of a noble heart. It is the love of Heloise which has rendered his glory immortal. If he sometimes discovered the truth, it was not out of love for truth, but, as Leibnitz remarks, owing to his desire to think differently from others.

The philosophy and theology of Abelard, form an almost arid waste, shunned by nearly all, even by the most adventurous thinkers. Light and life are, however beginning to be scattered over it; but of all those who, while traversing these deserted plains, have attempted to reunite the golden chain of philosophy, so long snapped asunder, very few, even by dint of patient research among these wild thorns of scholasticism, have succeeded in gathering any flowers of true science. The history of the human mind, of learning, and the church, with the entire history of thought in the middle ages, at last, again lives before our eyes. Much ridicule has been thrown on the art of the scholastics, which consisted of decomposing language and argument, and which rather descended to words than raised itself to ideas; but every system of philosophy has had a cause for existing, for reigning a year or a century. The Omnipotent has not permitted the human mind to arrive at science by a road free from darkness and danger.

Now that modern ideas have taken so rapid a flight toward regions more elevated than those in which the subtleties of scholasticism so long held philosophy enchained, Abelard owes his fame principally to his having so ardently combated for liberty of thought, and to his having been one of the first who, in that restless and courageous age, fearlessly entered the mysterious paths of the ideal world, and discovered that the Almighty, who spread darkness around man, does not forbid him to seek the light.

The star of Abelard—a star lost in the firmament of the learned, only glitters now in the quiet of the finest nights of summer. But how many once brilliant stars are there which no longer shed their light on us! Stars of Plato, of Aristotle, of Locke, of Kant, of Descartes, of Leibnitz, of Spinosa, where are you? Glory, rather than truth, form your rays. O Truth! Truth! shall we never repose an hour with thee under the tree of science? Will it be always necessary for the human mind to pass through the tomb, in order to know whither it is going?

THE DEATH OF ANDRE CHENIER.

Much has been written on the ride of Roucher and André Chénier to the guillotine, and much misconception prevailed in relation to the facts. I knew an old military intendant, M. de Soustras, who followed with an anxious eye the fatal cart, without losing sight, for a moment, of the two poet-martyrs. He was a worthy old gentleman, who had retired from the world—almost retired into the other world, as he used to say himself. He is, at this time, much more interested in thinking how he shall again join his friends above, than knowing men's opinion of them here below. He is not, however, entirely a stranger to our philosophy, politics, or literature, but now and then condescends to put on his spectacles and cast a glance over the *public prints* and the new books. He does not understand much of it; he is irritated at hearing such a noise about nothing; Paris seems to him a second Babel; he despairs of the French mind; I have more than once heard him commend himself to M. de Voltaire.

I surprised him one day reading André Chénier.

"Well!" said I, "what do you think of him? he is one of us."

He began to smile. "One of you? Really, you go somewhat far after your captains. André de Chénier is neither one of you nor one of us; like all men of genius, he was his own standard-bearer. Do not fancy that you will attain his purity and grace by breaking up your verses without measure, and giving yourselves the airs of the Greek muse. Take care, monkeys are only good at copying grimaces. Besides, this collection contains two thousand verses too much. Of what use is it to reproduce all these sketches, which have, as yet, but the semblance of design and color? Whatever may be the genius and death of a poet, nothing authorizes such carelessness. We may collect the fragments of an Etruscan vase, which was a masterpiece; but did the potter ever think it worth while to gather up the fragments of a broken jar?"

As I saw that M. de Soustras was in a humor for talking, I took care not to oppose his metaphor, for he would have closed the volume in a pet to return to M. de Voltaire. "You knew André Chénier?" said I to him.—"I have seen him twice—once in prison and once on the scaffold. I saw him die with other eyes, doubtless, than his biographers; I have not, therefore, written on his death. M. de Latouche is a poet: that is the whole story. Besides, I owe him thanks for having nobly executed the will of M.

de Chénier. I regret only that he should have deceived the world about the death of the poet—deceived it to such an extent, sir, that, only yesterday, my daughter was not willing to believe my account of the matter."—"What, then, has M. de Latouche said which is not exact? André Chénier died by the guillotine, I think."—"As to the main facts, he has spoken the truth; that part of the story is engraven on brass: but he is mistaken in the details. What would you expect? he was not present, I imagine; he can only have spoken from hearsay. I who address you have seen and heard."—"Well, tell me what you saw and heard. It is never too late nor too soon for the truth."—"Truth? of what good is truth, if it extinguishes the prismatic hues of falsehood? Is it not better to behold André de Chénier in the poetic death in which his memory has been draped, than in his death simply and actually as it took place?"—"Go on, I beg of you! I am listening. On this sombre theme, the truth can not but be poetic."—"I will tell you, then, without circumlocution, how he died."

M. de Soustras rang for his servant: "Philip, bring me my snuff-box with the portrait."

The servant instantly returned. The old man took the box and opened it—"Very good, there is plenty of snuff."

The box was full. "Whose portrait is that?" I asked.—"It is a portrait, nothing more. Fancy that it is Roucher's snuff-box. That also had a portrait in it. Whose? I was not able to learn."

M. de Soustras, standing by the chimney-piece, went on as follows, closing his eyes as if to look back better into his recollections; never had a great actor on the stage or a brilliant woman better prepared me to be a listener:—

"In those times, my dear sir, though I was young, careless, and a lover, I often, more often than at the present day, had my hours of sadness. I liked tragedy, I liked gloomy pictures. I scarcely dare to confess that I experienced a mournful but attractive charm, in following those red carts which passed from the prison to the guillotine. I seemed to be following the funeral of a friend. Among the condemned, who were looking for the last time at the sky, I sympathized most deeply with a youthful and gentle face; I went so far as to believe, in my sad fancies, that it was another self whom I was attending at his death-bed—that horrible death-bed! The 7th Thermidor, I was following the red cart for the fifth time. There was curiosity in this action, but there was also a mournful feeling of respect which should acquit me on the score of curiosity. The red cart was a bier which I, perhaps, was the only one who followed with a prayer to God. On that day I recognised among the victims the poor Baron Trenck, and the mournful André de Chénier. I was ignorant then that the latter was a great poet, but I did not the less pity him, for he was then the poet of death. As he looked at the crowd over the heads of the gend'armes aud the *sans culottes*, doubtless in the vague hope of meeting a friend, his ardent and melancholy glance met mine. We recognised one another; it seemed as if a ray of sympathy had touched us both at once. I saluted him mournfully, but we lost sight of each other. I broke through the crowd with desperate energy, and threw myself against the horses at the risk of incurring the threats of the guards: when I saw André de Chénier again, he seemed to be listening with resignation to some words of his neighbor, Roucher, you know—another poet whom death has ennobled. They were both on the first seat, in company with three or four unknown persons, gloomy and silent. Roucher was the most animated of the whole party; he talked incessantly without knowing well what he was saying, I fancy. He had in his hand a tortoise-shell snuff-box, very similar to this one; he rapped it with the ends of his fingers, opened it with a jerking motion, and offered snuff to André de Chénier. The young poet, more grave and more reserved, slowly shook his head in sign of refusal, either because he did not like snuff, or disdained to raise his spirits in this manner in his last moments. Roucher took a large pinch, twitching at the same time with his eyes. He recommenced talking. After some words, interrupted by the cries of the crowd and the rattle of the wheels, I found that he was speaking of Robespierre. His companion listened with an absent air. I saw well that he was listening to himself; and, in truth, how much he had to say to himself on such a day and at such an hour!

"I was suddenly pushed back into the crowd by a press of curious persons. When I raised my head to again behold the mournful spectacle of the cart, Roucher, always in excitement, rapped his snuff-box, opened it with a loud creak, and, without regarding the refusals of André de Chénier, offered it to him. The young poet again refused by a motion. This time, I think, I remember that Roucher spoke of his daughter; he raised his head and looked at the crowd. Not seeing a single beloved face among all these curious countenances, he took another pinch of snuff, as if to raise his spirits. He did not weep, but the most bitter grief was expressed in his features. André de Chénier was still pale, sad, and silent; he replied from time to time by a word, to all which the bard of the *Months* uttered. What can I tell you! I was not able to register their words in my memory; besides, I heard very badly, scarcely a word here and there amid the noise of the populace and the tramp of the horses. A third time Roucher placed his snuff-box before the poet, who again refused by a sign. For ten times, perhaps, did Roucher repeat this movement, without recollecting that his friend had refused. At last, André de Chénier could not refrain a smile at this obstinacy, but a smile of sadness, as if he had divined the trouble of mind with which Roucher was overwhelmed."

M. de Soustras, in order to paint Roucher the better, took a pinch every moment, taking care to spill plenty of snuff on his shirt-bosom.

"You see that my box is almost empty? Well, there was scarce a pinch or two in Roucher's when the cart reached the place de la Révolution. André de Chénier was the most pale, Roucher the most animated; the first imprisoned his heart, the second allowed his full liberty. In the animation of conversation, Roucher did not see that they were at the place of execution. For the last time he shook his snuff-box, opened it, and passed it before his friend, who no longer saw anything. As usual, Roucher took a pinch, not without some trouble, the box, as I told you, being almost empty. He raised his fingers to his nose, but his hand suddenly fell; he had seen the guillotine.

"At this moment, André de Chénier roused a little: far from overcoming him, this sight of the guillotine restored all his energies. He took Roucher's hand and spoke to him with emotion. I have no fear of being mistaken in repeating, among other words of his: "*Courage, friend . . . other shores.*"—"*But my wife! my daughter!*" exclaimed Roucher.—"*It is a dream which has come to an end,*" replied the poet.

"I heard some other disconnected words. A wave, pushed on by another wave, bore me, in spite of all my efforts, more than twenty paces from the cart. It was impossible to get any nearer; I contented myself with looking, hoping to gather their thoughts from their faces. Roucher could not conceal his grief and despair; he struggled, to the end, against the violent death which awaited him. André de Chénier rose above death, on some presentiment of his future apotheosis; it seemed to me that his glance saw further than the guillotine: I may be mistaken; but this much is certain, that at the moment when the rumor was spread about that Madame Roucher had just fallen among the crowd in a swoon, André de Chénier appeared to be preventing his friend, by conversing earnestly with him, from being overwhelmed by this heart-rending fact. Meanwhile the horrible *sans culottes* had made the summons. Privileges existed even in front of the guillotine, the privilege of dying first! The two poets were reserved for the last of the spectacle. André de Chénier mounted the scaffold gravely, passed his hand over his forehead, glanced at the sky, and committed himself to the executioner's assistants with resignation or torpor. I wished to see if his friend Roucher was watching him in his last moment. I do not think that he thought of doing so; he had lost command of himself, he struggled aimlessly like a wrestler who is fighting against death. I did not see the noble head of Chénier fall; I was apprized of the fact by the cries of the spectators. You know that Roucher was executed the last. He was led, or rather pushed on to the scaffold. He did not look above, but among the crowd. Chénier fled this world without regret; he asked an asylum in heaven like a traveller who is about to cross the boundaries of a strange land; Roucher was not one of those poets who find a country everywhere, but of those who are attached to the hearthstone beside which the children sport in their mothers' arms. Roucher had a wife and children who loved him: we should not, therefore, be astonished that his last glance was for this world."

M. de Soustras paused. This recital had somewhat fatigued him; he placed himself in his easy chair again, and adjusted his wig. "But the verses of Racine?" said I to him.—"The verses of Racine? what do you mean? do you believe that story too? There was nothing said about Racine on the road to death. But stay—I fancy I recollect—yes, I recollect that the portrait on Roucher's snuff-box was that of Racine."

Such is very nearly what I gathered from the old man. I will not adduce his gray hairs to consecrate his words. Can one, however, give full and entire confidence to recollections inscribed fifty years ago in a memory which has been a thousand times ransacked? However that may be, I have considered that it was a duty to reproduce this tardy testimony. Has it not all the tone of truth? I know too well that Truth is an adventuress whom each one dresses according to his fancy. How often, in the dread of showing Truth naked—or rather, in the dread that she should not appear sufficiently probable—have men thrown over her shoulder the many-colored scarf of falsehood!

THE MARQUIS DE SAINTE-AULAIRE.

AN ELECTION AT THE FRENCH ACADEMY IN 1706.

In 1706, the report was circulated about Paris—at the court and in the city, among the nobility, the men of letters and the clergy, that M. Jacques Testu, abbé de Belval had just died. Who was this abbé de Belval? A scholar, an historian, a philosopher, a grammarian, a poet? No, he was one of the Forty. Why did he belong to the academy? Ask M. de Sainte-Aulaire, one of the Forty of the present day. What is beyond doubt, is that the abbé Testu de Belval had succeeded to Bautru, and that he had been immortal for the last forty years. I do not know that he had much wit, I know that he always wanted to be talking, though he had lived at La Trappe with his friend M. de Rancé; this passion for talk, backed by a conceit of the first order, had given him the nickname of *Têtu tais-toi* (*Hold your tongue*). No longer listened to by men, he turned to the women, and among them, doubtless caught some sparks of brilliancy. This feminine delicacy of appreciation, has been adduced by D'Alembert as a proof of the subtlety of the abbé de Belval; he used to say of madame de Montespan and her two sisters, all three celebrated for the grace of their conversation: "Madame de Montespan talks like a person who is reading; madame de Thianges like a person of talent who is dreaming, and madame the abbess of Fontevrault, like a person who is talking."

The title of academician, was not sufficiently elevated for the ambition of the abbé de Belval: he wished to be a bishop; but Louis XIV. always refused, saying that the abbé was not a good enough man to lead others. In his extremity, the poor abbé took a desperate resolution; he went after Ninon de l'Enclos, not doubting but that if he succeeded in converting her, the king, touched by his eloquence would confer on him the first vacant bishopric. But the fair pagan of the seventeenth century, heard the abbé's sermons without gathering the bitter flowers of penitence. "He believes," said she "that my conversion will do him honor, and that the king will at least give him an abbey; but if he can not make a fortune except out of my soul, he runs a great risk of dying without a benefice."

When it was well understood that M. Jacques Testu, abbé de Belval, had departed for the other world, several ambitious literary men took the field in order to succeed him at the academy. There was a great agitation among the Forty, some being for one man, some for another. We will attempt to paint an election session at the French academy in 1706.

(*The scene represents a large hall in the Louvre. A table covered with velvet tapestry. Two urns. A fire on the hearth.*)

CHARACTERS:—*The Forty minus One.*

(CAILLIERES *and* BIGNON *enter together.*)

BIGNON. Well, my dear friend, we are the first on the ground.

CAILLIERES. We ought to have taken the longest road, like La Fontaine.

BIGNON. Do you know who has presented himself?

CAILLIERES. Don't they talk of Ménage?

BIGNON. My dear friend, you don't know what you are talking about; Ménage has been dead a long time.

CALLIERES. Ah! then we must nominate M. Fraguier.

VALINCOURT (*coming up*). It is now the turn of the nobility, they will nominate the marquis de Sainte-Aulaire.

CALLIERES. Ah! has M. de Sainte-Aulaire written anything?

TOURREIL (*saluting them*). Has M. de Sainte-Aulaire written anything! who is it asks such a question?

CALLIERES. After that, whether he has written or not, I shall not look into the matter so closely.

(*The abbé Abeille and the abbé Choisy enter disputing with one another.*)

THE ABBE ABEILLE. When I tell you that M. de Sainte-Aulaire will not be elected.

THOMAS CORNEILLE (*following them*). Then you are going to elect Regnard or Dancourt.

THE ABBE ABEILLE. Who are you proposing there? an actor and a farce-writer—the gravity of the academy—

THOMAS CORNEILLE. In truth, I tell you, you will sink by your gravity. For my part, I give my voice for Regnard.

A group of new-comers form near the door: among them are to be distinguished Mongin, Sacy (the lawyer), Malézieux, La Loubère, the abbé Dangeau, Chamillard, Renaudot, Cousin, Campistron, the abbé de St. Pierre, La Chapelle, Target, Genest, the abbé Tallemand (not Tallemant des Réaux), Clerambault, Mauroy, the abbé Regnier, Sillery, the abbé Fleury, Caumartin—that is to say, all the lower order of the Academy. The cardinal de Polignac, the cardinal d'Estrées, the duke de Coislin, Fénelon, the abbé de Lavau, and the cardinal de Rohan, stand near the fire, and salute with a patronising air the academicians scattered about the hall. Old Thomas Corneille walks about by himself, his hands behind his back.

FONTENELLE (*going up to him after having passed between the great lords and the men of letters*). Well! uncle, do you incline to the marquis de Mimeure, or for the marquis de Sainte-Aulaire?

THOMAS CORNEILLE. For neither one nor the other.

DANGEAU. Marquises who are not able to conjugate the verb *to know*.

FONTENELLE. Whom do you give your vote for, then?

THOMAS CORNEILLE. For those who are absent.

(*The Duke de Coislin, who is to preside on the present occasion, advances jauntily to the table, and makes a sign to the academicians to gather around him.*)

FENELON. M. Despréaux ought to be here; in this place, we can not but wait a little for him, who always holds the sceptre of Parnassus.

THE DUKE DE COISLIN. Boileau no longer attends all the meetings; he did not vote at the last election.

FLECHIER. It is so; but it appears that M. Despréaux wishes to give the academy a lesson to-day; he proposes to oppose with all his power, the election of M. the marquis de Sainte-Aulaire.

FENELON. However, the debate may commence, I hear the voice of M. Despréaux on the stairs.

(*Boileau enters, leaning on the arm of Dacier.*)

BOILEAU. Come, come, I will show them that my mind has not grown old.

THOMAS CORNEILLE (*taking the hand of the old

poet). You come opportunely, you remember that your contemporaries were named Corneille, Racine, La Fontaine, and Bossuet. Let those who love letters unite and open the doors of the academy to an author, and not a great lord.

FONTENELLE (*moving off*). I wash my hands of it.

M. DE COISLIN. The session is opened. The academy, you are aware, is called upon to elect a successor to M. the abbé Testu de Belval, our lamented brother. Among those who seek the honor of filling his chair, are mentioned M. the marquis de Sainte-Aulaire, and M. de marquis de Mimeure, two gentlemen who have distinguished themselves in our wars. There is also M. de Mesme, but —

THOMAS CORNEILLE. I request monsieur the president to read the entire list of candidates.

THE DUKE DE COISLIN. 1. M. the marquis de Sainte-Aulaire; 2. M. the marquis de Mimeure; 3. M. de Mesme; 4. M. Danchet; 5. M. la Monnoye; 6. M. de —

THE CARDINAL DE POLIGNAC (*interrupting*). What is the use of this litany of saints, to be fêted at a later period?

THE CARDINAL DE ROHAN. In the other world.

THOMAS CORNEILLE. I am going in my turn to nominate the actual candidates. I do not doubt but that all good men will salute their names as I read. (*The speaker seeks to catch the eye of Boileau, Fon-*

tenelle, and Fénelon.) They are as follows: 1. Rousseau; 2. Regnard; 3. Dancourt; 4. Bayle; 5. Malebranche; 6. Dufresny; 7. Lesage.

BOILEAU (*with impatience*). What is all this? The academy is not an asylum for atheists and actors.

THOMAS CORNEILLE (*indignantly*). It is Boileau who speaks thus! Atheists! I appeal to M. de Fénelon. Actors! I appeal to—ah! Fontenelle, you too turn away your eyes.

FENELON. No, those who seek the truth, those who mount the sublime height of philosophy, are not atheists, since they mount up to heaven. Because we have had neither Descartes nor Pascal, is that a reason for rejecting Malebranche?

BOILEAU A madman.

FENELON. The madness of some is often more productive than the reason of others.

BOILEAU. Truly, by following your advice, people would go to the academy, as they go to the Petites-Maisons.

THOMAS CORNEILLE (*bitterly*). M. Despréaux will at least tell us who his candidate is; since he likes neither Rousseau, nor Malebranche, nor Regnard, nor—

BOILEAU. I have only a moment left to live, I have nothing to conceal; I will say frankly, that all taste is lost. I have come expressly from Auteuil to protest against the nomination of M. the marquis de Sainte-Aulaire, in the first place, because he has put bad rhymes to bad verses, and in the second, because in these bad verses, he has outraged propriety. Still, as Malherbe said, if he had had the alternative of making these verses or being hanged!

THE ABBE DE LAVAU. I take the liberty, in the name of all fair-minded men, of contradicting M. Despréaux. The verses of M. de Sainte-Aulaire are "dictated by the Graces." I do not wish to compare them with those of M. Despréaux for I confess that I have not read them.

FONTENELLE. The abbé de Lavau is too mischievous to-day; (*maliciously*) we will pardon him to-morrow.

THE ABBE DE LAVAU. I maintain that M. de Sainte-Aulaire is a gallant man, who has good birth and talents.

BOILEAU. I do not contest his titles to nobility, but his titles to Parnassus; and as for you, monsieur, who think so well of the verses of the marquis, you will do me much honor and pleasure, by condemning mine.

THE ABBE DE LAVAU. Once more, I have not read yours.

REGNIER-DESMARAIS (*in a satirical tone*). There is a great deal of talk about the verses of M. the marquis de Sainte-Aulaire. Has he written any?

THE CARDINAL DE ROHAN. He has composed four.

TOURREIL. He has composed five, and these five are as follows: it was at the house of madame the duchess du Maine, who was a thorough cartesian, and used to argue passionately about the vortexes. One day when she had talked a great deal about subtle matter and attraction, she asked the marquis what he thought of all this. He replied to a well-known air:

"What, shepherdess, to you and me,
Are Newton and Descartes?
For two such fools as they must be,
Could never, I am certain, see
The bottom of *the cards*."*

THOMAS CORNEILLE. That is a passable song, but that is no reason why he should enter post haste into the academy, while so many real literary men are kept at the door. We should leave M. the marquis de Sainte-Aulaire to madame the duchess du Maine, especially since, as she has said, she can not do without things she can make no use of.

THE DUKE DE COISLIN. M. Thomas Corneille should remember, that he has come here to vote and not to make epigrams.

FONTENELLE (*smiling*). After all, if we should make our epigrams for ourselves, instead of letting them be made out of doors!

THE CARDINAL DE ROHAN. M. the marquis de Sainte-Aulaire has not only composed the five lines, but also four others—

BOILEAU. Total, nine lines.

THE CARDINAL DE ROHAN (*with impatience*). M. Despréaux does not count those which M de Sainte-

* Des cartes.

Aulaire has composed against M. Despréaux: that explains to us why M. Despréaux comes from Auteuil to Paris. Since the debate is becoming sharp, I will tell the whole truth. M. de Sainte-Aulaire has written an epistle in praise of the king, in which occur these two lines:—

"The satirists he drove away,
Who sought the jester's part to play."

I will not say that that is the whole secret of M. Despréaux's wrath, for M. Despréaux, who knows what satire is, is above its reach.

BOILEAU (*bursting forth*). What is a forgotten couplet to me? I live far from the court and courtiers. I shall have the courage to give my single vote, in favor of a poet worthy of the suffrage of all. I venture to play the braggart here: does any one suppose that my free and unbiased vote is not worth twenty basely begged?

THOMAS CORNEILLE. My brother the Roman could not have expressed himself better; but, once more, you, who refuse your vote to Malebranche, Rousseau, and Regnard, to whom will you give it?

BOILEAU. I will give my vote to M. the marquis de Mimeure.

(*Murmurs, bursts of laughter, whispers.*)

THOMAS CORNEILLE. It was worth your while to make your journey from Auteuil! You want to proscribe a poet of the court in favor of a poet of the court. Marquis for marquis: I like the first one the best. I have applauded your thoroughly republican freedom; but I see, with sorrow, that I am the sole representative here of the party of letters. Fontenelle himself, the nephew of the great Corneille, has passed over to the enemy. Fénelon, it is true, thinks as I do; but Fénelon does not dare to think aloud. Adieu! I am going and shall not return. (*He goes out.*)

THE ABBE DE LAVAU. M. Despréaux should be willing, in respect to M. de Sainte-Aulaire, to believe him on his word. I acknowledge, as any one else, that the author of the *Lutrin* is the legislator of Parnassus, but not at the academy. The academy is a tribunal which recognizes its own laws only. Every academician should consult his own conscience, and not that of another. I propose that M. de Sainte-Aulaire should be judged by his own works. M. Despréaux will plead against him, proofs in hand, and I will plead for him merely by reading his verses.

THE CARDINAL DE ROHAN. I approve of the proposition of M. the abbé de Lavau.

BOILEAU. I like that better; I have in my pocket the condemnation of the marquis de Sainte-Aulaire.

THE ABBE DE LAVAU. And I have his passport. (*With these words, the abbé de Lavau draws from his pocket a manuscript.*)

BOILEAU. Well! read.

THE ABBE DE LAVAU. It is your turn, rather; the defence after the accusation.

BOILEAU. By way of indictment, I will read the verses of the marquis—true nobleman's verses, savoring only of the wine shop of Parnassus.

THE DUKE DE COISLIN. Let M. Despréaux read first; he can criticise afterward.

BOILEAU. These are verses on wine.

FONTENELLE. Anacreon and Horace were not water-drinkers.

BOILEAU. (*Reads.*)

"All the pains of our life by good wine may be healed;
It surpasses the juice of all plants of the field.
When drunk in the morn, it will new strength impart,
And wine in its freshness will gladden the heart.
'Tis wine causes jokes round the table to fly,
'Tis wine, when it's good, make us witty and—dry!
'Tis wine causes man all his thoughts to disclose;
In a word, 'tis from wine that true poetry flows.
Apollo, I'm sure, had ne'er smiled on Corneille,
Were it not that his name is a rhyme for *bouteille;**
No one would have printed the works of Mairet,
But that his is a rhyme for the word *cabaret;*†
Because Baro's like *barrel*, he wonders achieves,
And Paris his lines perfect oracles believes;
And if praise is bestowed on the fair Rabavin,
It is only because her last syllable's *vin*."‡

(*All the academicians laugh and applaud; Boileau tears the paper with indignation.*)

THE CARDINAL DE ROHAN. My opinion is that M. de Sainte-Aulaire had been drinking good wine when he composed these lines.

* Bottle. † Wine-shop. ‡ Wine.

"'Tis wine, when it's good, makes us witty and—dry!"

FENELON. If I dared, I would applaud with all my strength this fine line:—

"'Tïs wine causes man all his thoughts to disclose."

CAMPISTRON (*with a tragic air*). I avow that I side in opinion with M. Despréaux: if good taste is banished from the academy ....

THE CARDINAL D'ESTREES. The question is about good wine, not good taste.

THE ABBE DE LAVAU (*almost overpowered with laughter*). Is it worth while to put in a defence?

TWENTY ACADEMICIANS. Yes! yes! yes!

THE ABBE DE LAVAU. Because .....

THE DUKE DE COISLIN. Read.

BOILEAU (*to Dacier and Campistron*). You will find that he will read passably good lines to them which they will condemn, after having admired that detestable trash which I threw at your feet.

THE ABBE DE LAVAU (*still laughing*). They are lines on wine.

FONTENELLE. He has repeated himself. (*To the cardinal de Rohan.*) The clumsy fellow, he is strengthening Boileau's side.

THE ABBE DE LAVAU *reads.*

"All the pains of our life by good wine may be healed."

SEVERAL VOICES. But these are the same lines.*

* D'Alembert. Notes to the eulogy on the marquis de Sainte-Aulaire.

THE ABBE DE LAVAU. As you say. (*Bursts of laughter.*)

THE PRESIDENT. The case is closed.

They voted. Old Boileau gave openly the famous black ball; the marquis de Sainte-Aulaire was elected without any other opposition.

He was not, however, a young aspirant; his years numbered sixty-three; but it was not long since that he uttered the revealing cry of Correggio. He was born in Limousin about 1643. He remained there during his entire youth, surrounded by gentry who made a parade of their nobility and their ignorance. Weary of the living, he took a fancy to live with the dead; that is to say, he cultivated the acquaintance of Homer and Virgil, Malherbe and Regnier, Rabelais and Montaigne, the poets, the story-tellers, and the philosophers. We are not told whether he lived in intimate familiarity with love. He was too much of a lover in his winter not to have sighed under the exciting dawn of April.

One day he tore himself violently from his seclusion to go to the wars. He did not lay down his sword until he had received the title of general. But at that time, every marquis who had seen fire had his golden spurs.

On his return from the armies he made his *entrée* in society. He went but seldom to Versailles, because there was then another court more frequented by great nobles enamored with poetry: it was the court of the duchess du Maine, who soon surnamed the marquis de Sainte-Aulaire her *old shepherd.* It was she who inspired him with the four lines of which the cardinal de Rohan wished to speak. He was supping with the duchess. He was thoughtful—which was at that time an impertinence.—"My Apollo," said she to him, "you are thinking of some rebellious Daphne. Pray tell me your secret." He replied with all the grace of an Italian improvisatore:

> "The deity who fain would see
> The secret in my breast contained,
> Were I Apollo, she should be
> Fair Thetis, and the day should end."

After all, Boileau was in the wrong. These lines are charming. Anacreon could not have done as well, nor Boileau either. For my part, I would give the whole of the treatise on the *sublime*, without counting the Ode on the taking of Namur, for these four lines. They are immortal. How many more famous poets would like to attach their works to these four lines to obtain a ray of the smile which will greet them for a thousand years hence.

The marquis de Sainte-Aulaire died at a hundred, like Anacreon his master—like Fontenelle his friend. A fine time that was, when one could make the tour of a century without meeting a revolution, when one became a general for having passed the Rhine, and an academician for having improvised four lines. No, it was not a fine time. How much better do I like our great passions, our serious follies, our tempests, and our shipwrecks! They were in the ebb, we are in the flood; they lived a hundred years reckoning by the almanac, we live a thousand reckoning by the heart.

Fontenelle said, as he died: "For nearly a century I have neither laughed nor wept." Let us pity, let us pity those who have never laughed; let us pity, above all, those who have never wept. Let us pity them: the early dawn did not crown their brow with its divine rays; the sentiment which brings us closer to God by unveiling to us the radiant beauties of the Scripture and of nature, those two immortal books of love and of liberty, did not make their hearts leap. In a word, they lived without loving. Let us pity them as Saint Theresa, that Christian Sappho who cast herself into the infinite from the high and rocky precipice of the passions, said of the devil.

COLLE.

A NUMBER OF HIS JOURNAL.

My name is Collé, I am a man of wit, such as you do not often find. I like the play, songs, and suppers; I am in good society, sometimes at the court, sometimes at the tavern. I have illustrious friends; some of them will be hanged if Heaven is just. Anacreon was not worthy to lift my dictionary of comical and merry rhymes, which I used when I was twenty-four, and the days contained twenty-four hours. I was born (I do not doubt that though I do the rest), I was born in the good city of Paris, and am the son of an attorney and a lady of the *bourgeoisie*, who did not fancy that they were to be so famous. At school, I began by admiring Racine, from Racine to La Fontaine, there is but a step. I forsook both to adore Corneille, that proud Roman, forgotten among the Gauls; but my last idol was Molière, Molière who had freed us from the ancients, and who will always be the genius of modern times.

I was born gay; I have always been the prodigal son of gayety, without exhausting that pious and divine treasure of life. I imparted my gayety to everybody; to the ladies of the court as well as to the actresses, to the beauties of the day, as well as the beauties of the night. And when I returned home to myself, it was to kill the fatted calf and to sing again.

It must be confessed, that I was born in an age beloved by Heaven, in which Sisyphus and Tantalus are no longer to be met. The rock of Fable no longer suffocates the passions of men; the golden fruits of life hang from every branch.

Noble age! Let any one talk to me now of Alcibiades and Aspasia, when I see Louis XV. leaning on the snowy shoulder of madame de Pompadour, to meditate on the destinies of France. We have, it is true, some rogues at the court, in the church and the academy; but the finest harvest is not without tares. I hope the future may reap many generations like our own. The factions say that the rabble are hungry: it is all prejudice; I go too often with Piron to the tavern not to know the truth of the matter. Truth does not live at the bottom of a well, but in a tavern. Whoever has seen people drinking, has seen humanity decked in antique garb. I have written a good comedy on this hint, entitled *Truth in Wine.*

My life can not be related, it is the life of all those who have lived, for there are some who have never lived. Fontenelle now numbers his ninety-seven years, but how many passions does he number? He has wished to number many years, according to the almanac. Well! for my part, if there were no almanacs, I should say that I was a thousand years old, and I should not deceive either myself, nor the gallery.

I have loved much here below. Fontenelle never had a perfect love for any one but himself; so, when he comes to die, he will embrace himself very tenderly, lock himself in his arms and say with tears: "Adieu, my friend, I never loved any but you, I regret none but you, I am in despair at quitting you."

For my part, I have poured out my heart like a cup which is always full; my whole secret, is to have wandered from one to another; like the ship with golden scales of the Piræus, I have contended with every sea, and touched at every shore, as long as Heaven has filled my sails. I have not belonged to any academy. The poets are not of the nature of little birds singing in a cage; they are eagles or if you will, geese, but they live on air and space.

I had forgotten: I belong to the academy of the cellar, which begins to be ridiculous now that vanity has effected an entrance into it. By way of parenthesis, I will state, that in those days, as we were supping together gayly enough, Crébillon and some others, three or four noblemen of the court, presented themselves, and asked permission to enter. We begged them to take seats at the table, but they refused, saying that they came out of curiosity. We left them standing, and supped like Sardanapalus, without saying a word to one another. They were waiting all the time for the show to begin. At last, they determined to leave, rather more foolish than when they came in. "Gentlemen," said I to them gravely (although I was between two bottles and two good bottles), "it is our custom to laugh at fools, but not to make fools laugh."

Let us pass on. I have had some little success at the theatre, on account of the *Hunting Party of Henry IV.*, and certain parodies. Like Homer and Molière, like all the geniuses of the first order, I have created a style. To every man according to his works; I have invented the *Amphigouris*.

I transcribe the following, because a remark of Fontenelle's has almost made it immortal.

"How happy to defend our heart
When Love has never thrown a dart!
But ah! unhappy when it bends,
If Pleasure her soft bliss suspends!
Sweet in a wild, disordered strain,
A lost and wandering heart to gain!
Oft in mistaken language wooed,
The skilful lover's understood."

These lines have so much the appearance of common sense, that Fontenelle hearing them sung at madame de Tencin's, fancied he understood something of them, and wished to have them repeated in order to understand them better. Madame de Tencin interrupted the singer, and said to Fontenelle, "Why! you stupid fool, don't you see that the lines are only a bit of nonsense?"—"It resembles so strongly all the verses which I have heard read and sung here," the wit maliciously replied, "that it is not surprising that I should have made a mistake."

But my especial claim is, that I invented the private theatre. I was the authorized purveyor for my lord, the duke d'Orleans. How much wit was thrown away in all those displays and parodies, destined to but an hour's life!

Now I am married—and have no longer anything to do. I have no longer to be busy about myself or my pleasures. My wife has thrown the bridle over my neck; but I have a bridle, I have no longer strength to take the bit in my teeth.

As I frequent Paris and Versailles, the church and the tavern, every place where the intricate comedy of life is played, I am going to write a journal of all that attracts my attention.

THE FIRST NUMBER OF MY JOURNAL.

FIRST PARIS.

(Paris was at Versailles.)

"There's a lass, they say,
Who has her own way
At the court to-day,
And turns it all upside down;
While the virtuous king,
Her praises doth sing;

> Such a very strange thing
> Has astonished the whole of the town."

Madame de Pompadour consoles herself for this song, by singing that of M. de Voltaire or that of the abbé de Bernis.

During the past year, there was quite a disturbance at Paris, made by the vilest of the populace, but without a chief. These infuriated rioters spread themselves about several parts of the city, and killed seven or eight members of the police, crying "*Death to the kidnappers*." It appears, that little vagabond boys, and particularly girls, are picked up with or without right. What for? No one knows. Where are they taken to? It is a state secret. Saturday the 23d, a man, highly esteemed as a spy, was massacred. His name was Parisien. He was very skilful, because formerly he had been a thief, and belonged to the gang of Raffiac, with whom he would have been broken on the wheel, if pardon had not been granted to him, on account of his having been of wonderful assistance in disclosing all the intrigues of these assassins. He was, they say, the best man in the world at finding out a thief.

Apropos to this sedition, M. de Fontenelle related lately, that when he was a young man, happening to be at Rouen, during a revolt which had commenced and which he witnessed from a distance, he asked on going out of his residence, of an old woman who was spinning very quietly at her door: "What is all this noise about, my good mother?"—"Sir," she replied with singular coolness, and continuing to turn her spindle, "it is nothing, my good sir; it is because we are revolting."

Three of the seditious persons who had taken part in the disturbance, were hung at Paris by decree of parliament. This execution might have taken place the day after the riot, and in the military style. So tardy a punishment does not make the impression on the people which is necessary for our quiet and security. All the watch, even the mounted force, was drawn out; there were also six companies of detailed troops, distributed in detachments, along all the approaches to the Place de la Grève; if they were pushed upon they had orders to fall back, join with other troops and fire on those who had pushed them: the soldiers were supplied with powder and ball. Nothing occurred, except that at the execution of the first criminal, some one among the populace saw fit to cry: "*A pardon! a pardon!*" This cry was followed by several others: the executioner who was fastening the neck of the criminal, even suspended his operations, but immediately recovering himself, continued to perform his office.

OFFICIAL NEWS.

The prince de Soubise has lately obtained the governorship of Flanders, vacant by the death of the young duke de Boufflers, who died the fifteenth of this month of the small-pox, at the age of twenty.

The count de Clermont, was not able to obtain this governorship of the frontiers, because the king does not bestow such on the princes of the blood, but he has obtained that of Champagne, formerly belonging to M. de Soubise.

On the 26th, madame the dauphiness was brought to bed of a princess, which threw the court into a consternation, similar to that which the loss of a battle which would open the gates of Paris to the enemy, would cause. The population of valets who inhabit Versailles, and there are many of them here, are afraid, apparently of wanting masters.

FOREIGN POLITICS.

Popular attention is very much occupied at Paris and London, with the prince of Wales, *the celebrated Pretender.* I am informed that he was arrested at the opera. Everybody knows the circumstances and the opinion of the public about this adventure; but everybody does not know that madame de Tallemont, who had one of her lackeys put in the Bastille with the Pretender's people, wrote the next day the following letter to M. de Maurepas:

"The king, monsieur, has just covered himself with immortal glory, by causing the arrest of Prince Edward. I do not doubt but that H. M. will have the *Te Deum* sung, to thank God for a victory which does him so much honor. But, as my lackey, La Prairie, who was taken on this glorious day, can not add anything to the laurels of H. M., I beg that you will send him back to me."

It is known that the prince was arrested by six sergeants of the French guards; and on this madame the princess de Conty remarked, that he was the sole Englishman whom this regiment had taken, since the commencement of the war.

RELIGION.

The curé of Saint-Sulpice, possesses a truly primitive simplicity. Lately, when he announced the jubilee, he announced from the pulpit to his parishioners, "that there would be exhortations delivered at different hours, for the various classes of persons connected with his parish."

"At six o'clock every evening," he added, "there will be a sermon to the people and to servants, religion will be treated in a very natural manner."—Very natural manner!

We are also assured, that some days afterward, in announcing the processions for the jubilee, he said: "We shall go first to Notre-Dame, then to Sainte-

Croix, thence to Saint-André-des-Arts, and end with the Petites-Maisons."

All this possesses a simple beauty.

I have met with the abbé de Boismorand, otherwise called the abbé Sacredieu, because he was the most accomplished swearer of his time. He was accustomed to play high. When he lost, he used to look up to heaven and say: "Ay, ay, I will send you souls, do you take care not to lose them!"

The famous gambler, Passavant, swore still worse than the abbé Sacredieu. Thus this winter, the latter having a continuous run of ill-luck, and at last at a loss for a new impiety to utter, exclaimed: "O Heaven! I can say nothing more to you, but I hand you over to Passavant."

DRAMATIC CRITICISM.

SEMIRAMIS, a tragedy, by M. de Voltaire. CATILINA, a tragedy, by M. de Crébillon.

"New blasphemy,
Old piety,
Cheap finery
And foolery;

"Naught comes amiss
In Semiramis;
There was ne'er, I wis,
Such hash as this."

I know very well that it does not become a scapegrace like me, to criticise M de Voltaire, but I am, in short, the glow-worm of Parnassus; my light is visible when no other is by. I shall say, therefore, that M. de Voltaire has not the manly pride of tragedy, and that he does not in writing, await the hour of inspiration.

I like Crébillon better. He had in *Catilina* a fine success at court.

Madame de Pompadour has taken the censor's scissors, and cut out these lines of Probus to Fulvia.

> "'Tis thus that ever, to your rage a prey,
> You and your like maintain imperial sway;
> For you have never loved. Your haughty heart
> Would make the lover play the minion's part.
> It seems to you but just that you should reign;
> And you the noblest lover would disdain,
> Unless unto your beauty's power be bowed
> Justice, the laws, his country, and his God."

Unfortunately for a tragedy or a comedy, whoever is armed with the scissors of the censor, is armed with those of the Fates or of the canon Fulbert.

Voltaire now takes a singular mode of attracting an audience to his pieces: he makes the play pay the public; he gives two thirds of the pit and boxes to his nieces, or some other women of his acquaintance; in a word, the players have assured Dutartre, that the success of *Semiramis* cost him eight hundred livres out of his own pockét, beyond the receipts of the fifteen representations.

FRENCH ACADEMY.

There is a vacant chair. The abbé Terrasson is dead. When they wished to confess him, he said with a weak and falling voice to the priest who presented himself for this pious office: "Monsieur, I am utterly exhausted, I can no longer speak, and I have besides entirely lost my memory, but there is Fanchette my housekeeper, who has lived with me for twenty years; let her confess for me, I beg of you, and you can judge afterward whether you can give me absolution." The fact is well authenticated, singular as it is.

Piron has presented himself; it is the turn of a poet: they will appoint a financier.

The last time they appointed a nobleman, the maréchal de Belle-Isle. He had the famous black ball which is a mark of infamy. It was some rogue among these gentlemen who gave it, so as to throw on Duclos the suspicion of having put it in. In truth, as he had been the only one who had expressed an opinion against the maréchal in respect to the visits, no one else could be accused with probability; but with a prudence almost incompatible with his vivacity, Duclos had taken the precaution to keep his black ball in his pocket; when he saw the one which had been placed in the urn, he threw down his own, and said, "Gentlemen, I have forgotten to give back my black ball, there it is." This proceeding confounded the person who had played the trick; the abbé d'Olivet is suspected of it, as he has already accumulated several charges of like meanness against himself.

POETRY.

ELEGY BY A WOMAN OF SENTIMENT.

"You have sworn to love me ever,
But so coldly you did swear,
All your vows, I fear, can never
Heal the anguish that I bear.

"Then your idle talk give over,
And the oaths that once you swore;
Be yet, if you will, my lover,
But I pray you, swear no more.

"We have acted a strange part, love!
Why do you my steps pursue?
Though no other claimed your heart, love,
I was never loved by you."

MISCELLANEOUS NEWS.

I WENT to Saint-Cloud on the 24th, to witness the representation of the *Philosophe Marié.* Madame the duchess de Chartres played the part of Céliante, M. the duke de Chartres that of the uncle (with more liveliness and truth than old Duchemin); the chevalier de Pont did well with that of the marquis du Lauret, whom no one knew anything of, as the part has always been abandoned to indifferent performers. Madame de Forcalquier played the part of Mélite tolerably well, imitating somewhat the style of Gaussin. M. de Montauban, who played the Married Philosopher, would make an excellent actor; but is he not one already?

The bailli of the palais, before whom madame d'Oppy had been sent, has ordered her provisional release; the husband immediately appealed from this sentence. Two of the three jades implicated in this affair have been imprisoned at Sainte-Pélagie, and the famous Gourdan, remaining in contumacy, has been ridden on an ass, with her face to the tail, according to the ordinary mode of punishment.

French gallantry has caused a great degeneracy here of the institution of the freemasons; scarcely any lodges are kept now except for women; and, quite recently, madame the duchess de Bourbon, having desired to play a part in this celebrated order, was received as grand mistress. A lodge extraordinary was held for this purpose in the Waux-hall of the sieur Torré, at which madame the duchess of Chartres, madame the princess de Lamballe, and many ladies of the court, were present. There was a brilliant illumination; they played at proverbs, and there was a ball.

DECLARATIONS OF BANKRUPTCY.

Gallet, grocer and song-writer, has become a bankrupt; it is fifteen years since I saw anything of him. He was a rogue who wanted neither wit nor literary skill; his songs are well known; he versifies like Piron, is as good a grammarian as Dumarsais; but that will not enable him to escape hanging.

DEATHS AND BURIALS.

On the evening of the 22d, Crébillon the younger lost the only child that he had had by mademoiselle de Stafford, one or two years before he married her.

On the 23d, M. Chauvelin, the only son of the keeper of the seals, was killed in a duel by M. Delagrange, an officer in the guards, brother-in-law of M. Joly de Fleury, acting attorney-general. They had a quarrel at Chambord, at the house of the maréchal de Saxe; they had been reconciled—or, if the truth must be told, Chauvelin had ignominiously begged M. Delagrange's pardon for what he had said to him. The latter made known this disgraceful transaction, and the friends of M. de Chauvelin then forced him to fight.

Madame de Tencin has departed for the other world, without leaving anything to this, except a philosopher, M. d'Alembert.

Madame Duchâtelet is dead also; she has left the fruits of her genius to Voltaire or to M. Duchâtelet, or to Saint-Lambert. They say that Voltaire and M. Duchâtelet have accepted the inheritance on condition that they should not be personally responsible for her debts.

ADVERTISEMENTS IN THE ENGLISH STYLE.

(1 livre, 10 sols the line.)

CAPRON, the tooth-drawer, who is the greatest fool to be found under the sun, was asked on Sunday how he occupied his leisure moments. "In composing the *Pensées* of La Rochefoucault," he coolly answered; "it amuses me, and furnishes a relaxation from my labors."

Capron lives in the rue St. Honoré, at the corner of the rue Richelieu. He gave me a dose of his literature; but I owe it to truth to say that he pulled one of my teeth out for me in a most skilful manner.

C. COLLE, *Editor*.

Read and approved by JOLYOT DE CREBILLON, *royal censor.*

It has been thought that it would be curious to show what a newspaper might be in France in 1750.

To some the world is like the sun to Joshua, it moves; to some others it is a sea which is tossed between its shores, losing at the south what it gained at the north. What is beyond doubt, is that men are always men. We have not attempted to be satirical on the nineteenth century, that age which is so disquiet, and which hangs over an abyss, like Pascal, by the recital of the joyous carnival of royalty and nobility; that would have been satirizing both centuries: we have simply reported, by the mouth of Collé, what composed a day of public and private life a century ago.

THE DAUGHTER OF SEDAINE.

Sedaine had marriageable daughters: one of them, the prettiest, who was called Hyacinthe, had cherished the strange fancy of marrying David. David was not exactly the Apollo Belvidere; his head had an inflexible severity; never had a ray of gayety played about it; his locks were bristling like those of the Cumean sybil. In his portrait, painted by himself, the beholder is struck by the antique expression of the countenance. But can we trust David, painted by himself? Did he not, on setting about to paint his portrait, suffer himself to be dazzled by the vision of some Roman faces of the times of Brutus. Now faces of this description, were not the ideal of marriageable girls about 1780, when the marquises and *mousquetaires* made such a gallant display. Mademoiselle Hyacinthe Sedaine had, however, allowed herself to be captivated by the fame of David, still more than by his face; what she loved in him was the artist; it is never the man as he is, that inspires the passion, but the man grafted on the man by chance, heroism, genius, destiny. Man, as he is, bears only wild fruit; the man grafted on the man, bears fruit of flavor. The first is the rude reality; the second the adored ideal. A man is seen and loved by the eyes of the mind.

David often went to Sedaine's to dinner. On those days, Mademoiselle Hyacinthe had a holyday smile and roses in her hair; she talked to David about his pictures with a siren's voice, for the sirens, before disappearing in the ocean, bestowed their voices on all the damsels who have beauty in their countenances, and love in their hearts. On that day, Mademoiselle Hyacinthe placed herself at her harpsichord, to play the sweetest airs of her friend Grétry. More than once had she found some new inspiration at that same harpsichord. David listened to the first air, said coldly, "*It is pretty!*" and threw himself back in his arm chair to take his siesta. Even if he did not quite go to sleep, poor Mademoiselle Hyacinthe was no gainer, for David was five hundred leagues and twenty centuries away, among the Greeks and Romans. Ah! had Mademoiselle Hyacinthe only been a beautiful antique bust of marble or bronze! but she only had her love, her wit, her youth, her beauty, her soul; David did not always understand such language.

The daughter of Sedaine however, pardoned his abstractions.

"Some day," she remarked to her father, with a hidden tear, "he will at last see that I am here."

David was, as the reader is aware, the head of a school celebrated from its origin. At every competition opened by the academy of Rome, it was always a disciple of David who was crowned; it was desired to decree a national recompense to the master. The king of France, who understood the royalty of Art, wished to have David lodged in the Louvre. That poor Louis XVI., surnamed the Tyrant, by David himself! When the painter at a later date, having become one of the kings of the Mountain, had to provide for the lodgings of Louis XVI., and sent him to prison, did he recall to mind that he was lodged at the Louvre, by the will of Louis XVI.?

Up to this time, David had not thought of marriage, he cared only for the children of his genius. He was forced, in taking possession of his abode at the Louvre, to make some arrangements with the royal architect, Pécoul. He had known his son at Rome. They had often conversed together about their absent family and country. The son of Pécoul had said to David: "I have sisters who are beautiful, you shall choose one, and we will be brothers." On the departure of the painter for Paris, he had given him a letter for his father, but more for the sake of giving him an opportunity of seeing his sisters. More than two years had passed, and the letter lay still untouched in a portfolio of drawings;

when he came across it. "Who knows?" said he, "there perhaps lies the secret of my destiny!" And then for six months he thought no more about it.

He at last presented himself at the house of Pécoul.

"Ah! you are David," said the architect, "you wish an apartment in the Louvre?"

"Yes, monsieur, the king has had the goodness to appoint me one."

"It is not his majesty alone," replied Pécoul, "who could have accorded you this favor; if you had come to see me, some two or three years ago, with a certain letter from Rome, which I am still expecting, who knows but that I might have lodged you at once at the Louvre?"

David had the letter with him; he drew it forth with a blush and handed it, with some agitation to the architect.

"Well," said Pécoul, "this letter can very well wait a little longer? come and dine with me, and we will read it at dessert."

"And the apartment?" said David.

"Some day, sooner or later," replied Pécoul.

David, to pass away the time till dinner, went straight to his friend Sedaine's, who was also lodged at the Louvre, and narrated to him his interview with Pécoul.

"I do not understand it," said Sedaine; "it is an imbroglio."

Hyacinthe was present; a sudden pallor had overspread her features.

"I understand it for my part," she murmured.

She went to her harpsichord, and sang for him the mournful elegy of Richard-Cœur-de-Lion. *A burning fever* . . . . .

A burning fever had seized the poor girl: she knew Pécoul's daughters; if they were not prettier than herself, they were more attractive. David went to dinner. All the luxury of coquetry was put in requisition, all the graces of sentiment brought to bear. Pécoul earnestly desired, that the glory and fortune of David should be the offspring of his house.

At dessert, between the champagne and the sherry, Pécoul took his son's letter and read it aloud. It was like a scene at a theatre. The silence was profound, the young ladies bent their heads with sidelong glances at David. David was questioning the Sphynx. Pécoul as he read the letter, sought to read the eyes of David. The mother alone thought of the writer of the letter, for her son was still at Rome.

This letter was not a long one, here it is:

"I present to you, my very dear father, my best friend; see that he becomes my brother. It is a simple affair enough: he is twenty-five, and you have marriageable daughters; he has genius and you have money."

M. Pécoul had finished reading, but they were still listening.

"You see, ladies," said David at last, as if he were taken by surprise, "that your brother arranges matters in his own way; I am overpowered by the good opinion he has of me, but he does not know that neither a daughter nor a sister are to be forced in respect to marriage. As for myself, who am the only one of my family, it is needless to say, that I shall be happy to people my solitude with beauty and virtue."

To this laborious phrase, in the style of the civic drama then in vogue, Pécoul's daughters replied by an eloquent silence.

David looked at both without well knowing which was destined for him, or which he had the right to destine to himself. The truth is, as to David, his true passion, his true poetry, his true wife, was painting; the other was to be only a superfluity of luxury, which would pass through his life without drawing him along with her.

There are two sorts of artists in this world: one class who display art in their lives, egotists who have a passion for themselves, who are true poets within the restricted horizon of the family; another class who display art in their works, who pour out their own existence, with a sublime self-denial, or rather with a higher egotism, since, after all their works are themselves, and their fame is the radiant metamorphosis of their personality.

The royal architect broke the silence by telling

David that he would follow his son's advice to the letter, since the glorious painter of *Belesarius* had made no resolution against marriage. The conversation again became animated; they talked gayly, they talked a great deal; but, when David rose to leave, he did not yet know which of the two girls he would marry. As he bowed his adieu, he caught at a rapid glance the two faces, and withdrew, asking himself if one was more attractive to him, in an artistic point of view, than the other.

Quite naturally, according to his habit, he went to pass an hour at Sedaine's.

Mademoiselle Hyacinthe was paler than she had been the day before; if he made no remark about it, it was because he did not notice it.

"Well! my friend David," said Sedaine to him, with his look of cunning good humor, "you look at once gay and anxious?"

"In fact," continued Hyacinthe, smiling to conceal her trouble, "there are two pictures in your face."

"Two pictures!" exclaimed David, "you have guessed it. I have been dining, you know with Pécoul; they have been talking to me of marriage. I marry! of what use would it be?"

"It is an old habit of the human race, which is always decided to be bad and always persisted in," interrupted Sedaine.

"I see no two pictures in all this," said Hyacinthe with impatience.

"Why," continued David, "to marry, one must have a wife, and I have two of them."

The poor girl breathed again. A last illusion, like those momentary returns of health at the hour of death, once more inspired her with hope.

"Yes, I have two of them," said David, as if looking into himself: "I do not love either one or the other, but I am on the point of loving one as much as the other; one is a blonde, the other a brunette."

Hyacinthe sighed, and raised her head to glance at her fair locks in the mirror over the chimney-piece.

"The brunette has the more marked lines, the more Roman profile; the blonde is of a more delicate type and more undulating contour; one might call her a Grecian marble softened down by a Coustou."

Hyacinthe was still looking at herself in the mirror.

"For my part," said Sedaine, "I liked better, when I was twenty, to loosen fair locks than black ones. Of what use is a Roman profile of the time of Augustus, to live with under Louis XVI.?"

Hyacinthe blushed, and hastened to say that she did not like light hair, and that she had always regretted that she was not a brunette.

"So," said David to her, "You advise me to marry the Roman type in preference?"

"Yes," murmured Hyacinthe;"besides, your sympathies are that way, since your genius is entirely Roman, like that of Corneille."

Hyacinthe was overcome by the beatings of her heart; it was impossible for her to say a word more; she felt herself on the point of dying for joy or of grief. She trembled lest he should decide for Mademoiselle Pécoul; she trembled, too, lest he should reply to her: "Since you recommend your rival to me, I will marry you;" for she had no doubt but that David was undecided between Mademoiselle Pécoul and herself.

Suddenly, David, who was walking up and down the saloon, approached Hyacinthe, and said to her, abruptly:—

"By-the-by, do you not know Pécoul's two daughters?"

"Yes," murmured she, completely overpowered.

"Well, since you know them, tell me at once which of them I should take."

Hyacinthe turned pale, muttered some words, and fell in a swoon; she at last understood all the bitter mockery of her fate.

The poor old Sedaine, who also understood, threw himself on his knees before his daughter and raised her head in his hands.

"What is the matter with her?" asked David with emotion; for, if he had never looked upon Hyacinthe with the eyes of a lover, he had always regarded her as a sister.

"The matter with her?" murmured Sedaine with a mournful shake of the head, "if you do not know, I will not tell you."

A death-like silence followed these words.

"Ah!" continued Sedaine to himself, "I thought that I had two children—am I to lose them both?"

David had taken the hands of Hyacinthe, and spoke to her with his somewhat rough tenderness.

She reopened her eyes and told him that she was touched by his anxiety, but that he need not think of it.

She rose slowly, dragged herself to the harpsichord, and recommenced the air, so sad and eloquent, *A Burning Fever*, which was like the *De profundis* of her love.

David married Mademoiselle Pécoul, the Roman type. Hyacinthe waited to die until old Sedaine should be dead.

PRUDHON.

I.

THE world, a philosopher has said, is the dream of God. Would it not be better to say, that God, having created the world and seeing it imperfect, but not condescending to recommence his work, dreamed of another world more beautiful, more dazzling, more worthy of himself, a new terrestrial paradise in which poetry, Eve before and after the fall, should walk in all the splendor of her beauty. Art is this dream of God.

The artist or the poet is therefore a privileged creature, whose high mission it is to realize this other world, which consoles us for the first. The poetically-endowed artist ought not only to study under the light of the sun, but to listen to that ideal voice which throws over nature its prestiges and enchantments. Has the divine beauty of the Madonnas of Raphael, ever been met with on the earth? Will the plaster-masks moulded from life, ever attain the elevation of the heads of Michael Angelo? Is the spring-time which we pass in France, in Italy, in Greece, as mild and fragrant as the idylles of André Chénier? Nature, beautiful as she may be, is somewhat wanting in tone and harmony; art completes the imperfect poem which we call the world, with the vague recollection of the heaven from which it is descended; hence is inspiration.

The artist ought to pursue his course here below proud, free, without caring for the noise of the world; it is not enough for him to study human passion on mouths which he sees smile, eyes which he sees weep; he must listen to his heart, which speaks out loudly in solitude; hence is sentiment.

Inspiration and sentiment formed the genius of Pierre-Paul Prudhon, as severe grace formed his talent.

In the seventeenth century, under the pompous reign of Louis XIV., two celebrated painters contended ardently to attain the royalty of painting; one had only his talent, but he had a determined spirit, always in the field, ready to get the mastery,to take the place by force of arms; you have recognised, Lebrun. For the struggle, the other had genius, but was of a timid and careful disposition, seeking ardently the solitude which inspires, and the silence which elevates; he was a simple, plain man, who loved painting and not glory, who asked from God the hidden joys of the artist, and not the trumpet flourishes of renown. He was a great painter, and yet he was vanquished by his rival, vanquished in life, vanquished until the day when time puts every one in his proper place; you have recognised Lesueur.

At the end of the eighteenth century, the same struggle was renewed; after the blue and pink landscapes of Boucher, when painting led by David, was retempered in the Roman soil, do we not see the appearance of genius surprise and strike everybody under the severe pencil of that perverse master, while true genius remains unrecognised in the humble dwelling of Prudhon? David, like Lebrun, made himself the painter of his times; his are the sombre forms of 1793, and the imperial pomp of 1812; his all that recalls the Romans, whom he wished to reanimate, the republican and the heroic virtues: Joseph Chénier is his poet, Napoleon is his hero, liberty is his God.

Prudhon, like Lesueur, inspired from a higher source, made himself the painter of all ages and of all countries. True genius is of no age, and has the world for its country, what mattered to him, that timid and simple Prudhon, all the noise which surrounded him, the saturnalia of glory, the saturnalia of liberty? Doubtless like every national heart, he was proud of seeing French heroism choose Europe for its field of battle, and proclaim liberty in every corner of the world; but alongside of Prudhon the man was Prudhon the artist; and there were plenty of things under the sun for the artist, which were worth more than Bonaparte or Napoleon, Robespierre or Saint-Just, than the guillotine or war; there was love, grace, beauty; there was God, there were infants sporting on their mothers' bosoms and lovers sighing at the feet of their mistresses. The field which he liked best, was not the field of battle, but the valley blest by Heaven, where the grain sheds its gold under the sickle, the meadow bordered by the willows over which the cattle were scattered, the blushing vine, bending with the clusters which the song of the vintagers still enlivened. What he loved, was Nature in her strength, her smile, her sorrow, seen through the prism of art, which is the second nature. The parallel may be pushed still farther: Lebrun and David had studied impetuously; they had drawn with a confident hand from all the springs of the great masters; they had become painters by dint of observing how the great painters had become so; in contrast to this behold Lesueur and Prudhon: they studied alone, following in no track, and acquired genius almost without suspecting the fact. Lebrun was the painter of Louis XIV., David was the painter of Napoleon; Lesueur and Prudhon were the painters for themselves, having no other inspiration than that which comes from on high.

It was seen from Prudhon's earliest years, that he was a predestined painter. He was born the sixth of April, 1760, at Cluny, almost in the same region with Greuze. These two men who have saved French painting, one in spite of Boucher, the other in spite of David, had the same youthful career. Greuze was the son of an architect, Prudhon of a mason; architect and mason in the country, are they not synonymous terms? Nothing would have been sadder than the infancy of Prudhon, if it had not been for his mother, who shed love upon his cradle: so it was with Greuze. Prudhon was born the thirteenth child of the mason; his father, poor pelican, who had torn his breast a thousand times to feed his brood, at last yielded to this life of labor and of sacrifice; he died in want, leaving to his desolated widow, God only for support. God graciously fulfilled his part of the testament; he made a little room in the sunlight for all these poor orphans. It was on Prudhon especially, that his bounty fell; but is the bestowal of genius a divine bounty to man? Is it not rather submitting him to rudest trials, is it not showing the sky to the bird who has lost his wings? In truth, it was by a mournful road, by another Calvary, that Prudhon bore the cross of genius.

Prudhon drew his powers from the tears of his mother. The first picture which this painter beheld, was that of a desolate mother who loves her children, and has often nothing to give them, but the love of her heart, and the tears of her eyes. Prudhon, therefore, saw life open in shadow, the life of the poor man, who has only labor for its support, and misery for its horizon. But there was at least in this melancholy picture, a mother whose sweet and tender face stood forth in a divine halo. This mother's face was always the most pleasing inspiration of the painter; it was from the recollections of his infancy that he drew the ineffable sweetness and angelic tenderness which are the soul of his genius. In good season, Prudhon went to the school of the monks of Cluny, we see him from his earliest lessons in writing, sketching, like Callot, a thousand fantastic profiles; instead of learning to write, he learned to draw. It is not with the letters of the alphabet that he *will express his thoughts*, and *will speak to the eyes;* instead of the ingenious art sung by Boileau, he will express himself with the art of Raphael. On his return home, turning from the games of his age, he takes a needle and traces the Passion of our Lord on soap or on stone. As he had a charming face, the monks of the abbey distinguished him, and became attached to him; he had the privilege of following them everywhere; at school hours he was permitted to wander through the vast dependencies of the monastery. He passed days in contemplation, before some dilapidated piece of sculpture, or some mouldy picture. There is the world to him; the work of God is not that which surprises him, for nothing is impossible to God, but the work of this poor creature who does nothing but display his feebleness here below. One day a monk, seeing his scholar in ecstasy before a *Descent from the Cross*, by some unknown painter, said to him, knowing that he liked to draw: "You will not succeed, for that is painted in oil." Prudhon did not reply, he left the monastery and ran over the fields, asking himself what was the way to paint in oil. In the first place, colors were needful; a thousand varied tints were requisite to reproduce this sky, these figures, draperies, and landscapes. In the meadow there were primroses and scabiuses, in the waving rye, poppies and corn flowers; along in the path, daisies and sweet-brier. "Here are my colors found for me," exclaimed Prudhon. He gathered flowers and plants, levying right and left, and re-entered the house as joyous and rich as a bee returning to the hive; he pressed out the juice of his bouquets; he experimented, he was mistaken; he attempted again, and was in despair; he returned to the fields; and brought back another harvest: his mother's house became a laboratory; they ridiculed him, pursued him with jokes; what mattered it to him! he is in chaos, but he will find light.

At the end of some days, Prudhon had discovered entirely by himself, the secret of painting in oil; he was thirteen, the age at which Pascal discovered mathematics. Prudhon returned victorious to the abbey, with his hands full of sketches. "That is painted in oil," said he to the monk, surprised at this flash of genius. "How have you managed it, my child?"—"I have sought and I have found; the horses have brushes in their manes, the plants contain colors." The monk spoke to his bishop about Prudhon; it was in the good times when every nobleman was born a protector of the arts. The bishop of Mâcon took the child from his mother, to place him in the hands of a provincial painter, Des Vosges, whose name has only reached us, because he had Prudhon for a pupil. The good man, however, was worthy of his mission: he had the good sense to be proud of guiding the child's pencil. He understood that that would be his sole task. Prudhon, free henceforth from all other studies, took the flight of an eagle in this realm of art. He was a pupil often rebellions to his master's lessons; he had his own peculiar ideas, understood beauty after his own manner, and had a certain mode of rendering the truth, which appeared to him more agreeable and beautiful than the style of others; so that it more than once happened that it was the master who took a lesson.

Prudhon passed his entire time in the studio; when he took a day's rest, it was to fly to his mother, his mother always tender, always sad, always anxious, his mother who was then seeing her numerous offspring deserting the nest and flying, at chance, as God pleased, from the safe shelter of her wing. The poor woman lived on little, like all who suffer here below; a ray of sunlight, the fragrance of the meadows and the woods, some crumbs of a fortune, long since scattered, the love of her children, these were her life.

The day when Prudhon dropped in upon her, without announcing his coming, was a day of joy; they embraced, they wept, they consoled one another. On that day, the supper was almost gay ; on the morrow, before parting, they breakfasted together, but the repast was saddened ; and yet nothing was more agreeable than this frugal breakfast, served at the window by a maternal hand, in front of the reddening vines ; but part they must! In withdrawing, the son turned back almost overcome, yet already almost consoled by the engrossing spectacle of the beautiful landscapes about him. Far off, at the turn of the road, he saw his mother leaning out of the window, immovable as a statue, lost in her love and sadness. Prudhon always recalled, with an ineffable charm, his poetical visits to his mother ; the journey and the return, the sudden approach, the silent surprise, the affectionate talk of the supper-table, the fire which was kindled on the hearth, that blessed hearth, at which God, passing over the earth, would have loved to have rested. He recalled, especially the sadness of the parting, the breakfast which to him was only the signal of farewell, and finally the sinuous path whence he could still see his mother. It was about this time, that when wishing to paint a fancy sketch, he was suddenly surprised and delighted to recognise his mother, his mother in the attitude in which she appeared at the window. It was a true portrait which satisfied the eyes and heart by its resemblance; there were the lines, there was the sentiment. Poor Prudhon, enraptured with his work, and not having the means of purchasing a frame, found it a simpler mode to frame with his pencil this beloved face in the window of the natal mansion. Thus far, Prudhon, then sixteen, had loved but two things: painting and his mother, a love blessed by Heaven, a holy and glorious joy, the morning delights of a scarce developed heart: a third love came to spoil the whole.

Prudhon was born to suffer; that which forms the happiness of others, was destined to blast his youth. The sky of youth is like the sky of April; cold showers pass over it in every direction; the heart of man, before experiencing the pure rays of love, gives birth to the deceptive clouds of pleasure; before love comes desire, the lip already trembles when the heart scarcely beats. Prudhon met in the town, he does not say how, a young girl more enticing than beautiful, more giddy than impassioned, who carried him away at once without his knowing how. She was not, certainly, the ideal of the painter of the modern graces, of the graces, still smiling, but who smile after having wept. While the soul of Prudhon wandered in the land of dreams, in the pursuit of the freshest, fairest, most adorable chimeras, his eyes, deceived by the delusion of love, rested on this girl who had nothing in her heart but caprices, such as God gives to all women, to moderate the worship of men for the creatures of this world. Thanks to the prism of youth, Prudhon was a pretty long time without being aware that he had deceived himself; he adorned his fair one with all the deceptive graces of which he dreamed, he judged of her heart by his own, he could not believe that any one could have reached seventeen, without possessing the poetry of that enchanted age; by degrees, however, the illusions dropped away like the roses from the brier-bush. Prudhon's hand found nothing but thorns. Bad women are as thorny as the holly; the young girl soon became a bad woman. The whole truth must be spoken; if Prudhon had given his heart, she had sacrificed her virtue; but was that in reality a sacrifice? The abyss was deep. Prudhon, who was yet but a child, was informed that he was about to become a father. This revelation was a terrible blow to his heart, and to his imagination. What was he to do? Fly from Mâcon, from his mistress, from his child, such was the counsel of his art; but what would become of him, an exile without resources? Would God bless the path of him who abandoned what he has loved, what he is to love? Besides, where was he to go? What would become of him? would he find a single friend? He consented to remain, that is to say to marry his mistress. Poor child! behold him married at the age when others, free as the wind, are essaying all the chances of life; behold him, who adored solitude and silence constrained to live with two, three, four, for what I know! Behold prose with its iron-heeled shoes, coming to trample down the green sward of his poetry. Marriage and love, as one of the ancients remarks, are the two wings of a bird, which bear him sometimes to the splendors of heaven, sometimes to the solitudes of the forest, sometimes over the rocks of the spring: for Prudhon marriage will have but one wing, behold him nailed to the earth, after having known the domains of the eagle.

Scarcely had he been married a year when he counted two children in his studio. These ill-clad children were not calculated to furnish any very poetic inspiration to their father; they, however, served him as models for those graceful groups in which his talent displayed itself in so graceful and natural a manner. In spite of the often devouring cares and the sometimes withering duties of family life, Prudhon remained tender, generous, and enthusiastic. The states of Burgundy had established a competition for a grand prize in painting, and sent the provincial laureate of each year to Rome. Prudhon, who was a competitor, went to work as usual with noble ardor. One day he heard, through the partition which separated him from his neighbor, lamentations, groans, and sobs; a pupil was in despair and indignant at his efforts. Prudhon at first smiled, afterward softened, and, forgetful of himself, detached a board, entered the apartment, and completed his comrade's composition. Generosity bestowed more talent upon him than he had yet possessed, so that his comrade obtained the prize: but, abashed at his victory, he acknowledged that he owed it to Prudhon. The states of Burgundy repaired the error; a cry of admiration was loudly raised; his rivals embraced him and carried him in triumph all over the city.

He set out for Rome, leaving his wife and children in the guardianship of his mother and of God, hoping to return from the Eternal City, if not rich, at least with sufficient talent to become so; he set out happy at recovering his liberty, dazzled by the prospect of the masterpieces he was about to study.

Arrived at Rome, he found a friend in Canova; this friendship was the most beautiful, the most noble, the most holy of his life: it included everything, even sacrifice; it consoled Prudhon for the want of love.

"There are three men here," said Canova to him one day, "of whom I am jealous."

"I know and love none but you," answered Prudhon.

"And Raphael, and Leonardo da Vinci, and Correggio," replied Canova; "you pass your whole time with them, you listen to them, confide your dreams to them; you go from one to the other, from this one to that; you have never finished admiring what they say."

Prudhon, in reality, studied incessantly these three masters, whom he sometimes called the three graces. Correggio, however, was the master he loved best.

If Prudhon had listened to Canova, he would have passed his life at Rome, far from France, which was ungrateful to him — far from his wife, who was unfaithful. The proverb says that the absent are in the wrong; to poetical imaginations the absent are in the right. In love, recollection preserves only the pleasing side; it is a magic mirror in which the bad pictures are never reflected. Then Prudhon had loved his country and his wife; through the prism of distance, both appeared more attractive to him than ever. He again beheld with infinite delight the beautiful landscapes of Burgundy: his wife herself had regained, thanks to absence, some lost attraction of her early youth. And he had, besides, left there a deeper love — his old mother, who waited his coming, to die. In spite of the persuasions of Canova, he set out, promising him soon to return. They did not see one another again, but they remained faithful to friendship — so far faithful that they died at the same period, as if to meet again above in the immortal gallery of the King of artists.

He arrived in France at an opportune moment: his mother was dead; his wife, as usual, in little of a conjugal humor. France was no longer a kingdom, and was not yet a nation. It was in 1789: the first rumblings of the revolution swept over the land like a storm-wind. It was a time of exile for the arts. Prudhon, who was always resigned, resigned himself to this. After embracing his wife and children, he set out for Paris, believing that at all times, even in those of revolution, it was still the best place in which to seek for fortune. He arrived at Paris with very little baggage, and took a lodging in a sorry lodging-house, not furnished in best style, until he could hire a studio. He found nothing to do, and consequently nothing to eat. This mode of life could not continue long; although proud and misanthropic, he thought of having recourse to the artists then in vogue. There were scarcely any except David, Greuze, and Girodet: he presented himself to Greuze as being of his part of the country; he confided to him that he had an entire family to support. "Have you talent?" asked Greuze.—"Yes," was the simple answer of Prudhon.—"So much the worse!" continued Greuze; "with family and talent, you have more than you need for dying of trouble. What the devil do you want to do with talent now, when there is no longer God nor devil, king nor court, rich nor poor? You know that I, who am speaking to you, am quite as great a painter as any other, and look at my ruffles."

Saying this, Greuze, who was a truly fantastic dandy about his dress, displayed to Prudhon a pair of ruffles in rags. "If you had not talent," he continued, "the evil would not be so great, you could daub portraits for the first-comer."—"Have I not told you that I have a family?" interrupted Prudhon; "I will paint signs, if needful—I will be a laborer as long as it pleases God."

In reality, Prudhon opened shop; he took miniature portraits, illustrated letter-sheets, concert-tickets, bill-heads, and ornamented address-cards and candy-boxes. "I do everything in my line," he remarked with a sad smile.

It was a labor full of anguish; he felt keenly that he was losing in this work his most precious time, the time blessed by Heaven, which youth bestows with his hands full of flowers. To console himself, he lived on little, and sent to his family the remainder of his gains. By dint of painting heroes at ten or twenty francs a head, he at last at the end of two or three years amassed a thousand crowns, which allowed him to become an artist again. The horizon already looked less sombre and less cold to him, the glory which he had lost sight of, began again to smile upon him. He resumed his familiar life with Correggio, Raphael, and Leonardo da Vinci; he wrote to Canova to confide to him his griefs, Canova sent him hope in his reply. Greuze also told him to hope; Greuze had sincerely and cordially recognised the genius of Prudhon. "That man," he often said, "will go farther than I shall" (and Greuze believed with justice that he would go farther than David and Girodet); "he will stride over two centuries with seven-leagued boots."

The thousand crowns however, were the milk-maid's pail. Madame Prudhon hearing vague reports that her husband was beginning to make a fortune, set out to join him with her children; it was necessary to receive her, and to live in community of heart and money: so long as the money lasted, that is during three months, all the rest went on well; but when misery again resumed its place at the hearth, all went ill. Madame Prudhon liked to shine, like all women who are not handsome. The poor painter was reduced to rocking and amusing his children. He had soon six of them, six pitiless mouths which were always crying give. Greuze often surprised Prudhon sketching out a picture in the midst of his six children, two on his knees, one on the back of his arm-chair, the others at his feet. He made no complaints; receiving all their cries, gambols, and tricks, with a smile of resignation which he had learned at an early period.

Poetry, however, came to him under the form of love, or rather under the form of Poetry herself. She is a fairy who is never weary of waving the golden wand of enchantment; you believe her lost without return, you have bid her an eternal adieu, you adore her as a pious recollection; but soon she is more than a recollection, she is still a hope; we behold her returning more rich and prodigal than ever, her hands full of illusions, her head crowned with roses. Every one has narrated the passion of Prudhon and Mademoiselle Mayer; I do not wish to deny the charm of this love, but I avow that another forgotten love, of which no one says a word, and Prudhon scarcely speaks, exhales a perfume far more pleasing to my soul. If the first has the odor of the rose, the other is pleasant to inhale as the sweet-brier.

II.

In 1793, between the death of the king and that of the queen, a young girl, who was not yet twenty, presented herself one morning at Prudhon's studio. "I have been told," she said in a low voice; "that you can take a portrait quickly; as I have but very little time, I have come to ask you . . . ." — "What kind of a portrait do you wish?" asked Prudhon. "Is it a drawing, is it pastel, is it an oil painting?" She smiled bitterly and said; "That lasts the longest." — "Yes," replied Prudhon, who had been looking at her; "but a portrait of you can not last too long." He took a small canvass and placed it on his easel. "Do you wish me to go to work, mademoiselle?" — "Oh, yes, monsieur, for who knows whether I can return," said she, turning pale.

Prudhon determined to paint her full face, with her head inclined. He went to work forthwith. The young girl sat like a statue, pale, immovable, and silent. Even while tracing the first lines, Prudhon sought to divine who was this mysterious model. As Prudhon was a philosopher as well as a painter, he read more readily than most in the eyes of men. He, however, could not say who this young girl was, whence she came, and whither she was going. She had not the appearance of a fine lady, but, although her garments were a little faded, she was dressed like one. She had a gown of blue silk, a kerchief of black lace, a bonnet of the simplest description which negligently confined her fair locks. She had no other ornament than these locks, some of whose rebellious ringlets fell on her neck. Her face was in the character of the time, graceful even to delicacy, coquettish in outline, of a type of beauty which we have lost, of that beauty formed for smiles, of which Mignard, Boucher, La Tour, and Greuze, were the painters in ordinary. Unfortunately, the young girl did not smile; no one smiled then: there was always a tear to shed or one to dry. But was she the less beautiful for that? Did not this sadness of heart stamped on her countenance, give her a more noble air? If less seductive to the eyes, she penetrated quicker to the soul; so that Prudhon after having regarded her for some minutes, felt full of compassion for this sister of misfortune. For three years he had painted plenty of sorrowful faces. In that fine time, when property no longer existed, a painter of portraits was a drawer of wills : for one could actually bequeath nothing but his portrait. Prudhon had preserved the recollection of a multitude of curious histories, in which his pencil, if not himself, had played a part. More than once he had well nigh fallen a victim to his willingness to paint aristocrats. One day among others, a cordelier came into his studio, to tell him that the republic did not regard with a favorable eye, his portraits of the late nobility.

Thus far, however, the noblest picture of sadness he had had to paint, was that of this young girl. Moved by a curiosity entirely fraternal, he could not refrain from questioning her a little. "Mademoiselle, do you wish your portrait to bear this expression of sadness and despair ?"—"What matter," she replied, "will it not still be my portrait ? however . . . ." She did not finish her sentence, Madame Prudhon having suddenly come in like a tempest. "Thank God," she exclaimed angrily, throwing a child at the painter's feet, "they are going on finely out there, I wash my hands of it. Don't you hear them crying and fighting ? It is a hell, I am not destined to that. Govern your house as you please, no money, no footman. See, here they come ; I shall be off." Saying this, she walked straight to the door. She paused to stare insolently at the young girl who was sitting ; but, fearing to have to quiet the children who were then rushing in in an undisciplined crowd, she forthwith departed without troubling herself about anything farther. Where did she go to? Prudhon did not know.

Meantime, the six children had taken the studio by assault; the poor painter humiliated and confused, no longer knew what to do: the young girl had no time to lose, but how could he work at this divine portrait, in the midst of all the noisy clatter which filled the studio, at the mercy of all these capricious little demons, who were gambolling about everywhere? Prudhon gave a supplicating look at the young girl: she had understood, and responded by a smile of fraternal compassion. "Go on," she added, "I like children."—"Pretty children," said the painter, "but such as those! besmeared, uncombed ragged as they are! what would you have, it is God who gives them, I do not complain, I only regret that God should have forgotten to put a heart in their mother's breast."

At this moment, a little imp began to play unceremoniously with the young lady's dress. Prudhon stamped and shook his finger. "It is no matter," she said softly.

She took the child's pretty head in her white hands and kissed his forehead. Prudhon continued the portrait in silence, exchanging now and then a tender glance with the stranger. After a sitting of more than five hours, a sudden flush took the place of the paleness of her beautiful face. She rose, saying she had not strength to sit longer. Prudhon hastened to open the window, but without waiting until a purer air could enter the room, she passed to the door, saying, "To-morrow."

She suddenly retraced her steps to see how far the portrait had advanced. "I think," said Prudhon "that I have caught your features and expression. Besides, I can work a little without you, you will no longer be before me, but I shall believe that I still see you; I have a well-trained memory; it is only indifferent faces which I forget at once; beauty impresses me a long time, I never forget it." — "Alas!" she murmered with a sigh. "However," continued Prudhon, "I do not know if I have been able in your portrait, to catch the grace of your neck, I have tied that handkerchief badly, if I dared, ... "—"To-morrow," said she, withdrawing.

The next day she did not come. His mind still completely filled with her remembrance, Prudhon finished the head; it must be said that he then painted his portraits more in the style of sketches than otherwise. He waited the next day, he painted and waited again; the entire week thus passed. He retouched the portrait more on his own account than that of the portrait, finding an ineffable charm in dreaming before this picture which was like a vision to him. The following week, some persons came to his studio to be painted in miniature; he laid aside this sad and charming portrait, not despairing of soon seeing the original again. Meanwhile, in spite of new faces, in spite of his wife, who had not exhausted her conjugal amenities, he lived, at least he suffered his heart to live on the poetic reminis cence of the young girl.

A month passed in this manner; paternal cares domestic annoyances, persevering toil, began to deaden this reminiscence, sweet as a dream of love. One day, seeking relaxation, he went out for a walk; he followed the quais; a great tumult drew him to the place Louis XV.: it was then a very common-place affair: they were about to guillotine twenty aristocrats "who had *conspired* against *the safety* of the republic one and indivisible," that is to say twenty victims taken at random from among the persons faithful to misfortune, to elegance, to the mind, and to God, which was still worse.

It was the second time that Prudhon had been present at a similar butchery; he followed with a compassionate look, the fatal car which progressed slowly, as usual through hedge rows of *sans culottes* and *bonnets rouges.* He gradually approached nearer; a form suddenly struck him: it was she, it was the young girl who did not return. *To-morrow*, she had said: on the morrow she had doubtless gone to prison.

Prudhon could not believe his eyes; he trembled, turned pale, his head swam. He approached still nearer; it was indeed she, always she, with her blue dress, her black lace kerchief, her faded bonnet and fair locks. She was as sad and resigned as on the day when she came into his studio; nothing had then changed for her? She, doubtless, even then saw death in prospect. "My God!" said Prudhon bitterly, "so she too has conspired against the republic. What has she done to be dragged to the guillotine with her fair locks and her twenty years?" As he thus muttered to himself, it seemed to him that the condemned victim made a sign to him; he wished to force through the crowd to approach nearer the cart, though he should be run over in the attempt; but his emotion had annihilated his strength, he could not make his way through the rude and ferocious crowd, he even lost sight of the cart. He was swayed backward and forward in the midst of the crowd, without being master of his movements. A mortal quarter of an hour thus passed. "I saw only the tumult," said he afterward, when recalling the fatal moment.

God once more permitted him to see the victim again: she slowly mounted the steps of the scaffold, repelling the services of an attendant of the guillotine. Before the executioner seized her she had time to look up to Heaven, and to make the sign of the cross. The executioner approached, she trembled and recoiled a step. Will it be believed? he scarce believed it himself! Prudhon did not feel himself a man only, before this lugubrious picture, before this funeral theatre, he was still the artist. Thus he recollected, on beholding the undulations of the young girl's neck, when she raised her eyes to Heaven, when she lowered her brow to sign herself with the cross, that in the portrait the head was badly attached to the shoulders. What a horrible idea! at the instant that this beautiful and noble head was to fall! when this virgin neck, which perhaps no lip had ever touched, was to undergo the hideous contact of the great monster of prostitution!

Prudhon returned home, sick; he was in a fever, almost in a delirium; he shut himself up in his studio, and passed the night devoured by anguish. They might have guillotined his sister, without touching him more deeply. Although without money, it was eight days before he took up a pencil. He more deeply than ever despaired of everything, even of his genius. The first time that he felt like work, the idea seized him of completing the portrait of the young girl, that is to say of working over again the neck, that beautiful neck, white and graceful as a swan's! He even one day accomplished the vision of Faust: he was alone, lost in his grief as usual, in contemplation before the portrait. "For all that, I must finish it," said he suddenly without knowing what he uttered. Impelled by an infernal hand, he ran to his palette, snatched his brush, and with a hand trembling before the canvass, he dipped it by chance in the carmine, he retouched the neck, he fancied that he saw a drop of blood fall; in his terror his brush vacillates it is no longer a drop of blood, it is the mark of the knife which mangles the entire neck.

Everything passes away in this world, even our recollections. After having so to speak lived with this strange portrait, after many hours of fever, of delirium and revery passed with the shade of this young girl, Prudhon, ended by forgetting or almost forgetting her. She was soon no more than a dream of the past, a lost love, a star in the night. The portrait remained in the studio, among the thousand and one sketches of the artist. Scarcely did he from time to time cast a saddened look upon it. He only experienced a mournful joy, in thinking that at a later period, when the hour came for him (if that hour was ever to strike) to take a little rest, and to live amid the fragrance of his youth, he could sadly revel in this adored remembrance. How many heart-treasures are thus amassed, never to be expended at a later time, in such haste are all to press onward!

In 1798, toward the end of the winter, Greuze introduced to Prudhon, a young man of noble family, who, during four years of exile, had sought relief in a love of painting. Greuze scarcely knew him, he was not even acquainted with his name, he had met him in a saloon, where he styled himself baron de Bergwald or de Hochwald, but that was doubtless a pseudonym, which sheltered him from ancient enmities. At first sight, he would have been taken for a

Frenchman; he had the accent and the manner; but Greuze did not trouble himself; artists are of no country. After a visit of half an hour, the young man asked Prudhon's permission to return; he did so a few days afterward. This time, seeing the willingness of Prudhon, he took occasion to examine the contents of the studio from the paintings to the cartoons. "It is very astonishing," said he on beholding the portrait of the stranger. "What do you find that is astonishing?" asked Prudhon, surprised at the exclamation of the young man. "Nothing, nothing," replied the other pale and agitated; "the sight of this neck all daubed over has almost terrified me." — "It is a truly melancholy history," rejoined Prudhon. "I am listening to you," murmured the young man seating himself.

The painter related in few words what had passed. After the recital, the young man pale and overcome as if he had been present at some terrible scene, or as if this story had recalled to him a page of his life, asked Prudhon if he would consent to sell him the portrait. Prudhon was restrained by the idea of profaning a beloved recollection. "No," said he, "I love this portrait, it is to me that of a sister, and besides, have I the right to sell it? The poor girl doubtless, foreseeing her death, was desirous of leaving this souvenir to her father, her brother, or her lover." — "You know that if they guillotined this young girl, they could have shown no favor to the men. But I respect your reasons; grant me only the favor of taking the portrait to show to my sister, it is almost her own face." — "Take it away! As you please. Give my compliments to your sister, especially if she resembles that noble and unfortunate girl."

The young man carried off the picture, without further ceremony, under his arm. The same evening, a very silent domestic placed in Prudhon's hands a rouleau of one hundred and fifty louis, without being willing to mention from whom it came. To all Prudhon's questions he replied in German. The painter, not being able to succeed in forcing the servant to carry back the money, promised himself to return it to the young man on his first visit. The young man, however, never returned. After waiting for a fortnight, Prudhon, losing patience, related his adventure to Greuze. Greuze had seen the mysterious stranger but once since; he soon learned that he had returned to Germany; and he could never inform Prudhon whether he was the baron de Bergwald or de Hochwald. Prudhon experienced a truly heartfelt pang at being separated from his dear and melancholy portrait. More than once did he surprise himself painting in his heads of the Virgin the adored features of the divine model, who had sat to him in his studio and at the guillotine!

III.

Meanwhile, time, far from smoothing down the testy temper of Madame Prudhon, made it the more irritable. The gale was always blowing on the fire; angry at losing, as she grew old, the slatternly graces which she had received from nature, having neither virtue, nor talent, nor maternity, for a refuge, she became still more acrid and mischievous, "bristling all over," as Prudhon said. Although he had in this respect the good humor of La Fontaine, he at last lost patience. After eighteen years of such intercourse (one might have lost patience in less), the painter took a violent resolution; he separated, in bed and board, from Madame Prudhon. It was separating paradise from hell. As he was a gallant fellow, he bestowed a pension on his late wife, and chose to take charge of all the children. Must it be said? suicide had often tempted him; more than once had he been near terminating all his miseries. He was, however, always resigned to life on account of his children. Separated from his wife, he breathed again; the sky appeared more clear to him, nature more smiling, and the men better: it is needless to say that the women gained by the change also. From this time, Fortune was less rebellious; she more than once came, if not to dwell, at least to pause at his abode. He had not yet his fair place in the sunshine, but he was no longer in the shadow; his genius began to loom above the horizon, not yet a cloudless one. All enemies of true talent, the mediocrities of all kinds, the abortions and the fools, endeavored to obscure the rising sun. Some, because he was severe, denied him grace; others, because he was graceful, denied him severity. It was so long since a painter at once severe and graceful had been seen in France! In spite of the envious, Prudhon had arrived at that point of his career where all that is said for or against a man's talent adds to his fame.

Glory and fortune, however, were late-comers for a man of genius who had grown pale, for more than forty years, in misery and obscurity, amid family cares and conjugal troubles. Although still young, Prudhon no longer felt his youth about him; his heart was sombre and devastated; it was like a wilderness in the night; not a ray, not a flower; even hope, a flower which grows on graves, no longer bloomed for him. God, however, doubtless touched by his tears and his labors, restored him his youth. It was permitted to him, as by miracle, to hope and to smile again, to find a long spring-time of love, or rather to traverse an autumn full of flowers and sunbeams, of shade and paths.

Greuze was dead. It was in 1803: his best pupil, Mademoiselle Mayer, wishing to recover the graces of her master, went straight to Prudhon's studio. The latter painter, to whom solitude was the best company, consented with reluctance to go and give lessons to the pupil of his old friend. Mademoiselle Mayer was, however, very seductive: she was a lively brunette, enthusiastic, always smiling, always impassioned. She was far from possessing the beauty which Prudhon bestowed on his faces of nymphs or virgins; but, in spite of her tawny complexion and prominent cheek-bones, she possessed attractions which impressed the most philosophical. Her eyes and her lips scattered fire; if her face was not moulded by the graces, it was evident that Cupid had had a hand in it. Prudhon, more insensible than all others, could not help feeling from the first a secret pleasure at the sight of this ardent and expressive physiognomy, which was ennobled by the religion of art. The lessons by degrees became longer; Prudhon did not notice it, and Mademoiselle Mayer did not complain. Love was soon of the party, sometimes giving, sometimes taking a lesson, and love was not the worst of masters. The painter and the scholar at last loved one another, the one with a rejuvenated tenderness, the other with all the ardor of her twenty years. About this time, Mademoiselle Mayer, having lost her father, took refuge with Prudhon, not supposing, in the purity of her heart, that there would be any great harm, in the sight of God, in replacing a wicked woman who had left only desolation and ruin in her steps. She had a small fortune, and devoted almost her entire income to Prudhon's children. Among them was a girl of twenty, who became the inseparable friend of this second mother. The world—which never looks with a favorable eye on a new mode of exercising the Christian virtues, especially when we brave the laws which it has made—could not find a single epigram against Mademoiselle Mayer. It was because she had not blushed on entering Prudhon's house, because she had passed the threshold with head erect, her heart full, and with virtue for her companion. Woman's virtue is not always vain modesty, it is sometimes humble charity. Mademoiselle Mayer soon received more proofs of esteem than many ladies of quality, married before notary and priest. The world understood that there was something more between her and Prudhon than a vow and a piece of stamped paper. They were met at the ball, the concert, the promenade, looking like persons who are happy and proud to live together. They were visited, fêted without hypocrisy, and asked without irony how the young family were. Mademoiselle Mayer was the true mother of Prudhon's children—for, is it not love which makes the mother? In fine, this marriage of a new style appeared legitimate to everybody, even to Napoleon and his government; so that, when the artists were dislodged from the Louvre, Prudhon and Mademoiselle Mayer each obtained an apartment at the Sorbonne. At a later period, the day when Napoleon placed with his royal hand a cross on the breast of Prudhon, two pretty Anacreontic pictures by Mademoiselle Mayer were bought, in delicate gallantry, in the name of the emperor.

The reign of Napoleon was very favorable to the artist; he took the portrait of Josephine, and gave lessons in painting to Maria Louisa. He has left several portraits of the king of Rome, and M. de Talleyrand. The famous diplomatist was never weary of sitting in the studio of the painter, provided that he was able to enliven himself with the wit of Mademoiselle Mayer. More than once did Prudhon store up charming repartees passed from one to the other, so that he said on finishing the picture, "Nothing is wanting to it, but the wit."

Prudhon had the genius of allegory. The city of Paris called upon him for designs, for the cradle of the king of Rome. It is curious, at the present day, to examine this cradle, on which the artist had in some sort predicted the future. It rises on four cornucopias; it is supported by Force and Justice; golden bees are scattered over it; at its feet an eaglet is ready to take flight. It is shaded by a lace curtain strewed with stars. Two bas-reliefs decorate the sides; on one, the nymph of the Seine, resting on her urn receives the child from the hands of the gods; on the other is seen the Tiber, and near him the she-wolf of Romulus; the god raises his head crowned with reeds, to observe a new star in the horizon which is to restore to his banks their ancient splendor. Like all oracles, Prudhon strangely deceived himself. Where are the Force and Justice which were to have traversed the world with the king of Rome? Where are the cornucopias, which were to scatter abundance over the four quarters of the globe? And the golden bees, whither have they flown? And the stars, in what sky have they been awaiting him, this king whose sceptre was but a reed?

After having painted the cradle, he painted the child; he painted him sleeping in a grove of palms and laurels, illuminated by glory, protected by two stalks of the imperial flower. The king of Rome, even under the pencil of Prudhon, is neither as beautiful as a Cupid or an angel, nor as his father or his mother; he is simply a puffy child stretching out his hand to his nurse.

Prudhon, who had slowly reached happiness after the rudest trials, detached himself day by day from human vanities: splendor and noise disturbed him; he liked better the crackling of the fire, the evening when the silvery voice of Mademoiselle Mayer with those of his children reached his heart, than all the delusions of glory. He adored painting for the sake of painting, so that the day of his nomination at the institute, completely preoccupied by the face of a nymph which he had just created, he led one of his friends before the canvass with the simple pride of a child. "But," said the visiter, "have you not then been nominated by the institute?"—"Ah, it is true," said Prudhon with some surprise, "I forgot to tell you." His happiness was that of those who love retirement, silence, and melancholy. It was a happiness shaded by recollection and presentiment. According to an Arabian poet, the purest happiness is like a sky of spring traversed by light clouds. He who is under the sky of happiness, seeks only to see the clouds; he follows them from north to south, east to west, in constant hope that the sky will become clear; but the horizon incessantly impels new clouds; Prudhon, like all men, saw the clouds rather than the sky. Between the horizon of the future and of the past, God, Mademoiselle Mayer, his children, in vain displayed to him the azure where live the blest: he persisted in seeing the clouds.

In spite of her natural gayety, Mademoiselle Mayer at last, by degrees, covered herself also with the veil of Prudhon. These two lovers had lived together for twenty years, with the same ideas and the same passions. Twenty years of love! From lively gayety, Mademoiselle Mayer passed to still smiling melancholy; from melancholy to sadness is but a step; in taking this step, Mademoiselle Mayer who did everything enthusiastically, went as far as desperation. She began to cultivate with a funereal joy, the pale flowers of death. In vain was she asked the reason of her sadness. She made no answer; if I must do so for her, I should say that on the day when she saw youth fly far from her, with the mocking Graces, a phantom visited her and spoke to her of the tomb, the tomb which buries wrinkles and gray hair. This phantom we have all seen, since the two past generations, and we call it Suicide. He spoke for a long time in his funereal tones to Mademoiselle Mayer, he did not even give her a year's grace, styling her *Mademoiselle* with an air of raillery while speaking to her of her forty years. She had a vertigo; for three days she lived side by side with death, although Prudhon dwelt beside her. The abyss was about to open, she could do naught but fall in.

It grieves me here, that the end of this story which would be fittingly terminated by a page of poetry, must be drawn from a page of the *Gazette des Tribunaux*. The morning of March 6, 1821, Mademoiselle Mayer was alone in her apartment; she had on that day seen no one but her physician and a young pupil. The evening before, she had bid Prudhon good-night with tears in her eyes. A heavy sound was heard by the people of the neighborhood, they assembled and rushed in and found the poor woman bathed in her blood, beneath a mirror, in which she had doubtless studied her death. In a word, she had cut her throat with Prudhon's razor. Why must it be told? Why must an explanation be given, of the sad end of this life, full of grace and feeling, art and love?

Prudhon survived this terrible blow but a short time; his agony however was slow. He grasped his pencil proudly until the last, saying that he wished to die in the breach. When death seized him, he abandoned himself to the beautiful inspiration which he has left in his *Dying Christ* in the *Musée.* "Death has come two or three days too soon, but I was expecting it," said he to his friends. He had in fact at that time, purchased the six feet of earth where he reposes at Père-la-Chaise, opposite to the grave of Mademoiselle Mayer. He often went, in his last days to muse over these two tombs, "the one which is closed without me, the other which opens for me alone." To the friends who were present at his death, he said with a smile of resignation: "Do not weep, I am not about to die, I am about to depart." This letter, which is a last adieu, shows him to us extending his arms to death. "Oh! how heavy is the chain of life! Alone on the earth, who still detains me here? I was held to it only by the cords of the heart, death has snapped them all. My life is a blank; hope does not in the least dissipate the horrors of the darkness which surround me. She who should survive me, is no more! Will the death which I await, soon come to bestow upon me the calm which I long for? It is to thy tomb, my beloved! that all my thoughts tend." It will be seen, that in spite of his genius, Prudhon wrote in the style of the literary men of the empire; a man always belongs in some way or other to his time. Prudhon belonged to that sad period, which denaturalized Ossian and Voltaire: but if he held the pen badly, what mattered it! he was a man of genius with his pencil in his hand.

Pierre-Paul Prudhon (he had been christened with the names of Rubens) died on the sixteenth of February, 1825; Géricault had died in 1824. In less than a year, France lost the two, perhaps most illustrious painters of the nineteenth century, the two truest representatives of beauty and sentiment.

Prudhon and Mademoiselle Mayer always had the intention of taking each other's portraits; but it was not executed. On a day of leisure, however, when alone together in the studio, resting from their weightier labors, they each took up a scrap of coarse paper, and in the same sitting, Prudhon made a charming crayon sketch of Mademoiselle Mayer, while she drew in a few bold lines, the noble and pleasing face of her lover. Prudhon, in his sketch, with a single tint, heightened with white, has caught all the attractiveness and fire of this creole physiognomy. He had dressed his mistress in the costume of the empire; but, thanks to the painter, the costume is charming: it is easy to see that her head-dress is by him; her locks, escaping from the Greek band, fall in abundant ringlets over her cheeks; Homer could not have done better by Diana the huntress: the whole antique grace is there. Unfortunately, Mademoiselle Mayer has muffled up Prudhon in the costume of the empire ; it is a caricature. She has well caught the character of the face she loved to enthusiasm. The face, very strongly marked, is sad, gentle, yet severe ; thought rests on the brow, a smile softens the lips, but it is truly the smile of resignation of a wounded heart which hides itself.

IV.

THAT which especially characterizes Prudhon, is his exquisite poetry ; he is as much poet as painter, for he paints for the eyes and for the soul ; while tracing the most graceful undulations of human forms, he does not forget to reproduce the sentiment which issues from the heart to illuminate the brow, the eyes, and the lips. A materialist said, on seeing one of the adorable female faces created by Prudhon : "It would be capable of making me believe in the immortality of the soul."

However, to judge this great artist properly, must we not follow him into his works ?

In the *Dying Christ* of the *Musée*, Prudhon has showed himself worthy of portraying the celestial sorrow of a God expiring for men. Truly, this grief has nothing human about it ; a dweller of the skies alone could display this sublime resignation and supreme patience. Prudhon had been at the true school, at the school of misfortune : in order to paint the Christ upon the cross, had he not himself borne on his forehead the thorny crown?

Crime pursued by Justice and the Celestial Vengeance, is a savage and gloomy allegory in which the artist has displayed all his powers. It is the work of a master in thought and execution. The mode in which Prudhon obtained the first idea is known; it was like an illumination. He was dining with the prefect of the Seine; a picture for the hall of the *cour d'assises* was spoken of; a poet recalls these verses of Horace:—

> "Raro antecedentem scelestum
> Deseruit pœna....."

Prudhon leaned his forehead on his hand; for his part the picture was already complete; he called for a pen and paper, to the great surprise of those present. At the end of a quarter of an hour, on issuing from the closet in which he had shut himself up, he produced a sketch in which his entire idea was already resplendent. It is truly the representation of the first crime committed in this world. Night is spread over the uncultivated earth; Abel has just been immolated by Cain; but night is never dark enough for crime; the moon tears away the cloud and strikes the murderer with its beams. It is the eye of God which sees all. You know that the picture of Prudhon was worthy of this sketch; the inspiration did not abandon him. The painter who until that time had found only the fresh colors of the Graces on his palette, found the dark and rude tints which this stern poetry demanded.

There is also at the *Musée*, a ceiling painted by Prudhon, *Diana imploring Jupiter.* Although he was forty-five years old when he produced this work, the artist did not yet possess the full freedom of his style. He did not dare to rely on his genius; it is evident that the two characteristics which form his strength, govern him by turns; he passes now to one and now to the other. He might be styled a cavalier, who has two horses to manage, and can not make them preserve the same pace. This indecision did not last long; Prudhon mastered the rebellious coursers (and pardon me for this allegory in his own style), harmony rides behind him. This ceiling of Prudhon's, is in a warm and luminous tone; his Jupiter has perhaps more the appearance of a father of a family, than the terrible god of Olympus; but his Diana! what an adorable creation! with what simple confidence does the huntress ask from Jupiter permission to light the world during the night in order to contemplate on Mount Lathma, Endymion sleeping under the foliage!

Allegory was the language which Prudhon loved best. He loved it too much; we must regret the sometimes whimsical fancy which inspired him with pictures, such as *Love seduces Innocence, Pleasure entices her away, Repentance follows Pleasure.* And what is to be said about his allegories on Liberty, Equality, and Fraternity? Often, however, thanks to allegory, he displays on the canvass all the depths of his mind; as in the *Soul taking its Flight to Heaven.* Is it a paraphrase of these words of the psalmist, "Would that I had the wings of a dove?" Or is it the representation of a dream of Prudhon's? He has represented the soul, under the form of an angel held down to the earth; the angel spreads his wings, raises his arms toward Heaven; but like Prometheus, he is chained on this storm-beaten rock, which is called the world; at his feet are scattered all the flowers of life, all that forms the joy of pride, and all that forms the joy of love; but, among these sceptres and crowns, a serpent raises his head: it is the demon, it is the spirit of evil, it is sorrow, that old eternal tenant of the world.

The *Musée* of the Louvre will open from day to day, I doubt not, to Prudhon's pictures; meanwhile one does not know where to study his genius. I have seen in a gallery an *Assumption of the Virgin,* over which Prudhon has successfully spread the joy of heaven. The Virgin, is like all those which he has painted, adorable in sentiment; it seems as if Raphael, Leonardo de Vinci and Correggio might have inspired the picture.

Prudhon is scarcely to be found at the print-room. The burin has not deigned to reproduce this great artist's work. Perhaps it has feared its inability to translate the whole of the exquisite charm, all the ineffable sentiment and severe grace which characterize him. Are the best days of engraving, then, passed? Shall we not again behold those laborious families, who shone in the seventeenth and eighteenth centuries? Prudhon has scarce found any but lithographers; his works are comprised in a thin volume, where are to be found a few of the sacred subjects and a few of the profane ones. The latter, his youthful works, are most numerous; the religious sentiment did not impress him until his latter years.*

Prudhon himself engraved *Phrosine and Milidor*, for the works of Gentil-Bernard. One of his sons engraved *The Arts* after him. The head of Poetry is simple and beautiful; it is the very muse who inspired André Chénier and Prudhon.

* I have seen in this volume a beautiful group, *The Abduction of Psyche;* a pretty cupid, *the cruel fellow laughs at the tears he makes us shed;* a chaste face, which is a good representation of *Innocence;* we see that she has never looked at the devil, even at a distance; *The Fates with the Distaff*, so attractive that one would like to go and meet them: it is evident that death was never dreaded by Prudhon; *Love and Venus;* it is not Venus alone, but a woman who loves; *The Family in Distress*, the terrible drama, commenced by Mademoiselle Mayer and completed by Prudhon. It is a family without bread and without hope, the ravages of suffering are seen in the faces of all; at the sight of this picture, we feel that life departs and death comes, or rather that life is no longer present, and that death has not yet come. *Truth Descended from Heaven and led by Minerva;* beautiful *Groups of Children*, the painter's children when he cradled them on his knees; *Diana Imploring Jupiter;* a divine *Head of the Virgin; Venus and Adonis:* nothing can be more sweet to the eyes, if not to the heart; *The Abduction of Psyche by the Zephyrs:* like Correggio, Prudhon had marvellous skill in painting figures in the air.

M. Charles Blanc has published a catalogue of the works of Prudhon, at the end of his very remarkable work on this great painter.

The works of Prudhon are scattered no one knows where; and yet they are innumerable. Prudhon, dreamer as he was, has scarcely taken time to cast here and there a glance before or behind the domain of Art. He traced out path after path, ever ardent in cultivating the ungrateful soil which produces so few golden ears in time of harvest. His portraits, drawings, pastels, water-colors, miniatures, and vignettes,* are innumerable; his pictures are his only works which can be counted, for his pictures were so to speak, the production of the intervals of his wretchedness.

Prudhon had not only the instincts of Art but also its science. It will be remembered, that he discovered colors at the age of thirteen, in the weeds and flowers. He did not limit himself to this: he has left in his letters, pages worthy of being reproduced, which prove that he was not one of those ignorant artists who attain to genius without knowing the reason why.

* * * * * * *

"Nature gives the example of the richest variety, and if she has modelled the human race on a similar

* Like all the men of the first order, Prudhon displayed genius at every page of his work, even at the feeblest. A vignette of Prudhon was sold for 500 francs to Sir —— Johnston. At the present day, the pictures of Prudhon are disputed, like those of Correggio. The cabinet of M. Marcille contains, among other beautiful things, a masterpiece of a foot square, *Venus and Adonis*.

Among the fervent admirers of Prudhon are remarked, Lord Yarmouth, M. Ledru-Rollin, M. le marquis Maison, M. de Rothschild.

type, has she not also infinitely modified color, forms, and shape? And you wish me, a daily witness of its variations, to adopt, in order to express what I behold, a style foreign to their nature [this was a hit at the school of David]. It would be as well to adopt in a picture, the same face and the same sentiment for all the men and the same beauty for all the women. I neither can nor will see with the eyes of others; their spectacles do not suit me. Liberty is the strength of the arts. Because Racine and Corneille produced masterpieces, are we no longer to speak and to write except in Alexandrines?

"In France we must adopt the silvery tones of Vandyck, Velasquez, and Teniers, the yellow tones are useless under our skies. To provide against the ravages of time, the artist must overlay his carnations with fresh and lake-colored tones, heighten his shadows with vigorous but transparent tones, spread an harmonious surface over the flesh and drapery, and thus secure the duration and harmony of a picture. Time destroys the freshness of color, while vigorous tints, on account of being underneath, resist these attacks longer; we thus see the old pictures despoiled of their freshest tones, while their vigor and effect still remain."

* * * * * *

Prudhon possessed all the delicacies of color; his pencil, in turn and at once, pure, pleasing and smooth, had the freshness of a rose. He said that it was necessary to have the ideal rather than the reality of color; but he was both ideal and true.*

Certain backgrounds in Prudhon's pictures incontestably proved that he was a great master in landscape, although he always sacrificed it to figures. What can be more aerial than those skies! was it not with the pencil of Correggio and of Claude, that he produced them? Prudhon succeeded better than any one else in giving a body to the Zephyrs. Have you seen these gods of the air, grouped in the clouds, balancing themselves in the groves, admiring themselves in the surface of the waters? Would you not call them dreams which were melting away? Breughel de Vlour was not more light or vapory.

Prudhon may be said to be the son of Correggio in a direct line.

During the first campaigns in Italy, a Leda by Correggio was sent to the Louvre by Bonaparte; thanks to awkward soldiers who treated it as an enemy, when it arrived, it was but a fragment of the work of the master, that is to say, a Leda without a head. Prudhon happened to be called upon to restore the picture. He trusted to his first inspiration and rediscovered beneath his pencil, as by enchantment, the head painted by Correggio. It has the same roundness, the same grace, the same freshness.

* On beholding a picture of Prudhon, M. Ingres, who often, by a single word, paints a man as well as with his palette, exclaimed, with enthusiasm: "Prudhon, what a beautiful delusion!" Is not this beautiful delusion the truth in the arts?

Bonaparte on again seeing the Leda on his return from Italy, saluted it as an old acquaintance, little suspecting that a French artist had picked up the pencil of Correggio, to reproduce the head.

According to Shakspere, life is a fairy tale, which we hear for the second time. Yes we have in ourselves recollections of another life; this thought of the English poet contains profound truth for lofty minds. How many times, here below, has a man continued the work or the action which death had interrupted in another's hands! How many times in turning over the annals of history, in consulting the life of an ancient, has a modern exclaimed: "It is myself." It is the same heart and the same mind, the same wisdom and the same folly; in a word, it is the same soul, for the soul is all this. Prudhon said, with the accent of conviction: "I am the shade of Correggio." In his infancy, when at school among the good monks at Cluny, he ventured into the library to look for pictures. A book was open on the table, he looked at it and was lost in astonishment at a design in red, after the Danae of Correggio. Steps were heard, and the pupil, as if he had feared discovering a secret, took to flight, muttering between his teeth, "Correggio! Correggio!" A few days afterward, while Danae was still alive in his young imagination, on his return from school, he picked up on the road, a folio page which the wind was tossing in the dust. Oh, unhoped for joy! the first word which caught Prudhon's eye, was Correggio, Correggio, which seemed to him, written in letters of gold or in lines of fire. He ran his dazzled eyes over the page, he scarcely knew how to read, but he understood before having read; now, here is word for word, what was written on the second page of this leaf, which he always preserved among his archives:—

"For Nature, who paints herself in her works, had made him a painter at his birth; he received his pencil from the hands of the Graces; without having consulted the great masters, without having studied the antique, or ever having gone beyond his own country, he straightway achieved creative genius. He painted almost always alone, at Parma or in Lombardy. His exclamation is well known, after having a long time regarded, in profound silence, a picture of Raphael: *Anch'io son pittore.* A great taste in design, enchanting color, a delicate manner, infinite charms scattered over all his works, closed the mouth of the critics; it is scarcely noticed that there is a little incorrectness in his contours, and a little oddity in the turn of his heads, his attitudes and contrasts; he lived poor and charitable; he was a great man and was ignorant of the fact. The prices paid for his works, were very moderate, which joined to the pleasure of helping the indigent, caused him to live in poverty. One day, having been to Parma, to receive the pay for one of his works, they gave him two hundred livres in copper coin : it was during the warmest weather ; Correggio set out with this load ; he would have liked well to rest, but his family were waiting for him. He arrived in time to succor his children, but a fever had seized him on the road, and he died of it. His Virgins are especially esteemed, as are also his children and his......"

After this precious windfall, Prudhon lived often on the remembrance of Correggio ; he saw him in his dreams, bent under his load of coin, toiling on, toiling on ever, like the dead in the ballad, taking no time for repose at the fountain or on the shady side of the road. "Ah," exclaimed Prudhon, "how I should have liked, at the risk of catching that fatal fever, to have carried the two hundred livres in copper coin, to that family who were waiting for it, to preserve from death, that man of heart and genius." In his gloomy days, Prudhon found a thoroughly poetic consolation in re-reading the page which he had miraculously found on the road. Correggio was not only a master for him ; but a friend whose joy and anguish he had shared in. Prudhon was not the shade of Correggio, he was Correggio himself, returned in another century and another country, with his ever-fresh and ever-pleasing graces. If the ancient Correggio succumbed under the cross of the poor man, and of the artist crowned with thorns and not with glory, has not the modern Correggio also undergone, without complaint, the same crown and the same cross? The first died for his children, did not the second suffer life for his?

Is not Prudhon, the son of Correggio, a brother of André Chénier? Does not his genius really consist in the alliance of antique grace and the sentiment of modern ages? Prudhon was at once Greek and French. He rediscovered the art of Phidias, and like Prometheus, brought down the fire of heaven to animate his statue. His imagination loved the country of Homer, but his heart inhabited the country which Christ founded with his blood. In the first days of our century, in the time when Louis David passed for a great painter, Prudhon was disdained, as an artist without force, character, or style. The Romans being in fashion, Prudhon found himself overshadowed by Louis David, as André Chénier was by his brother; but by degrees the fallen stars were eclipsed: André Chénier and Prudhon, the regenerators of poetry and painting, have thrown into the shade, Joseph Chénier and Louis David.

BLANGINI.

HERE LIES THE SOUND OF THE WIND.

A MUSICIAN has just died in silence, oblivion, and neglect, still holding in his arms a broken violin—a musician who has had his days of festivity, of love and poetry; who has passed his youthful days with kings and queens in the courts of France and Germany; who was, for at least three weeks, the lover, or the wooer, of the most charming of profane princesses, the princess Borghese. He was besides a man of talent, unsophisticated as a child, enthusiastic as an Italian, infatuated with music, loving painting without knowing anything about it, loving the women with all the gallant delicacies which Benserade has sung.

Blangini was born at Turin in 1781. His father passed his life at the bar, and left at his death, as the sole fragments of a settled fortune, a portfolio full of notes, demonstrating his rights to the domain of Toricella. Blangini renounced the inheritance, and threw the notes in the fire, liking better to run over the gamut than to pursue Italian palaces which were worth little more than castles in the air. This, it is well known, was not lost time. His mother, of a noble family of Genoa, was attached to the princess Félicité of Savoy. She was extremely hospitable to the French exiles of 1792. "By this hospitality," Blangini used to say, "she opened to us in a worthy manner the doors of France."*

Blangini made his debut in music like Grétry, of whom he was always a pleasing though feeble echo. At seven he became a chorister-boy of the cathedral of Turin. A Latin-master and a music-master were given to him. Of what use was a Latin-master to one

* Among the exiled nobility who had recourse to the heart and the purse of Madame Blangini, a few words must be said of Madame de Saint S——. She had, during this very exile, married, at Turin, M. de Tro—. The young couple, completely carried away by the honeymoon, were desirous of returning to France. Madame Blangini furnished, in her noble poverty, a hundred louis for their perilous journey. They set out, one by land, the other by sea, resolved to risk all hazards in order to again behold their dear country in the intoxication of their love. They arrived at Paris in the height of the reign of Terror. They found one another, but soon separated, in the fear of death, or rather of the guillotine. Madame de Saint S—— disguised herself as one of the common people, to work in full liberty in a seamstress' establishment. M. de Tro— went no one knows where. The poor wife soon regretted that she had not been able to brave the guillotine alongside of her husband: the seamstress in whose house she was, read the newspapers; one day she learned that M. de Tro— had just been condemned to death by the bloody tribunal. She ran and presented herself before Fouquier-Tinville. "My husband is to die to-morrow, I wish to die with him."—"That is a good trait in a woman," said the president. "Citizen, go and have your hair cropped." She went and rejoined her husband, they passed their last hours together. The favor was granted to them of going to execution in the same wagon. They died without a murmur, with a funereal pleasure.

who was to speak the universal language of music? The abbé Ottani taught him the gamut; he studied with so much zeal, that at the age of twelve he composed, and had performed at the church of the Trinity, a *Kyrie* of some character.

He was seized about this time with an ardent love of the violoncello, which was to his death his most dear and faithful love.—"See," said he to me, seizing the bow with vehemence, "it is in this violoncello that all my hopes and all my passions have gradually taken refuge; there are souls in this violoncello that I can reanimate as if by miracle; my whole life is there, for my life is no longer aught but a recollection. If I wished, I could, at the first stroke of the bow, cause to reappear the adored form of Pauline."

The court of Turin was very devotional: Blangini was brought up amid sacred chants and the fumes of incense; he never regretted it. Happy are those who learn to love God in the dawn of youth; this love perfumes the whole of their lives; they occasionally return to it as to a dear refuge in their days of sorrow or weariness; they pass on to death with a firmer step and a calmer heart. There was, however, alongside of the church, a theatre, the *Carignano*. Blangini concealed himself, in order to go there, in the cassock of the abbé Ottani, one evening when the *Amor imaginario* of Fioraventi was performed. He was enchanted with the sweet, smooth, and unctuous music. The *Amor imaginario* long remained his musical breviary. "Nearly half a century afterward, I still knew it by heart; in my hours of solitary leisure, when I suffered my fingers to wander over the keys of the harpsichord, I was completely amazed to hear the beloved airs of this opera." After Fioraventi came Paesiello, after the *Amor imaginario* came *Nina.* He thought it ravishing.—"It is to these operas that I owe the little harmony I have scattered here and there. I have been simple and natural from the remembrance of these masterpieces. I could have made a little more noise—in my music—but I was afraid of disagreeably awaking the shades of those great masters who never made harmony an exercise of artillery."

Blangini has written his memoirs—quite like Jean-Jacques and Chateaubriand. He had a certain picturesque and poetical tone in relating his life. "How is it that, while I scarcely recollect what I did yesterday, the remembrances of my childhood reanimate themselves by enchantment as under the wand of a fairy? My memory is so complaisant for those times, that I can at my will, when I resume my linen robe, replace myself in the cathedral of Turin before the pulpit, where I used to sing with my clear, chorister's voice; I amuse myself in rehearsing how I passed from point to point on Easter-day, when I sang the Epistle; here are the twisted columns of the high altar before me, the royal family of Sardinia in their gallery hearing the divine office with pious attention. The illusion is so great, that the incense burnt in the magnificent silver censers still perfumes the air I breathe."

At sixteen, Blangini went to Bologna to pursue his ardent dream, when a general called Bonaparte suddenly appeared to turn all Italy topsy-turvy. Madame Blangini, soon without asylum and without resources except a good heart, resolved to depart to France, trusting in God. She was a musician, and hoped to give concerts with her six children in the cities of the south. The whole family set out on a Friday, in spite of Blangini's supplications, who always had a dread of a Friday (he died on a Friday). The journey went on very well for two days; but at the summit of the col di Tenda, in place of a hospital open to travellers as on Mont Cenis, they met with a rather disagreeable adventure. They were about to re-enter their vehicle, after having walked nearly five hours, when the vetturino began to whistle, and to whistle out of tune. "What a position for a musician!" exclaimed Blangini. They soon heard cries of *Ferma! ferma!* Blangini, who had assumed the courage of the head of a family, quickly descended. He suddenly found himself before three men in masks, armed with guns. They aimed at him forthwith. All descended from the carriage. The brigands pillaged pitilessly, after which they made Blangini kneel down in order to shoot him. "One may well have some ill-will to Fridays." At last, thanks to the tears and cries of his mother and sisters, they contented themselves with stripping him to his shirt, rolling him a little in the snow, and laughing immoderately.

At Nice, the family gave their first concert. An audience collected, somewhat out of curiosity; they wanted to see this poor mother, who was going into exile, dragging in her train, half a dozen children almost at the breast, all musicians, singing or playing. They embarked for Marseilles, after having picked up enough to pay the passage. They also gave concerts at Marseilles, Montpelier, Lyons, all the southern cities. The pilgrimage lasted a long time; it was blessed by God and by St. Cecilia.

They at last ventured into this palace and desert called Paris. Blangini, always inclined to superstition, augured well from the hotel at which the little caravan halted: it was the *hotel de la Providence.* A little time after the arrival, they established themselves in the *rue du Cherche-Midi*, in the old abbey of the Premontorians. They lived then on the past, that is to say, on little; they thought of giving concerts at Paris; they studied, loved one another, prayed to God with accompaniment of piano, guitar, and violoncello.

"Every evening, between nine and ten o'clock, I heard with an unusual charm, certain sounds of an old tune escape from the room above me." This music, which often seemed to come from another world, continued to the middle of the night: they were old airs of Lulli and Rameau. At the loud sound of the instrument, he recognised beyond doubt, a spinnet of the time of the regency. He contented himself a long time with listening to the music, without troubling himself about the musician; but at last his gradually-sharpened curiosity, carried him almost in spite of himself, to the door of his colleague in harmony. He knocked with a trembling hand. He was not very much surprised at being received by an ancient lady, of more than eighty, dressed *à la Pompadour*, having still the smile, the wit, and agreeable manner of the gallant reign; she was the marchioness de Saint-Simon. She took the young musician under her protection, taught him something of the science of the world, praised him to every comer among the fragments of the nobility, which was about to flourish once more. She was so to speak, the first article of his journal.

From the *rue de la Cherche-Midi*, the little caravan went to live near the Madeleine; it was in 1799. So far Blangini had done little more than practise, but after this year, his name may be inscribed among true musicians. He gave concerts every tenth day, in the morning. He was talked about, the misfortunes of his family, were related; either by chance, curiosity, or for the sake of the music, they went to his concerts. He became the fashion in the gay world, when but scarce eighteen. There was therefore bread for the morrow at his mother's, which had not been seen for a long time. In 1800, he commenced the collection of his romances; it is from that period that those charming serenades and graceful canzonets date, which more than one heart still recalls with a thrill of delight. From romances he rose to the comic opera by *la Fausse Duègne:* but, finding that a romance was more productive, to him at least, than a comic opera, he resumed his light labors. Certain of Blangini's romances have made the tour of the world, as do all light productions which come from the heart and go to the heart. M. le Comte Ségur, has remarked somewhere, that he had heard *Il est trop tard* in Siberia. Blangini was soon much sought after to give lessons in singing, or to sing. Never had a musician so brilliant a school. The queen of Bavaria, the queen of Westphalia, the queen of Holland, the princess Pauline, the duchess de Berri, the princess Poniatowski, the countess d'Appony, the *maréchale* Ney, the duchess de Rovigo, the marchioness de Polignac, the duchess de Broglie, in a word, almost all the women of his time, celebrated for birth, beauty, or intellect, sang with him. He had no longer an hour's liberty; he devoured time; he devoured space; he went into ten saloons during the same evening; he returned wearied and broken down, having only strength enough left to embrace his mother and his young sisters, who wept tears of joy and thankfulness. It was, he said, "the most delightful and glorious hour of the day." He scarce took time to sleep. During the four or five hours of the night which he passed in his room, he often kept awake on account of a romance, a serenade or a canzonet, or even sometimes for an opera. The opera, however, was always beyond his powers; he needed simply the soft breeze of the rustic path; the mountain wind broke his pleasant voice. An opera was not to be made off hand, with a little melody and a graceful air here and there. For an opera, time and quiet are needed. Blangini was always in motion, in the midst of the noise of the world. His serenades were his true glory; everybody has sung them, at Paris and in the provinces, at the theatre and in the street, at the court and in the garret.

"Why," I asked him one day, "do you stop your ears?" — "It is at the recollection of a period in my life, when I could not move a step without hearing my music. You understand that one should stop his ears at the least."

He did not thus go about the gay world, among these women so beautiful or graceful, these queens of the world and of fashion, without leaving fragments of his heart here and there; but, like a true disciple of Plato, he saw in love only an archangel with white wings, scattering into our souls the chastest perfumes of divine sentiment; it was better than Plato, it was

Petrarch. Were not his canzonets and his serenades inspired by some one or other of his fair scholars? He loved in silence, not daring to say anything, even in a look. He was loved likewise in the same mystery, and all this exhaled in song; but was it not enough to sing a duett of the heart, to mingle his voice in the divine harmony? How many persons there are who would do well to confine themselves to song! Blangini recalled especially, among the most beloved, mademoiselle de Montpezat and the countess de Lubersac.

In 1805, the little caravan was somewhat dispersed; a sister who played on the violin, had left for Germany; another who sang like an angel, had returned to Italy. In his turn, Blangini was desirous to travel, to rest himself a little from all this Parisian hubbub, of which he had his ears full. He went to Germany, where he met, singing his serenades at the court of Munich, the king of the Belgians, who was then a duke of Saxe-Cobourg. Blangini was soon appointed chapel-master. After having sung with all the great personages of the court, he returned to Paris, prouder of his costume than of his success. The elector had given him the true dress of a maestro, a green coat with crimson collar and facings, a three-cornered hat with a golden tassel, an officer's sword and sword-knot. On his return to Paris, the doors of the grand opera were opened to him. With his cocked hat on his head, he was no longer doubtful of anything; he composed the music of *Nephthali* with a great deal too much carelessness, as if it had been a serenade for two voices. The libretto was bad, considered as the libretto of an opera; nevertheless, in spite of the libretto and the music, *Nephthali* met with an enthusiastic success; the curtain fell amid great applause, the authors were called for; that was not all, scarcely was the name of Blangini uttered, when the cry resounded from all sides, "*Let him appear! let him appear!*" He was behind the scenes completely overcome, not having heard a single note of the music. Laïs and Rolland led him on the stage, in obedience to the audience. At that flourishing period of the empire, everybody wore their hair *à la Titus*, it was like a universal flattery to Napoleon; but Blangini had not cropped his locks, which fell over his shoulders like weeping willow boughs, powdered with hoar frost. At the sight of his pretty, terrified face, half lost in this forest of black curls, the pit received him with a hearty peal of laughter. "I wept like an infant, I was never so happy in my life, except when I embraced my mother." All this was, however, but a transitory success; at the end of six months, naught remained of all this music but a single air, sung by Madame Branchu, and greatly admired by Mèhul: *Votre cœur est-il inflexible?*

From the grand opera, he returned to Feydeau with the *Femmes vengées*, which, thanks to Ellevion and Madame Gavaudin, had good fortune. Other comic operas followed this, without any too great success. Blangini could however dispense, without complaint, with the honors of the opera, as one who figured so well on so many other stages.

About this time, he became one of the musicians of the court of Napoleon. M. de Ségur, grand master of ceremonies, M. de Talleyrand, prime minister, Napoleon himself received him like a child, spoiled by the women and by genius ; but he was still better received by the beautiful princess Pauline. He ventured to fall desperately in love with her ; the princess was far from complaining of it, she smiled on all his inspirations. "It was the most beautiful duet of my life." He wrote under the eyes of the princess, the serenade which was so much sung : *Se son lontano dal mio diletto ;* that romance, the words of which were by herself : *Il faut partir, le ménestrel vient de l'apprendre ;* in a word, a great number of fresh and graceful melodies destined to live for a morning or so.

The princess appointed him her musical director ; Josephine to vex her, appointed Blangini the day after, composer of her chamber. What was to be done? Serving two masters might be got along with, but to serve two women, was running a great risk of spoiling the concert. Blangini voted according to his heart. The princess left for Nice ; he soon followed her like a lord, in a court carriage. In spite of all his love, there was some vain satisfaction in his mind at reappearing in his native country, in this splendid style.

The sojourn at Nice, under the enchanting glances of Pauline, was the most delightful oasis of his life. He scarce dared to believe in his own happiness; he was almost terrified at it. How many a delightful promenade on the seashore or in the palace-garden! how many evenings deliciously wasted in revery or song beside Pauline!

It was almost like living at a château: they rose early; after a gay breakfast, they took a ride, a stroll in the garden, or a sail on the sea. There was a charming absence of ceremony. If there were any Excellencies of the department, or who were passing through, to receive, she put on the most serious air in the world; but her friends knew that she was laughing in her sleeve; she reigned more by the empire of her graces, her beauty, and her brilliancy, than by the empire of her brother. As to her husband, the prince Borghese, no one ever thought of him. Everybody enjoyed the freedom of the little court of Nice; they amused themselves, not with all their might, but with all their heart. In the evening, Blangini had enough to do: music, always music; it was the staple of conversation. Did a dignitary of Nice enter, a ritornello of the gayest kind was called for; if it was a great lady, forthwith a serenade. Everybody was received by the order of the gamut. The archbishop of Genoa, the cardinal

Spina, grand almoner of the princess, was saluted like the rest, by strains of secular music. On Sunday, an altar was erected in the saloon for the celebration of mass; Blangini took the piano to counterfeit the organ; Pauline, carelessly reclining on a sofa, heard more or less of the music or the sermon. It is impossible to be so beautiful without being a little profane. However, in this palace filled with music and love, which was almost a palace of fairies, Blangini was not without disquiet: happiness is always tremulous. He knew very well that, if Napoleon discovered the mystery, poor Blangini ran the risk of being favored with a sub-lieutenant's commission, in order to sing his serenades in Spain with a cannonade for accompaniment. On the other hand, the princess was whimsical, and must be incessantly amused. To amuse a pretty woman, who has nothing to gain and nothing to lose, is a labor for a genius of the first rank; and Blangini could say, oftener than Titus, "I have lost my day." She wanted him to sing only for herself. She heard one evening that he had gone to sing at the house of the prefect of Nice; she despatched a footman after him, with orders to interrupt him and bring him back. The order was obeyed in every particular.

"What song were you singing, monsieur?" said she to him on his return.—"I was singing, if it please you, madame, this air of Nephthali: *Nous le touchons, ce fertile rivage;* but I was not able to finish it: they fancied at the prefect's that your palace was on fire, the valet made such an uproar."—"The palace on fire would have been nothing; the secret is, I was overcome by ennui; continue the air at the note where you broke off."

He must needs obey.

The princess had all the caprices of a beautiful woman. Another time, when she wanted something to do, she summoned Blangini.

"This evening, maestro, we will disguise ourselves to visit, incognito, the gipsy whom they talk so much about. Be ready to follow me. I am somewhat desirous to know whether I am destined to a throne or a cottage."—"What matters the throne or the cottage? will you not always be a queen?"—"I want to have the answer to the enigma of my life, that is all. Take the dress of a monk; for my part, I shall disguise myself as a Benedictine nun."

In the evening, the princess and the musician silently left the palace. They went on foot to the house where the gipsy prophesied. They announced themselves as connected with the church, brother Pancratius and sister Agnes. The gipsy was not deceived, although a prophetess. She recognised, if not Blangini, at least Pauline, who was a princess to the tips of her finger-nails. "Oh! ho," said she, "this sister is not so catholic as she looks. You can not tell such stories to me."—"I do not ask you who

I am, I want to know what I shall be," said Pauline, abandoning her hand to the gipsy.—" What you will be, what you will be," said the old woman, studying at the same moment the lines of the hand and the features of the face—" you will not be, I fancy, a saint of the calendar."—" Have done!" replied Pauline impatiently.—" What do you want me to tell you? it is a sad thing to tell . . . You will die on the field of battle, that is, in your beauty . . . See, the line stops before the point of fifty."—" And where shall I die?"—" In Italy."—" I want to die in France."—" I can do nothing about it."—" You do not know what you are talking about; I am soon going to return to Neuilly, where I wish to live to the end of my life: is it not so, Brother Pancratius?"

Blangini approached a little nearer.

" And I, where shall I die?" he asked the gipsy.—" Where do you want to die?"—" In Italy, in my true country."—" Well, you will die in France," said the gipsy as she consulted her basin of sand.—" I see very plainly," said Pauline, " that Fate does not agree with us: she always arranges so as to disappoint our most cherished wishes. Nothing is so easy as to predict the future to those whose desires are known; all that is necessary, in order to hit the matter exactly, is to predict the opposite of what they expect. That, however, is not all; I wish to know, by the virtue of your magic, why I shall die at forty." —" Alas my beautiful lady, you know, as well as I, that in this world we often die in consequence of our sins. Besides, a beautiful woman has no longer anything good to do after she has found a gray hair among her black ones."—"But what will force me to go and die in Italy?"—"My art is very limited; I can not well divine small causes. He who will force you to return to Italy will doubtless be the prince, your august husband."—"Pshaw!" said Pauline, "I shall not do so, unless I go to get rid of him."—"Well, well, my beautiful lady, it will not do to say too often, 'Fountain, I'll not drink of thy waters.'"

The princess departed very much discontented with the gipsy, who by chance had predicted almost the exact truth. The predictions for Blangini did not turn out so correct: she said that he would die in exile; he died in his own bed, exiled, doubtless, from glory; but the prophetess did not utter metaphors.*

During his sojourn at Nice, Blangini went to Milan, hoping to gather some musical ideas there. But what did he find? He was informed that the

* Blangini had collected some very curious notes upon the court of Nice. He recounted simply, without commentary, what the princess said or did; her caprices; her jealousies; her hatred toward the prince Borghese, who had no other fault in her eyes than that of being her husband, but which was, by-the-by, a fault of the gravest character. I have turned over all these notes at my leisure, and reproduced the most curious, those especially which display any trait of the musician; I leave the rest for the chroniclers of the imperial family.

son of Mozart was a resident of that city; out of reverence to the father, Blangini was desirous of paying his respects to the son, hoping besides to find a worthy echo of the great musician; he mounted to his apartment, entered, bowed: a rather ill-favored gentleman, buried in figures, answered him in monosyllables.

"But really, monsieur, are you indeed the son of the great Mozart?'"—"Yes."—"You have come to this land of the arts protected by the shadow of your father . . . ."

Mozart, second of the name, did not understand.

"I hoped, monsieur, to have found you alone with a piano or violin."—"What the devil are you prating to me about? I do not like music."—"What! you are not a musician?"—"Me! what do you take me for? I am a banker, monsieur. See here! this is my idea of music."

M. Mozart took a pile of crowns in his hand and made them ring on his desk.

Everything went on as smoothly as possible at Nice: Napoleon, however, a little scandalized at the duet, gave orders to recall one of the performers to France; Pauline, however, was not willing to let Blangini go. "I improvise the words, and you the music, of a serenade which does not concern his majesty my brother. I will not yield except to the force of bayonets." Napoleon, knowing the bad temper of his sister, contented himself with sending her husband, the prince Borghese, to her; which was a great deal worse than the bayonets. The prince himself, husband as he was, wanted to be of the concert and the party. Here was a husband well set to work! The princess, hearing of his arrival, wanted to brave him to the last moment: she got into a barouche with Blangini and rode about the town, nonchalantly reclining toward the musician, who dared not object, though he trembled like an Italian in misfortune.

The husband managed his affairs so well, that Blangini was soon forced to go and sing elsewhere. He returned to Paris in very poor condition with some morsels of interrupted melody. He set to work again.

He was unfortunate in finding poets of romances and operas; it must be confessed that he flourished under the empire. His best words were inspired by the women. La Grassini, among others, inspired him very agreeably by this song, after his own style:—

"Adora in cenni tuoi questo mio cor fidele
Sposa sarò se vuoi non dubitar di me,
Ma un sguardo sereno ti chiedo d'amor.

La Grassini was to sing the *Cleopatra* before Napoleon; she was in his good graces; she had introduced this interlude in the opera. As she sang, she turned her amorous glances toward the emperor's box. It was Cleopatra again before Cesar.

Blangini returned to Germany as musical director to the king of Westphalia; he kept up great style at the court. At the end of a year, the king, discontented with his chapel, gave him a mission to seek, with 100,000 francs, in France and Italy, for three musicians. Blangini had a charming trip, following the route of the scholars. He returned alone and was disgraced; but, at that time, the king himself was disgraced: it was in 1814.

Blangini belonged to all parties, except the party of non-paying kings. He returned to Paris. For what king was he to sing? Was he himself to become a Frenchman, remain a Bavarian, or resume the Italian? Ingrate! he began to sing for the English, with the *Cleopatra* who passed from Cesar to Pompey. Blangini sinned in this. Talent as well as courage needs a country; Blangini had no country: in that lies the sad portion of his life.

In 1817, Louis XVIII. appointed him superintendent of his chapel; a little while after, the duchess of Berry appointed him director of her music. A little wearied with his travels, he settled down in every way. He married one of the prettiest and most charming women of Paris; but his reputation, if not his happiness, had reached its termination. We can not always sing the same song.

The princess Pauline had not forgotten him. She wrote to him that she expected him in Italy. How could he avoid rejoining so much beauty and love? But how was he to leave so much love and beauty? He stood firm to marriage. More than once, however, must he have followed in his dreams her who had deigned to descend as low as his heart.

Like all those who derive their renown from fashion, after a day of chance and good fortune, Blangini passed out of fashion; the renown which was so brilliant, by degrees melted away; the name which was pronounced in song by every lip fell almost into oblivion. A man can not always be composing serenades and canzonets, nor be always the lover of the princess Pauline: all this is the business of youth, and youth must pass away. The grand opera soon handed him over to the comic opera, the comic opera to the vaudeville, the vaudeville to the romance, romance to forgetfulness. He consoled himself a little with sterile honors. Louis XVIII. gave him titles of nobility; this might still have passed, had these titles been accorded by Mozart and Palestrina. The poor man! he felt himself, in his last days, so pleased by the glories of this world, that he sought with ardor that of adjunct to the mayor of a small village of La Beauce. Music, happily for him, had not entirely deserted him; it was still, as in his youth, his dearest and most delightful refuge. Music to this fallen musician was a mistress still adored though faded; he did not dare to take her any longer into society, where her whitening locks were commented upon: he walked with her in solitary places, drawing from her some scintillations of the olden time. I have often heard poor Blangini, abandoning himself to his still ardent inspiration, recover now and then some melodies worthy of the lover of Pauline. His eye was reanimated by the sacred fire; he heard with an amorous sadness those melodies which he had not taken the trouble to note down—those melodies which died away in the air with his last hopes. Sometimes he rose overcome by agitation, let his arms fall, hung his head sadly, and seemed to say: "For all this, it is still music!" Benserade, also, who had had his days of festival at the court of Louis XIV.—Benserade, the favorite of glory and of fortune—ended at last by no longer being able to find a printer for his pretty verses; but he, at least for his part, had a bit of charcoal left to write them with on the walls of his room, where people came to read them. Blangini would no longer note down his songs: "My wife herself has plenty of other songs to sing." There is no sadder spectacle than that of a poor artist who witnesses the last agony of his glory when he feels the fire still in his heart.

Blangini was a humming-bird Grétry: grace always without force, the delicate gentleness of the birds. The solemnity of the church chants had left no echo in his soul. He had studied the somewhat quiet music of Fioraventi; he had aimed at the simplicity of the great masters; but simplicity almost requires genius ; and Blangini's simplicity did not often attain that character. He was poetically gifted ; it was his success at eighteen that ruined him ; he wasted in vain sounds, serenades, and canzonets, all that was in his soul ; he wasted with lavish hands, his scarce-created melodies ; he shook the tree for the blossoms, without even waiting for the fruit. The tree itself became barren, but Blangini at least was intoxicated with delight with the spring-flowers.

One winter evening, some seven or eight years ago, I met Blangini in society, which he frequented with great difficulty ; we passed the evening in talking over Mozart, we parted with our hearts in our hands, as we gave one another the hand. He was wearied ; he had lost all his friends ; he beheld with a happy smile, a poor rhymer of twenty, living on lost time. The friendship progressed on his part rapidly. I was awakened the next morning before day, by hearing my door open.

" Who's there ?"—" It is Blangini who has come to carry you off."—" Carry me off ? And where to ?" —" My hermitage."

I lit a candle, looked distrustfully at Blangini, but found him in the most reasonable mood in the world ; he was equipped more like an English than an Italian traveller. I had no difficulty in deciding to follow him. Some minutes after, I got into his post-chaise ; fortune had not entirely forgotten him. We went to his country-seat, in the centre of the beautiful forest of Orleans. Our journey was pleasant in spite of the snow; we passed two months in the forest, in the society of the wolves, a neighboring curate, and a pretty Orléanaise. His retreat was noisy enough: piano, violoncello, and hautboy, each urging their claims. Even at night an Eolian harp sang to us most funereal strains.

Blangini had thus retired from the world to the forest of Orleans, with his beloved recollections, his sweet violoncello, and the pastel portrait of the princess Pauline. He was a most hospitable hermit, and greatly beloved by all around; the poor turned two leagues out of their way to pass by his door.

I met Blangini for the last time, a year ago, at a curiosity-shop. I had somewhat lost sight of him. He was still the same man, sad yet smiling, restless, extravagant, agitated, his eye full of fire. "Well, my dear Blangini how are the canzonets?"—"The canzonets? alas I am at my *requiem*."—"And your dear violoncello?"—"Ah, my violoncello, I have shed many a tear over it since our excursion to the forest. I hope that God will give me strength to break it at the hour of my death; for," continued he, pressing my hand with a tender and sad smile, "I do not wish that another shall possess the secret of the follies of my heart."

Blangini was not a musician, but a poet who wrote his hymns with his bow on the violoncello, that eloquent book which includes the gamut of the passions and responds to every beating of the heart. *Here lies a poet, here lies a soul that sang, here lies the sound of the wind*, as Antipater said over the tomb of Orpheus.

AN UNKNOWN SCULPTOR.

Nicolas Maillefer, was born in 1760, in the Vermandois, which favor he owed to a poor carpenter of La Thierrache. His mother was a sweet and pensive Fleming, living in the love of God and of her children. But he, who next to her God, rewarded her the best for her pains, was Nicolas Maillefer.

Nicolas Maillefer was born in a château. He thus related with charming simplicity, his first quarter of an hour of life:—

"I was born in the château of Marchais. At my first glance, I saw my poor mother, who did not look as if she were at a fête, although she was lying in a beautiful bed, decked with roses in gold embroidery, and shaded by velvet and silk; a lady soon appeared more delicate than a fairy, who took me in her arms and cradled me on her bosom. Ah! what a charming pillow. In truth, I was very easy about my condition; one could not commence life better; but alas! for me, great dreamer that I was—I was already dreaming. The dream was not long: a man of bad figure and rough manners, badly clothed and his shock of hair badly combed, opened the door of the room, advanced in silence to the fire, and put upon the hearth, a pot of, I don't know what. 'Monsieur Maillefer,' said the beautiful lady to him, 'you have got a fine boy there.' At that moment my brow darkened, for I at once perceived with whom I had to do, I was no longer marquis, but a clod-hopper like my father. My father, however, came to the bed, bowed slightly before the great lady, and gave me a tap on the cheek by way of caress, which I by no means thanked him for. *I should like right well to pay him back*, said I to myself. But at that moment I was startled, at noticing a sad smile which was interchanged between my father and my mother, a smile which revealed many hidden joys and sorrows, a smile which seemed to say: 'Ay, wife, let us console ourselves, poor devils that we are, we have courage as long as it pleases God.' I already felt a tear which came from my heart, roll down my cheek. I resigned myself to life, to the life of the poor, full of labor and of tears. But why are there poor? I said to myself at that moment."

You see by this, that Nicolas Maillefer had an original mind. At fifteen he read Jean-Jacques; at seventeen, he did better than that: he loved his wife; at twenty he did still better, he supported his family by his art of sculpture in wood.

The critics have never thought of throwing a little

light on that lost race of carvers in wood, who have left us so many masterpieces, scattered here and there in churches, châteaus, and monasteries. Nevertheless, nothing would be more curious to relate, than the history of these laborious, unrecognised artists, who had no newspapers to sing the praises of their works. Nicolas Maillefer will not be unrecognised; there is still time to save him from oblivion; moreover, thanks to the French Revolution, he has left too many recollections not to survive.

As I run over his life on the rapid wing, I will take at hazard, the first chapter which comes to hand.

In 1787, already the eighteenth century, which had commenced, by singing little arias like this: "*Come and dance beneath the brake*," was preparing to finish by songs like this: "*Let us dance the Carmagnole*." Nicolas Maillefer had been married ten years. He planted trees in his garden, he carved in his workshop, he cherished his wife in the chimney-corner; he gave alms from his threshold, not forgetting to moisten the alms with a drop of claret: "Here, my brave fellow, drink;" and when the poor man had drunk, he poured him out a cup of philosophy into the bargain.

Nicolas Maillefer was beloved by all the world, except M. the curé and M. the count (a count such as there were few, one of those who almost justified 1793). He preserved his free mode of conversation with them: so he took the trouble of warning them of the danger which threatened the nobility and clergy in France. "Yes, monsieur the curé, yes, monsieur the count, take care, the philosophers of whom you speak so ill have sown the ideas of deliverance, of which we shall gather the harvests. In the seventeenth century, men studied the arts: the tree was in flower; in the eighteenth, they studied humanity, the tree bore fruit. The hour of knowledge has arrived, it is the hour of liberty. I have my fears that that hour may strike unpleasantly on your ears. What matter? We are approaching a grand and noble contest. Abel rouses to attack Cain." M. le curé, and M. le comte would have liked right well to have driven the philosopher far away from them, but the church and the château could not dispense with the carver.

Thus in 1787, on a fine April morning, a footman from the château came to the workshop, to say to the carver, "M. the count wishes to see you."—"I am glad of it! Go and tell your master, that I am visible at any hour in my shop, which is without an antechamber."

At the report of the footman, the master was in a fury; but the fury over, he must needs pass by the shop of the carver. He went there one evening with his gun and his dogs, as if returning from the chase; Nicolas Maillefer was seated before his house, on a stone bench, with the last ray of the sun shining on him—the sun, his sole master.

After this visit, the sculptor went to the château. At dinner-time they called for him in vain; at the hour of lunch, as madame the countess was passing on horseback through a path in the wood, bordering on the château, she was very much surprised to meet the carver, side by side with a beggar, dividing like brothers, and each eating with the best appetite in the world, a piece of bread.

The next day, very much impressed with the artist's mode of life, she ventured into a hall where he was at work. "You are a very queer man, Monsieur Maillefer; so you like better to live in the woods than to live at the château."—"I wish to live neither with footmen, nor with masters, madame. A little bread, the bread of labor, the water of the spring, a little sunlight is enough for me, to say nothing of the fragrance of the forest, which is for me the best of desserts. In a word, madame, I like to live on the air of the time."—"It is rather a frugal repast," said the countess, somewhat out of her reckoning, "nevertheless, I saw yesterday with great pleasure, that you found the means of giving to the poor the crumbs of your table."—"Our kind Creator, madame, has permitted the joys of charity to his poorest creatures."

The countess blushed: they gave alms at the château, but that might be called, throwing away alms.

Toward evening, as the sculptor was departing, he saw on the threshold of the vestibule, the pretty hand of the countess, over the coarse hand of a poor man. "Ah! madame the countess," said he, "that hand if it continues to do thus, will efface many sins; it is by that hand that Saint-Peter will conduct you to paradise. Meanwhile, allow me to thank it after my fashion." Thereupon, without other preamble, Nicolas Maillefer kissed the hand of madame the countess, who did not trouble herself much about getting offended. After all, the sculptor was as handsome as he was proud; she loved to see this dreamer sometimes sad, sometimes gay, according to his mood; having at times his soul in his eyes or on his lips as at the moment of the kiss. There were plenty of countesses of the eighteenth century, who would have given him both hands.

The countess was a beautiful woman, who reminded one at the same time, of the portraits of Greuze and the pastels of La Tour; she was, it is true, the countess of the eighteenth century, but a little too far removed from the gentle atmosphere of the court, and having already a presentiment of the whirlwind, which was to scatter the leaves of the roses in her bosom. Thus with a gayety almost licentious on her lips, but at the same time with a pious thought in the bottom of her heart, a heavenly image, some restoration of banished virtue, in a word, madame de B.... who counted her thirty-four years, had commenced with love under the shadow of the screens of her grandmother, the marchioness of R.... ; she thought of ending with virtue, under the shadow of the great trees around her château. Until then, following the tradition of certain châteaux, she had divided humanity in her mind into two species: the children of the bountiful Creator, that is to say, the nobles, and the animals of the bountiful Creator, that is to say the common people. Nicolas Maillefer's kiss singularly modified her ideas in this respect.

At night, as the remembrance of this occurrence prevented her from sleeping, she called the count, to inform him that the sculptor was a man of mind and a man of heart, worthy of a better position in the world, to which the count replied, that "Nicolas Maillefer, in spite of his pretence of philosophy, was in his proper situation, that God had given him his hands to work with, and for nothing else, that he knew nothing of the science of humanity, that he was as ignorant as a schoolmaster." The countess wanted very much to reply, that Nicolas Maillefer had the eyes of a poet, and the mouth of a man who had read deeply in every chapter of humanity; but seeing that she would talk to no purpose on this subject, that the count had his reasons for not being of her opinion, she made her defence of Nicolas Maillefer to herself.

Some days after, the sculptor having finished his work, left the château without saying a word. At the door of the park he stopped, to salute the countess: "Are you going? Are you through already?" "Yes madame."

The count came up at the park gate: "I must pay you, Monsieur Nicolas Maillefer."—"No matter about that monsieur, I have repaired a work of art after a fashion....."—"You have worked for me," interrupted the count, who no longer feared to offend the sculptor, "I do not wish to be under obligations to you."—"As you please, monsieur."—"Return to the château, I am going there myself, and we will finish matters."

Nicolas Maillefer saluted the countess a second time, who by her sad look seemed to say to him: "If I had the management of this, it should not end thus."

At the château, the count clinked five crowns in his hand, in offering them to the sculptor. "You have worked five days, Monsieur Maillefer."—"I have not counted, monsieur, but as I am to be paid, I am well content to let it be so. It is not a crown, but a louis a day. So give me five louis or give me nothing, I care not which."—"You are a fellow unworthy of my favors."—"I am content, monsieur-count."—"Take care, no impertinence at any rate, if you please."—"Come, monsieur-count, no bluster; you know very well that I am not at all afraid of you. But as you choose to pay me with bad words, I will give you a receipt and be off."—"Wait, wait, once more I tell you, I wish to owe nothing to a man of your sort. Here, I will not haggle with you."

With these words, the count threw, rather than placed, five louis in the hand of the sculptor—one dropped on the floor. "You have only given me four, monsieur the count."—"And the one which dropped."—"I do not count that."—"Do you think that I am going to pick it up for you?"—"Do you think that I will do so?" said Nicolas Maillefer, energetically.—"But here comes one of your servants, just at the right time. John! John! come here."

And John having come—

"Pick up that gold piece."

The servant looked at him all agape; the count was ready to burst with rage; finally the servant, accustomed to obey, picked up the gold piece.—"Very good, my friend, keep it for yourself," said Nicolas Maillefer, turning on his heel. "Turn that rascal out of doors!" roared the enraged count.—"It is not worth while to take the trouble, monsieur the count, I am going but too willingly."

While descending the staircase, he contented himself with repeating: "Wo unto you who join house to house, and who add land to land, so that there remains no place for the poor! Are you, then, the only inhabitants of the world?"

During the same season, if we are to believe certain indiscreet reminiscences, the sculptor met several times, by accident, madame the countess in the shady paths about the château; these two minds comprehended one another marvellously; the flower of love bloomed in their hearts and embalmed them; but the historian has naught to say thereon—it is a mystery which the autumn wind has carried into infinity.

In 1792, power had changed hands a little in France. Nicolas Maillefer was commissioner of the republic; that is to say, the sovereign judge of the entire region. Thanks to this power, he exercised charity quite at his ease. Monsieur the curé had raised the cry of terror in the church, but without carrying off kind Providence with him. Nicolas Maillefer had succeeded him in the pulpit to preach the new religion. Monsieur the count had come to hear him like a courtier; having met him in the nave, in the middle of the crowd, who were offering him their hands, he said to him: "You really speak like an attorney, but you have no pity for us."

And while speaking in this manner, monsieur the count slipped a purse full of gold in the hand of the new-made tribune. The sculptor was, for a moment, overcome by a noble indignation; but, immediately restraining himself, he took the purse, advanced to the poor's box, emptied all the gold into it with a smile, and forthwith returned to give the purse to the count.

"We are lost!" exclaimed the count. "There is no longer anything to be done with this rabble."

Some days after, monsieur the count had gone to join monsieur the curé at Coblentz, with the countess and his two sons. But the decree followed which sequestrated the entire property of the emigrés to the use of the nation. Nicolas Maillefer received from Paris the order to sell the château and all its dependencies.

Soon, in due form, he had notice given that the sale would take place on the first Sunday in October, in the old hall of justice, at the set price of twenty thousand livres.

The evening previous, at eleven o'clock at night, as he had just gone to sleep in peace alongside of his wife, he was suddenly awakened by the sound of a footfall in the adjoining apartment. As there were no bolts to his door, a person could enter without hinderance. "Who's there?"—"Hush, if you please, I am the count de B...."

The sculptur lit his lamp and approached the count. "What brings you here so early, monsieur the count?" Monsieur de B.... was as pale as death. —"Alas! I have come to cast myself at your feet; I am a lost man, but you can save me: if they sell my château, I am without resources!"—"An honest man is never without resources, monsieur the count." —"Ay, but at the same time I am for ever banished from France."—"What matters that? it is no longer your country, monsieur the count."

The sculptor's wife, who was rather tart, came, scarcely clothed, into the room. "Ah, Nicolas, do not think of yielding; you are here as the representative of the people. Think of your duty."—

"My wife, go to bed; I am here the representative of my heart."—"Remember that that citizen there would have driven you away from the door of his château like a dog if you had gone to ask a favor of him."—"Well, for my part, I shall teach him how to live."—"You will do better to teach him how to die."

Nicolas Maillefer seated himself at his desk, and wrote in silence this certificate, which might be his ruin:—

"I certify that the citizen Adolphe D...., formerly count de B...., has not quitted the national territory as was here supposed. He is, moreover, a charitable man. He gives half his fortune toward the fund for carrying on the national war, and, if necessary, will convert his château into an hospital for wounded soldiers. Consequently, the sale announced will not take place, and, until further orders, the said citizen will enjoy all the rights of a French citizen.

"Given and executed at B...., by us, the undersigned, commissioner of the republic.

"NICOLAS MAILLEFER."

"There, monsieur the count, if you wish my certificate."—"The devil!" said the count to himself, "the half of my fortune for the national war! Pshaw! I will do nothing of the sort. I will bow my head during the storm; but the storm once over, I shall raise it higher than ever."

After this determination, M. the count spoke as follows to Nicolas Maillefer: "You are my savior; allow me to press your hand. I was unworthy of you; but this good deed will be a lesson for me."—"Be off, be off, citizen, it will not make you any better," said the sculptor's wife as she closed the door.

The next day, madame the countess of B.... inquired for Nicolas Maillefer. As soon as she was alone with him, she threw herself into his arms—"Ah! I thank you," said she with a sob.

Nicolas Maillefer, completely softened, looked at her affectionately; seeing two tears in her beautiful eyes, he dried them with his lips. She departed, and she herself carried away with her on her bosom two tears of the sculptor's, two burning tears, which she felt until death.

She died some few years after. The sculptor often went in pursuit of her adored shade to the woods of the château.

The time came when the count also thanked Nicolas Maillefer, but after his own fashion. At the fall of the empire, the commissioner of the republic was imprisoned by order of the count, who had regained his power in the country. Nicolas's generosity weighed upon his heart; he found a cruel pleasure in striking him with hard words. According to him, the sculptor's hands were still red; he had buried treasures; he had offended God and the devil. The truth was, that Nicolas had not a drop of blood on his conscience, nor a sou in his pocket; the truth was, that the most offensive act of his life had been the certificate given to the count.

Nicolas Maillefer died at eighty years of age, without fear and without reproach, leaving nothing here below but good works. He has gone to find elsewhere his friends, Condorcet and Camille Desmoulins. In spite of the outcries of the count, he was, up to his death, venerated by all. He had preserved to his old age his thoroughly French philosophy. "Let us laugh," he used to say—"let us laugh, since we have no longer anything good to do. Let us laugh; it is the summing up of wisdom."—"Go," said he to the poor, "go and dance; go and shake off your misery under the windows of the rich, to discourage them in their egotism. For my part," said he, "I have taken up my violin again, and I intend to give my best salute to the parting sun."

Every evening, in fact, he went up on the mountain in front of the château, and abandoned himself to his beloved recollections of 1792. He played with enthusiasm the air of the Marseillaise. The count raged with fury; but, in the fields, the peasant rested on his hoe or on his plough to listen. And when the peasant was an old soldier of the republic, he applauded while he wept.

VANDYCK.

Time which devours all things, has not attacked the works of Vandyck; his portraits have preserved all their light and freshness; perhaps it is time itself which has scattered over these immortal canvasses, the harmonizing dust, the magic texture which gives old pictures the mysterious appearance of consecrated works, in which the hand of man is scarcely recognised.

The Flemish school condemned itself, by its principle always to descend, from the ideal to the real, from poetry to truth. If this tendency was fatal to the great works produced at Bruges, Antwerp and Brussels, may we not affirm that it was favorable to the works of Vandyck. If nature is to rule anywhere in full force and liberty, is it not in the portrait, provided that the painter, like Vandyck, knows how to shed over it the light of heaven, and the light of intelligence?

Portraits are the most faithful page of history; for the study of the characters and passions of an epoch, I should recommend a gallery of portraits in preference to a library; during the last three or four centuries, a gallery has been gradually created, with the deliberation of genius, in which are found all the great physiognomies which have governed the Christian world. The painter may deceive himself, but he is still more faithful than the most faithful historian. If the head which he shows you is that of any kind of a king, king by bravery, genius, birth, or talent, you will gradually see the halo of this royalty shine out on his forehead, or in his glance. The soul of every strong man, is incessantly passing over his countenance; it is of no use for him to mask it, for it will make itself visible in spite of himself. But to seize this soul as it passes, to fix it on the canvass by the magic of color, nothing less will answer than a painter of the first rank, Titian, Vandyck, or Rembrant, who has the gift of creation in his touch. For one such master of the Deity's own school, how many unintelligent painters have we, who copy the material covering, without thought of the intellect which lies beneath the brow!

Anthony Vandyck, whose family was originally from Bois-le-Duc, was born at Antwerp, in the last year of the sixteenth century. According to Houbracken, his father was a painter on glass, and his mother a proficient in lace-embroidery. Painting on glass was already declining: cathedrals were no longer built, protestantism ruined Gothic art; without doubt, the lace-embroidery contributed more to the education of Vandyck, than the art already lost of the painter on glass. Vandyck had at first his father for his master, but the latter, soon acknowledging that a painter on canvass could not be produced, on the principles of a painter on glass, took his son to Van Balen, who was his friend.

Van Balen had made a trip to Rome and Venice, he had studied all the traditions of his art, he was a learned artist as well as a good painter. An intelligent pupil like Vandyck, might have issued from his studio, with his talents fully developed. Vandyck had however, seen Rubens' pictures; to his eyes, Van Balen was a painter in good repute, but Rubens was the monarch of his art. He went and knocked at his door: "Who is there?"—"A child who understands your genius." Rubens recognised the same day, that he was a child of genius.

If we are to believe the story-tellers, Rubens became jealous of Vandyck, but not in the studio. These story-tellers, assure us, that the young painter was beloved by Isabella Brandt. Vandyck without possessing the beauty adored by the Greeks, perhaps with his bold yet tender, chivalric and amorous features, possessed the ideal beauty of his country and his age; for it must be confessed, that beauty changes its character in accordance with countries and periods.* As these passions are only written on the

* In France, the present beau ideal of refinement resembles little the beau ideal of the court of Louis XIV. What a difference there is

winds, and painted on the waves, we can affirm nothing here, but neither can we deny anything. That which is indisputable, is that Vandyck quitted his master about that time; their farewell was that of two brethren in arms, and not of two enemies. Vandyck offered Rubens, as a mark of high and profound regard, those of his pictures which he most esteemed, an *Ecce Homo*, a *Christ in the Garden of Olives*, and a portrait of Isabella Brandt. This portrait was perhaps painted with passion; but a fact which gives little probability to the report already mentioned, that Vandyck adored Isabella, is that Rubens placed this portrait in his saloon himself, and showed it as a masterpiece to all his visiters, as well as to all his friends. "If you were not about setting out on your travels," said Rubens to Vandyck, "I would take you into my cabinet, and say to you: choose. But of what use is it to give you pictures, since you are going to Italy, the country of masterpieces; I prefer offering you the best horse in my stable." Vandyck set out; his father, his mother, and a hundred friends escorted him on his journey. Although his horse was impatient to rush forward, he turned him round every moment to see the last

between Rotrou and Racine, who were both considered fine-looking! What similarity is there between the pretty rakes of 1740 and the pale dreamers of 1840? The mask becomes modified according to the passions of an epoch. Thus, in the eighteenth century we had Vanloo and La Tour; at the present day we have Delacroix and Scheffer.

signals of farewell of his mother, who had chosen to go farther than his friends. At last he could see only the spire of the cathedral of Antwerp. "I, too," said he with a holy enthusiasm, "will one day paint my *Descent from the Cross.*"

He scarce made a halt at Brussels, quitting the city of the arch-dukes in the morning, under a fine July sun. Scarcely had he advanced two leagues, when seeing a village, he halted to drink a pint of beer. He remounted his horse, but destiny awaited him there. A young girl, a peasant, more fresh, more fair, and more rosy than all his visions of twenty, appeared at the threshold of the inn, and said to him with a smile, which displayed teeth as white as those of a young wolf: "And the stirrup-cup, monsieur?" Vandyck pulled the bridle of his fiery travelling companion. "The stirrup-cup?" said he; "I shall not leave." He descended to examine more closely this artless beauty, so striking and so unexpected, who was to be his third master. She was clothed pretty much in the style of the time, with naked feet, short petticoat, loosely-laced bodice, her hair loose to the wind, and her neck exposed to the sun. Vandyck entered the tavern. "Where were you going, monseigneur?"—"To Italy; but if you please, I will not go so far." In fact, what was he to do in Italy? See the women of Raphael and Titian. Were they then more beautiful than this miller's girl of Saventhem? In the life and career of

Vandyck, the heart was to play a more important part than the head. Peasant maiden though she was, this miller's girl of Saventhem realized the ideal of Vandyck. Since he had found his ideal, he had no desire to quit the country. He boldly installed himself with the family of his mistress. Thus did Vandyck, already celebrated, habituated to polished society, born with an instinctive love of grandeur, content himself with a rustic shed in the shadow of a mill for a studio, as did Rembrandt at a later period.

His mistress, desirous to obtain pardon for their amorous joys, begged him to paint two religious pictures for the parish-church. Vandyck's passion was undoubtedly serious, for he obeyed his mistress. Any one else in his place, would have contented himself with painting the fair maid of the mill twice, once for her, and once for himself, after which he would have continued his journey, with a laugh over the adventure; but Vandyck was as fervent a lover as he was a fervent artist. He painted the two pictures for the church of Saventhem. The first represented *Saint Martin dividing his cloak with the Beggar*. The St. Martin was Vandyck. As he had represented himself on horseback, he had painted his fellow-traveller, who although pasturing like a veritable miller's horse, had lost none of his heroic spirit. In the second picture *The Family of the Virgin*, he represented the old miller, his wife and their daughter. "All who have seen this picture, assure us that the peasant-girl sufficiently justifies by her beauty, the attentions of the young painter." It is Descamps who thus speaks.*

Meanwhile, the report had spread from Saventhem to Brussels, and from Brussels to Antwerp, that a young painter who had started for Rome, had been stopped on the journey by the fine eyes of a miller's maid of twenty, who inspired his masterpieces. Rubens fancied that he recognised Vandyck; he set off for Saventhem. On his arrival, he heard the neighing of the horse which he had given to his disciple. He surprised Vandyck on the steps of the mill, nonchalantly reclining at the feet of his mistress. "I thought," said he to him with a smile, "that you would henceforth dispense with a master." Vandyck had already thrown himself upon Rubens' neck. "And Rome, and Venice, and Raphael, and Titian, and Michael Angelo, and Veronese?"—"I will start to-morrow," replied Vandyck with sudden enthusiasm. He did so. This romance of his life winds up here. His historians do not say whether he consoled himself soon. What became of the fair maid of the mill, his freshest inspiration? Did another come and wipe away her tears? She was made to love much: she consoled herself.

*The *Family of the Virgin* has disappeared for more than a century from the church of Saventhem. The *St. Martin* had also disappeared in favor of the Louvre; but in 1815, Saventhem again beheld her masterpiece.

Vandyck went straight to Venice; he studied with ardor the luminous tones, the air of the head and the draperies of Titian and Veronese, but without losing sight of Nature; he corrected truth by art, without ever smothering her beneath ornament. From Venice he went to Genoa, where he studied a long time. From Genoa he went to Rome, where he had been summoned by Cardinal Bentivoglio, to paint his portrait. There was at that time, a colony of Flemish artists at Rome, who had abandoned their primitive genius, that is to say, vitality, brilliancy, and freedom, to copy servilely the Italian masters. Vandyck at first thought that he should find friends among his compatriots; but they all violently exclaimed against him when they recognised in his portraits, the bold and luminous touch of Rubens. These Italianized Flemings, who had renounced their national genius for servile imitation, did not wish to admit, that a Flemish painter nourished in the robust principles of the Flemish school, had arrived in Rome with endowments, which were to throw their own into the shade. Vandyck might perhaps have obtained pardon, if he had consented to lead a dissipated tavern-life with them, but he had acquired more noble tastes in the school of Rubens. The Flemish colony organized so powerful a cabal against him, that he abandoned the Eternal City almost immediately after his arrival. He passed into Sicily, where he painted among other portraits, that of Philibert of Savoy;

from Palermo he returned to Genoa, and thence finally to Antwerp, where he found Flemings more Flemish than those of Rome. He alone after Rubens saw his name inscribed in majestic characters on the tablets of the corporation of St. Luke.

He had, however, in spite of Rubens' testimony in his favor, to struggle desperately to make known his talents. The canons of Courtray ordered an altar-piece from him. He painted a *Christ on the Cross* in a grand style and with much feeling. He called together the canons, when his picture was placed in the church, counting upon their admiration. His surprise was great, on beholding the contemptuous bearing of the entire chapter toward the painter and the picture: "What a daub! what a dauber!" Vandyck wished to defend his picture, but the canons all exclaimed against it together. The sum of their eloquence, was, that the *Christ on the Cross* was but an ignoble masquerade. "Vandyck was left alone with a joiner and some sacristians, who fancied they were consoling him by recommending him to take away his picture, and assuring him, that it was not an entire loss, as his canvass could be used for screens." Vandyck, who knew his powers, haughtily ordered the joiner to hang his picture. The day after, he returned to the canons, and told them, "they had not seen his picture in a proper light." They all exclaimed that they did not want to see the thing a second time; they paid him for it, to avoid scandal, but with so bad a grace, that the artist was thoroughly indignant. Soon after, certain connoisseurs, passing through Courtray, loudly expressed their admiration of the work as a masterpiece. The news of this spread from mouth to mouth; admiring crowds gathered before the picture, and Vandyck then made known the incident. The canons were regarded as ignoramuses, "too moderate an expression," parenthetically, remarks the artless Descamps. The canons convoked a chapter to repair their mistake. They wrote in formal session, to Vandyck, begging him to paint them some more pictures. "You can find daubers enough in Courtray and the neighborhood," was his answer; "for my part, I have resolved to paint henceforth for men, and not for donkeys."—"It is pretended," says artless Descamps, "that this term was to some extent a formula for the chapter." Vandyck, moreover, never had reason to congratulate himself, in reference to religious corporations. He had painted a *Saint-Augustine* for the Augustines of Antwerp; when the subject of pay was broached, they declared that he had dressed their saint badly, that they wanted him in black and not in white. Vandyck, in the hope of being paid, changed the saint's garments; but the monks then said they had no money. "However," one of them timidly suggested, "if you will give us a Christ from your own hand, we will find the means to pay for your Saint-Augustine."

Although indignant at their knavery, Vandyck gave them the Christ to secure the pay for the saint.

According to Houbracken, Rubens, about this time, offered his eldest daughter to Vandyck. Vandyck refused her, because he was still an ardent admirer of the mother. The imagination of the anecdote-mongers, no doubt, plays an important part in this story. Vandyck made but a short stay at Antwerp: Rubens absorbed too much of the sunshine to leave any for others. He left for the Hague, where the prince of Orange, Frederic of Nassau, paid him in better money than the monks. He was lodged at the court, and painted there more than twenty portraits of princes, dukes, and embassadors. From the Hague he passed to England, and from England to France, harassed, at that time, more by the love of gain than the love of art. It was, however, written that a thousand obstacles should be cast in the way of the wheel of his fortune. He passed through London and Paris as a stranger, without finding a being to notice his talents. He was (will it be believed?) forced to return to Antwerp to paint for the monks again. Happily the order of Capuchins treated him better than that of the Augustins.

His evil days were, however, soon to be over. Scarcely had he quitted England, when several of the portraits which he had painted at the court of the prince of Orange passed to that of London.

Charles I. became an enthusiastic admirer of the fine character of Vandyck's portraits, and was desirous of attracting him to his court. Vandyck, however, not forgetting the inhospitality of Great Britain on his first visit there, vowed that he would not return there. Sir Kenelm Digby, however, carried him off to London, in spite of himself, and presented him to the king. Charles I. received him with as much favor and deference as if he had been Rubens. He gave him his portrait set in diamonds, attached to a gold chain. Vandyck respectfully placed the chain around his neck. Charles I. afterward created him knight of the bath; and, desiring that England should become his second country, bestowed a large pension on him with two residences, one for summer and one for winter. He told him that his entire court should be painted by him, and fixed the price of his portraits: a hundred pounds sterling for full-lengths, and fifty pounds for half-lengths.

These were his best days. Like Rubens, he possessed a royalty of the highest and most genial stamp—that of perpetuating the work of God. The most beautiful women of Great Britain came, as to a fête, to sit before his palette, charged, for them, with roses of immortal bloom. Fair locks were loosened for him in wavy ringlets; fair shoulders, whiter than the summits of the Alps, were unveiled before his pencil. Like the Maréchal de Richelieu, he could style himself, to some extent, the husband of all the women. When the beautiful princess de Brignolles, half naked, sat so complacently in his studio, when Vandyck painted with a trembling hand her dazzling neck, the masterpiece of nature, did he not fancy that the Great Master had created that neck for him?

Vandyck lived in familiar intimacy with Charles I. He was insatiable; he cost the king more than a prime minister. One day, when Charles I. was sitting to the painter (perhaps for the admirable picture which the burin has immortalized), the king, who had just been consulting with the duke of Norfolk about the bad state of his finances, turned toward Vandyck, and said to him, with a smile: "And have you too, Sir Anthony, known what it is to want for five or six thousand guineas?"—"Ay, ay, sire, an artist who keeps open house to his friends and open purse to his mistresses, is but too often sensible of a void in his strong box."* Vandyck indulged in in-

* The queen Margaret de Bourbon, daughter of Henry IV., sat to him one day. As he lingered a long time over the hands of the princess (he excelled in painting the hands and feet), she asked him in a gay tone, why he caressed her hands more than her head? "Madame, it is because I hope a reward from those fair hands worthy of her who bears them." Descamps cites this as a happy reply. We hope, for the honor of the painter, that it is another of the many anecdotes without foundation. Another remark of Vandyck would prove that he was somewhat candid in his character. He was reproached for painting more negligently at forty than at twenty. "Formerly," he replied, "I worked for my reputation; now, I work for my pocket."

credible expenses; he enriched his mistresses and servants, but ruined by degrees his talent and health. In his excess of luxury, he did not, like Rubens, build a palace; but he did build a laboratory, for he had fallen into the fanaticism of the alchemists, and beheld all the gold which he had created, as if by magic by the pencil, evaporate in the crucible.

It was owing to his friend the duke of Buckingham that he was led into the folly of undertaking great schemes. The proud favorite of Charles I., seeing that he had almost ruined Vandyck, was desirous of repairing his otherwise involuntary injuries. He snatched him from his mistresses, and married him to the daughter of Lord Ruthven, a Scottish nobleman. She was one of the most beautiful women in England; but she brought him no other portion than her illustrious name and already celebrated beauty. Vandyck, as soon as he was married, gathered together the fragments of his fortune and set out for Antwerp, hoping to be at last received there with enthusiasm. That, however, was decidedly not the field of his glory. He made a second visit to Paris: he had been told that he could re-establish his fortune by painting the gallery of the Louvre; but Poussin had anticipated him. A second time did he quit inhospitable France; he returned to England, but his career was ended: he had abused his powers; though still young, he had neither vigor nor courage. He fell sick and did not revive again.* His wife had given him a daughter, who died at two or three years of age. This was a final blow to his heart.

He died, without leaving many mourners, aged forty-two, with the sad and holy hope of being buried in St. Paul's cathedral, where his daughter was already laid. Maria Ruthven remarried, but died shortly after.

Vandyck was but the Virgil of Rubens, with less genius and greater attractiveness, less of the grand and more of the noble, less enthusiastic and more perfect. It must be remembered that he died young and lived a hap-hazard life, always in love, and therefore always mad. Besides, were it not always a settled thing to place the pupil in the shadow of the master, the same fervor would often be excited before the great compositions of Vandyck as before those of Rubens. To those who deny him genius, we may reply by his famous picture of *St. Martin*, painted at the age of twenty in the little village of Saventhem, where he was alone, without master or precedents. He has left admirable works in Italy, which will not yield to those of Rubens, or even of Titian.

He had, like Rubens, the poetry of color; his tone

* The king was always warmly attached to him, notwithstanding his greediness for money and his prodigality. During the painter's illness, he promised three hundred guineas to his physician, if he could cure Vandyck.

is less spirited, but still more harmonious; his chiaro-oscuro is the triumph of art, since art is not therein apparent. What is especially to be admired in Vandyck is his firm, broad, and deep touch, which does not exclude a marvellous delicacy. We can still less comprehend this perfection, when we remember that he painted a head at once upon the canvass and with the same palette. He usually commenced a portrait in the morning, kept the sitter to dinner, and finished it in the evening. It is apparent that those who sat to him did not find it wearisome. In truth, Vandyck had at his disposition players, jugglers, musicians, dancing-girls, everything that contributes to noise and display. By skilfully heightening his lights and shadows, Vandyck always attained a grand and simple effect. He took only from nature that which truth demanded, and added to it the splendor of art. His heads are in such strong relief, have such vitality, that in beholding them we almost forget that they are portraits.

Vandyck, as a portrait-painter, is on a level with Raphael, Holbein, Velasquez, and Rembrandt.* Life is resplendent in all his portraits; he seizes on the reality at the moment when the mind is radiant on the countenance: hence his ideal perfection, even

* Joshua Reynolds, the great English portrait-painter, styles him the first of portrait-painters. The Marquis d'Argens calls him the finest painter in the world. Among the great portrait-painters, Rigaud and Hals are not to be forgotten.

in his precision. Besides, when mind is not apparent in the features, Vandyck throws his own into them from the point of his pencil.

Vandyck is, perhaps, the painter who has best comprehended the beau-ideal of his age; his luminous portraits, tinged with the reflection of the new dawn which was spreading over the earth, have all, with their chivalric and intelligent pride, a trace of Spanish and romantic poetry. We may also say that they recall the heroes of Tasso, who are more amorous than sanguinary; all are imbued with a chivalric air. We feel that the romance of their lives has passed through their hearts. The portraits of Vandyck are therefore, besides being masterpieces, also animated by the expression of the face. They have always a family. How many times has the portrait even of an ancestor been removed to give place to one painted by Vandyck!

Vandyck closes the cycle of the great painters of his country. Flanders exhausted her powers in her sublime children. Genius, like the golden grain, will not spring from the soil until after it has lain fallow and been made fruitful by the dews. The genius of the north sought an exile farther on amid the fogs; it was to flourish at Leyden, Harlaem, and Amsterdam. The school of Rubens was gradually dispersed and became extinct. We find, after this splendid harvest, here and there a green shoot; after this dazzling light, we perceive, with the gathering night, traces of the luminary which is disappearing; the sunset retains awhile its tinges of purple and flame; but, by degrees, nothing is visible but the stars in the heaven of art.

A LOST POET.

We meet here and there in the solitary and silent life of the mountain and the valley, with poets, painters, sculptors, musicians, who have not been able to expand on a large scale, but who have preserved in this world, a certain indescribable rustic perfume, which is worth quite as much as any other. I knew a miller, who played on the violin like Paganini, a schoolmaster who was a poet like Hugo, a shepherd who sketched with the feeling of Delacroix. I should like to narrate the history of these artists of the open air, a history always simple, but for all that more picturesque than that of many great geniuses, who shine in the gas-light of Paris. Trust me, these poor ignored artists are none the less the privileged children of God, although they have no other halo than the sun's rays.

At this moment, I remember especially an old schoolmaster of Vermandois, who left as his whole heritage in this world, an unpublished volume of verses and a pretty daughter; but this work of the schoolmaster is no longer unpublished; it has had many editions, revised, corrected, and enlarged. This schoolmaster was called André Durand; a name well known in the canton of Sissonne, from the church to the tavern. André Durand was born near Guise, at two steps from Flanders, about 1760, a little before Camille Desmoulins, with whom he played truant, in the most delightful manner possible. He was a lively youth, adventurous, careless, moving on without knowing where, at the grace of God. His father who was a hard-working blacksmith, witnessed the first steps of his dear André with sorrow. "There is a boy who will never be good for anything," said this brave fellow. In fact, André Durand turned out a schoolmaster, but before falling upon this grotesque throne of science in roundabouts, André Durand had been a poet, of the good stamp, a love poet in wooden shoes, a poet like Uhland.

It was thus that poetry and love took possession of his heart, without his mistrusting the fact; like the savage, he found with dazzled eye, two pearls on the border of the sea. At sixteen, he began to hammer iron like his father; as soon as he could escape from the forge, he took to his heels, with a beloved book, toward the Bois aux Loups, which still cover the western side of the hill of Montigny. He peopled his imagination as he best could, until he had something better, that is to say, the fair and smiling countenance of mademoiselle de Froidmont which almost put to flight all the others.

Mademoiselle Lucy de Froidmont was twenty; she had inhabited, since her return from the convent, the small château of Froidmont, in company with her mother, who, since her widowhood, had preferred not to revisit Paris. Hers was a calm and beautiful youth, which bloomed in the sunshine, among the flowers and sometimes in ennui. She was to be married in a short time, to one of her cousins, a guardsman, a philosophical coxcomb, who devoted two hours every morning to the arrangement of his hair, and declaimed every evening behind the scenes at the opera, against the frivolity of his age. Lucy fell in love with him, I know not why, perhaps because he was a guardsman, perhaps because the guardsman sent her by the post, kisses in verse, in the style of the *Kisses of Dorat.* However, in those times, kisses in prose were preferred.

The château of Froidmont is built at the end of the valley of Montigny, on the border of the Bois aux Loups, which is one of its dependencies. Toward the end of his life, the vicomte de Froidmont had almost made a park of this wood. He had planted, in the cleared spaces, roses, acacias, jessamines, lilacs, and statues; he had lopped the large trees, watered the turf, adorned its borders with cornel trees, elders, sloes, white thorne, in a word, with all the wild shrubs which cast their flowers to the wind.

It was in this park, open to every comer, that our blacksmith delighted to wander. He chose the most shady paths as if his heart, which already had a presentiment of love, would have fled from the sun. One summer evening as he heard, without listening, the warbling of the little birds, he saw pass near him, on the other side of the hazel-trees, Lucy, the beautiful Lucy, who was dreaming of her cousin the guardsman, as she caressed in her bosom a letter, which she had as yet read but twenty times. André Durand was so charmed at this apparition, that he assumed the most beautiful smile of beatitude that ever was seen. "Ah, heavens! how beautiful she is!" he exclaimed, bowing unconsciously. At this strange voice, Lucy turned her head and rapidly retraced her steps toward the château, but not without turning around. André sighed when she disappeared; he pressed with a timid and agitated foot, the sward over which she had passed, he looked with a vacant gaze at the dilapidated towers of the château! "What a pretty little blacksmith's wife she would make!" said he with a little bitterness.

He returned to the paternal roof later than usual. On again beholding the forge and furnace, he heartily wished that his father had been a marquis, or at least a baron. He supped with bad grace enough at the rustic table, he slept indifferently on the truckle-bed of his garret. The next day he did nothing of any consequence; the day after he listened from morning till evening, to the little birds of the Bois aux Loups ; a week after, he announced with a gape that he was not made to hammer iron. The father, irritated with good reason, told him to go to the devil, and the poor André not knowing where to go (when he did not go to the Bois aux Loups), entered, at his own risk and peril, as prime minister to his schoolmaster, hoping in time to shake the tree of science, that is to say, to rise to the higher regions of the world, where shone in such mild radiance the fair Lucy de Froidmont.

Love has its strange and sublime caprices : it turns aside at its will, the natural course of our life, it incessantly sets us adrift on the troubled sea of the world ; it is an absolute king who reigns and governs without shackles. He beats down the strongest and raises the feeblest, according to his fancy; he impregnates some with splendid enthusiasm; he extinguishes the divine fire in others. Love possesses all the golden keys of our soul, which he opens and closes at pleasure or by chance. There are poor children of the lower classes, who appear to be condemned to die without having lived; lost in the depths of some hamlet, sheltered by a mountain, which separates them from the world, they move on to death in the shade, bent down by labor, without taking time to raise their eyes to heaven, without breathing on their course the intoxicating perfume of those charming flowers, which God has sown over the earth with a smile and a tear: poetry and love! To animate these living marbles, a look only is needed, the tender glance of Juliet upon Romeo; a word only is needed, the word spoken so well by Francesca and Manon Lescaut; an apparition only is needed, such as all the poets have seen, an apparition in the morning at a window, in the evening between the bushes along the path, at night in the whirl of the ball-room. The heart asks so little with which to commence the romance of life, whose first chapter is a poem, the poem of the angels! Thanks to this look, this word of love, this charming form which appears to them like a recollection of heaven, the statues become animated as by enchantment, a veil falls from their eyes, a chain from their hands, they behold the splendors of heaven and the wonders of earth, they stretch out their hands to embrace life. After having seen the purple of the grape, they will press it to their lips; they will not die at least without having plucked flowers in the valley, and fruits on the hill-side.

Thus did André Durand seem condemned to that painful every-day labor which weighs down and extinguishes the soul. Thanks to love, his soul shed a radiance on his body; thanks to love which lent him his wings, that soul derived like the most noble gifts, from God, elevated him to poetry. André Durand did not take from choice the road to the school of Montigny, and in truth he had to undergo many torments in the midst of all those noisy children, who did not leave him time to listen to the first motions of his heart. But there was his means of support: he resigned himself to it. And then in the evening, after having rung the *Angelus*, he bent his steps toward the Bois aux Loups; and how many consolations did he not find at every step in that Eden! Here the elegy of the nightingale, there the white and scented berry of the hawthorn, before him the clump of hazels where Lucy had appeared; everywhere, in fine, happiness, happiness—that invisible image, the perfume of the heart, the echo of heaven which comes to you at the morn of youth, with a gentle breeze, when you are in an amorous solitude. André Durand was happy, without knowing why or how, in the Bois aux Loups; happy in the memory of Lucy; happy in a confused hope; happy to behold the sky through the trees; happy, in fine, as a man is when life is yet but a smile. He did not behold Lucy again; but often, at twilight, did he wander in the avenue of the château, listening intently to the low sounds of a harpsichord. And when he looked upon those lofty walls, which formed a barrier between her and himself, he raised his head with pride—the pride of the poet—and swore to overleap everything in order to die at Lucy's feet. Pending the execution of these chivalric resolutions, he humbly ruled the school of Montigny.

He came out of the wood a lover and a poet. It

was there that he dreamed of poetry and love. Mademoiselle de Froidmont was not at first touched by this rustic homage; but by degrees, thanks to poetry, love rose very high; and, thanks to love, poetry disengaged itself from all grosser matter. André Durand undertook to rhyme some verses. When I say rhyme, I mean measure, for André Durand had at that time no great rhyme or reason.

The beautiful dream of André Durand soon vanished, but left fruitful traces: the following winter, the guardsman came and married mademoiselle de Froidmont. André wept over the ruins of his happiness. She knew that he was in love; she paused one day before him with a divine smile of compassion. He consoled himself in poetry, perhaps even in love. Lucy quitted the place, to be absent for a long period. "She has not utterly departed," said André, "she has left something of herself in the Bois aux Loups, and a flower and fragrance of youth in my heart which I can not describe:" and, as usual, he betook himself to the woods to find her.

It must be confessed that he was not always constant to this archangelic love. His lips opened one day to ask something else. The schoolmaster had a daughter who was quite good-looking, and did not show herself very cruel to André. The poor poet went the way of the world—he married. Once married, the halter once over his head, with no other prospect than the chimney-corner or the graveyard, he must needs bid adieu to all his wild chimeras, and put a stop to some of his vagaries. André, however, remained a poet. At the end of a year of marriage, as he must needs support his increasing family, he resigned himself to the charge of an obscure village-school, not knowing of anything better to do. He had some thoughts of trying his fortune elsewhere; but he was of a timid disposition, loving silence, avoiding hubbub, content with little provided he always enjoyed sunshine and verdure.

I knew André Durand, the schoolmaster of Montigny. He was at that time a fine old man, full of gentleness and patience: in his worn features, resignation was the prominent characteristic. I saw that he went a little too often to the tavern: he was not happy under his own roof. He had been indulgent toward his children, and they, to use his own expression, poured a great deal of bitterness into his cup. His wife, almost always sick, had become querulous and discontented. In a word, he had to live alone, having no one to understand his good and noble disposition. And at sixty, instead of seeking solitude in the Bois aux Loups, in the shadows of the good time past, he sought it at the tavern before a bottle of claret.

I saw André Durand again last year, amid the snows of December. He received me with a smile. He had read some bad book or other of mine. "My young friend," said he to me, shaking his head, "you must know that I am not so much of a schoolmaster as I seem to be; I have only wanted a publisher to be a poet like so many others. Do not laugh at this confession, which I have as yet made to no one. Yes, I have carefully preserved in my heart the secret of my poetry; I have sung in a low tone, and to no audience but myself; no one has found anything to say against my songs. Ah! good Heaven, when I think of those beautiful seasons of my life which I passed in the depth of a wood!..."

He sighed and bent his thoughtful brow. "Come, come!" he continued with warmth; "it is a fine winter's-day, so I may as well return there before I die, and I have no great time to lose. If I were to wait for spring, it would perhaps be too late."

We went together to the Bois aux Loups. The edge of the wood once past, he leaned against an old oak, shook off the snow which covered his shoes, and looking at the whitened roof of the chateau, "Ah yes!" said he, "yes, I too was a poet." There was a whole revelation in his voice. "Alas!" he continued, "my first muse, my only muse, fled too soon! Do you guess? It was mademoiselle de Froidmont: she was married to her cousin de Bussy. I have scarcely seen her three times during half a century. But what do I say? have I not seen her a thousand times a-day in that other world of the imagination in which the poor poets take refuge with so much happiness?" The old schoolmaster cast upon me a sad glance.—"It is well," said he, "you at least understand me." He told me, in a gay tone, of his poetical triflings; he recited to me his first verses; he confided to me his love history. All this was simple and sincere; I listened with all my heart. When he had finished, he again glanced around him. At the sight of the snow and the bare branches, "Ah!" he said to me, stretching out his arms toward the shadow of his youth, "be always twenty; think that winter will one day come for you. Twenty! love, green branches, poetry, singing-birds, blooming roses; and, besides these, Lucy, who comes some evening like a fairy to display her sweet face between the hazel boughs . . . . ."

The poor schoolmaster wiped away two tears. "Do not let us stay here long, for soon I shall not have strength enough to return to Montigny; and in spite of all, I wish to die like a good Christian, and repose in the graveyard beside those for whom I have sung the *De Profundis*."

We returned to Montigny, turning over, by the way, the volume of memory.

It was the last time that the schoolmaster was in the Bois aux Loups. He died gently at the end of February, some days after having written me a short letter which ended with these words: "I will not forget you in the other world, but do not forget the old schoolmaster in this; tell your wits that where my heart was, there was a poet."

HANDS FULL OF ROSES, FULL OF GOLD, AND FULL OF BLOOD.

A PHILOSOPHICAL STORY.

I.

This story will appear strange to you: but it is written by truth itself.

Men were breathing the bitter odor of the bean—that odor which intoxicates some persons even to madness. The traveller disturbed with his foot the strawberry-leaf, and scattered the fragrance of the strawberry already ripe. The school-girl amused herself on returning from school in blowing, with her maiden lips, the flowering plantain, with flowing locks and powdered like a marquis. The school-boy amused himself with the architectural delicacy of the thistles, he gathered the bristling dandelion, he ventured to suck the juice of the nettle, whose white flower reminds one of the band of the priest. All was joy and festivity on this beautiful evening. The earth sang her hymn to God by the voice of men, of forests, of harvests and birds. There is nothing down to the potato-beds, which does not yield to the wind, the plebeian odor of its green shoots, starred here and there, with those poor despised flowers which no fair hand has gathered, and no muse has sung. I salute you—oh potatoes!—verdant hopes of future Spartans.

A young man of twenty, was passing on horseback, along a little valley of the Vermandois, bordered by meadows, woods, and ponds, overshadowed by a mountain, on which four wind-mills were turning noisily. The sun was bidding adieu to the pointed spires of the church; the angelus did not sound as in the romances, because the schoolmaster was watering his little garden, bordered with box, where the onion flourished side by side with the dahlia. The silvery cry of the frog, that sweet poet of the marshes was heard. The cuckoo and the blackbird, who had already made their bed in the branches, replied only at rare intervals.

The young man was going, I know not where. The horse completely intoxicated, by the green and savory odor of the mown grass, moved as buoyantly as youth. He skipped over the grass and devoured space. The cavalier went still more quickly; he was travelling with loosened rein in the ideal world, which opens to those at twenty years, its doors of gold and azure. Where did he come from? College. Thus far he had not lived in life. He had known only the Greeks and Romans. Study had chastely watched as sentinel over his heart, like the ancient vestal in the temple of Juno!

He was at last to live! Passion was coming to him with dishevelled locks, with her divine frenzy and her fiery grasp. He had learned to read, but he had scarce half-opened that sacred, that infernal book in which God and Satan have written their poems. As he believed only in God, he opened the book with confidence. He entered life with the pious fervor of a Christian, who crosses the threshold of a church, with the reflection that there at least, under the gaze of the angels, the virgins and saints, who smile in the stained windows or the pictures, he is sheltered from the wicked.

Georges Arnault—that was his name—was the son of a country gentleman, who destined him for everything. It was therefore a thousand to one, that Georges Arnault would come to nothing.

He was, after the summer, to set out for Paris, Paris the great devourer of men, Paris, which swallows up a thousand ambitious men, to form a single dwarf. While awaiting this rude combat, he lived without care, enamored of the dawn and the twilight, the ray that descends and the sound that arises, confiding his dreams to the clouds and the stream of the Oise.

On this evening, after having skirted along a hedge of hawthorne and elder, on which the bind weed suspended its little whitebells, he suddenly paused at the grate of a wooded park, where through the fresh foliage of the avenue appeared the front of the Château aux Grives, a small brick château with stone quoins, with peaked slate roof, in the pure Louis XIII. style.

Georges Arnault, born with a vague sentiment of art, was in an ecstacy.

"Ah!" he exclaimed sadly, "if my father lived in such a château, I would be glad to live and die there, without disquieting myself about the golden apples of the Hesperides! Can not one find here better than at Paris the joys of the heart, the festivals of heaven and nature?"

He had dismounted, to lean his burning brow against the gate. He would have given some good days of his life, to have been able to tread in full liberty, the turf of the park. "Such must life be," mused the young philosopher: "temptations which show you their naked breasts, but forbid you to approach them."

At this instant, he saw, as in a dream, a young girl dressed in a white robe, who issued from an avenue of linden-trees, and came toward the gate with a pensive air. She was as beautiful as if she had come from the hands of Correggio; pure as if just from her Creator. Praxiteles, who was never able to find his ideal, would have bowed before her.

Although she appeared to be in deep meditation,

she suddenly paused before a playful butterfly which was fluttering its wings, as if to applaud this vision. She was desirous to seize these wings all gold and purple, and began to run like a school-girl among the trees and branches. Her locks, scarce knotted together, flowed over her shoulders and veiled from him her eyes. Her dress blown about by the wind, caught on every rose-bush. Twenty times was she on the point of seizing the butterfly, which seemed to understand the sport, and wished to scatter a little of the gold dust of his wings on that virgin hand.

She uttered a cry, which went through the heart of Georges like an arrow of fire; she had torn her hand upon a rose-bush; the blood flowed like drops of wine. She began to laugh that she might forget to cry; she snatched a white rose and tinged it with purple, like Venus of old, when sporting with the Hours.

She had forgotten the butterfly; she gathered roses of all colors; she attempted to make herself a crown, and looked into the water to see if she was more beautiful, with roses in her hair.

I can not relate the thousand and one sports with which she enlivened her meditation. Georges Arnault was still at the gate. He would have remained there yet longer, if a neigh of his horse had not startled the young girl. As soon as she found herself surprised in her solitude, she took to flight like a dove, among the foliage. Georges Arnault saw no more but the waving branches, which she had brushed against in passing.

He remounted his horse, thoroughly resolved to come every evening, to ramble in this enchanted park.

As he spurred on his horse to reach his father's house by dinner-time :—

"Take care," said a peasant-girl, almost buried under a load of freshly-mown grass, "you were on the point of throwing me into the brook."

"I did not see you," said he.

"Where were your eyes then? Would any one say that I was an ant, carrying a straw to the ant-heap?"

"My eyes were......Who does this château belong to?"

"To the *Sleeping Beauty*."

"What do you mean?"

"The château belongs to the estate of an old general who has no heirs. Since he died, a year ago, it has been inhabited by no one but his dogs, his cats, and his gardener."

"And that young girl whom I saw just now dressed in white like a communicant?"

The peasant-girl looked at Georges Arnault with an air of ridicule.

"Are you a visionary?"

"I saw a young girl of from eighteen to twenty, running after roses and butterflies."

"It is a fiction. The gardener is my cousin. Yesterday too, I was all the afternoon cutting grass for my cows, in twenty places in the park, close to the doors of the château; there was not a soul to be seen."

Georges Arnault would believe nothing. He left at a gallop, resolved to return the day after.

He returned, again and again. The vision had disappeared for ever. He questioned every one; the gardener opened the gate to him, and conducted him everywhere. He could not find even the imprint of the feet of this beautiful girl, with flowing locks, the Eve of this terrestrial paradise.

"Nevertheless," said he, as he embraced the empty air in his amorous arms, "I have seen her—and I have loved her."

II.

Georges Arnault, set out for Paris when autumn arrived.

On the eve of his departure, he went to the cemetery to gather *immortelles* on the tomb of his mother.

As he sadly kissed these flowers of the sepulchre, he thought that he must also carry away a rose—though a faded one—from the Parc aux Grives. At nightfall he mounted his horse, and let him wander with slackened bridle like the lover of Leonora.

The old gardener was smoking his pipe in the avenue of the château. Georges begged him to take care of his horse, and ran into the park toward the grate.

As he sought for roses with his hands, rather than with his eyes, for the night was dark, he saw pass under the black trees, that adorable white vision, which had enchanted his heart. He rushed forward to seize her, but she disappeared like the phantom of a dream.

At Paris, Georges Arnault studied law as all true students do. He rose at mid-day, under the excuse that he went to bed at midnight. He went to study at the café with a female neighbor, who replied to him with politics, as he talked to her of love. He expressed great admiration of Lycurgus, while smoking at the Chaumière or the Château-Rouge; he extolled Lacedemonian broth after dinner, and declaimed against money as he thought of his debts.

Now and then he went to the law-school; they once spoke to him about party-walls: he returned in all haste to repeat his lesson to his neighbor aforesaid.

Another time he met on the threshold of the law-school, a daughter of Eve, who was asking her way.

"Where are you going?"

"I don't know."

"Well then, since we are going to the same place let us go together."

And so they went.

Georges Arnault therefore passed his first examination, as Cæsar passed the Rubicon, as Louis XIV.

passed the Rhine, without shrinking. His enemies, the law professors, did not succeed in demolishing him with their heavy artillery. He made them a discourse on the detention of the body, in the style of a man who had deeply studied the subject. One of the three oracles went to sleep, the second burst out laughing, the third wiped away a tear: total, three red balls.

In the amorous hurly-burly of the Latin quarter, Georges Arnault had forgotten his country—the country of his mother. Did he still kiss with a respectful lip the *immortelles* which he had gathered from the tomb, that had opened too soon? Life had become for him a masked ball, an endless carnival, a descent almost into *la Courtille*; he went on without turning his head, intoxicated by all the ardent follies of blooming youth, throwing his heart like his money, out of the window, to all the chances of love.

One evening he arrived alone, contrary to his custom, at the Château-Rouge.

He was attracted to the battle-field of the dance, by the engaging exterior of Mademoiselle Pochardinette—a Taglioni well-known at the opera of the open air.

But suddenly, while a hundred eyes were following passionately the light gambols of this illustrious dancer, he grew pale and trembled.

He had just seen a figure pass amid a crowd of

new-comers, a form which was well-known to him. It was that of a young girl of perfect beauty in its full bloom. She threw herself with infatuation into the midst of the quadrille, and danced with passion. Never did Fanny Elssler display her leg with more impertinent coquetry, never had so beautiful a neck wearied a more noble bust. She was beautiful from her life, her youth, her luxuriance. Her slightly golden hair and her eyes, which had stolen a ray from the sun, recalled Violante, the mistress of Titian. There was the same bloom, the same exuberance, the same power of human beauty. But of divine beauty, naught. She had forgotten heaven for earth. However, when she was at the end of her mad cachucha, she bowed her head with a tone of melancholy — as if a recollection had touched her heart.

But, at the same moment, a profane smile passed over her lips; she placed her joined hands on the shoulder of her partner, and appeared to beg him to carry her again into all the giddy joys of the cachucha.

Georges Arnault had recognised the young girl of the Parc aux Grives. It was the same face, with three springs more, three fragrant springs, crowned with pinks, fruits, ears of wheat, and cherries, like a bacchante of Jordaens. She was still fresh, but already touched by the first ravages of the passions. Her mouth, formerly pure as the bloom of a peach, had no longer the adorable artlessness of an ignorant mouth, which had, as yet, only laughed to itself: the knowledge of love had come to it.

"It is she, however," said Georges, advancing toward the gay dancer. "I recognise that beautiful careless neck, which I have only found in the Psyche of Praxiteles. And those eyes, so proud and so gentle! And this profile, cut from pure marble! There is no doubt of it, it is she. She shall at last explain to me this strange mystery."

"Who are you soliloquizing about?" Georges Arnauld was thus interrupted by an intimate friend, whom he had known since the evening before.

"Listen: three years ago, in a park in my native country, I saw pass, like a vision, a beautiful girl, whom I am still in love with, and whom I have never been able to approach, under the pretext that it was only a vision. To-day the vision detached itself from the blue sky; I have found it dancing at the Château-Rouge. See that striped dress, that bold yet pretty bonnet, that scarf of which she makes a serpent, that girdle of purple which is well worth a great name."

"You are making fun of me, my old friend; I see neither dress, bonnet, scarf, nor girdle. Are you a visionary?"

"How?" exclaimed Georges Arnault with impatience; "you do not see that distracted dancer who scatters about her an odor of youth in its bloom?

One might style her a bacchante savoring of the vine-branch. Watch me well, as I rush to her and bear her off with all the force of my passion."

Georges advanced to seize the dancer; but, as he believed that he already touched her, she disappeared in a flood of superannuated beauties which Brididi was leading on her steps.

For more than an hour, Georges Arnault ran through the garden to find her again. He fell exhausted into the arms of his friend, who offered him an ice, and threw a glass of ice-water over his head, all the while resolving to consign him to Doctor Blanche.

"I am not mad," said Georges passionately, falling on his knees—"I am not mad, but I am afraid."

III.

Georges Arnault did not, however, pass his second examination. He had taken too literally the thought of the philosopher, who says: "The man without passions is a vessel which waits for the wind, with sails spread, without advancing an inch." He had summoned to him all the winds—those which come from the tempest, as well as those which come over the fields of wheat. He had been dashed against the rocks—he was leaking everywhere; a few more tempests, and he is wrecked without a plank of safety.

Dissipation had taken possession of him from the head to the heart. He had entered into the labyrinth of passion. When the soul, suffocated under impure embraces, has no longer a ray to lead the body, the student of yesterday is but the idler of to-day, who lives on the hazards of play and love.

I shall not relate all the degradations of Georges Arnault. One sole sentiment raised him above himself: it was his love of country. He had preserved until twenty the republican virtues; he had lived a long time in intimate familiarity with Lycurgus and with Saint-Just; dissipation had not been able to lead him astray on that side. The native land has, like the mother, this that is good, it can preserve a man from the last degradations, and even raise him to the heights from which he has fallen.

Georges was not preserved: he fell to the bottom of the abyss—the abyss without a bottom.

Like Figaro, not knowing what else to do, he had taken up a pen—between two bottles—to scourge this society built upon money, living for money, adoring money. He had been acknowledged at first sight as a vehement satirist, poetically inspired in his patriotic and savage rage. Some journals gave him enough to drink and smoke. One of his friends had become a minister. They met, they understood one other: Georges Arnault was inscribed among the honest people on whose hearts are marked these two odious words, *secret service*. The day before, he had abused royalty; the day after, he administered his blows to France.

This crime of treason to the nation was not his last. He had a mistress, a woman of society, a devotee who had married a Voltairian, and had metamorphosed him into an imbecile devotee. She felt every night the purse and the pulse of the old man. She succeeded in despoiling his family, who were poor, by a will made in her favor; when it was signed, Georges Arnault bore his part in this infernal work—some grains of arsenic to sweeten the cough-mixture.

The widow is still inconsolable.

Two days after the death of the old man, Georges Arnault bought a horse and cantered in triumph along the Champs-Elysées, followed by a groom got up in excellent style.

"I greet you on horseback," cried one of his friends on foot to him; for one always has friends; as the proverb says, one is never alone on a road.

Georges Arnault deigned to bow and check his horse.

"How have you obtained this unexpected luxury? I am not aware that you had an uncle in America. Is Madame * * * a widow?"

"All the women are widows for me," said Georges with impatience; "my father has killed the fatted calf—that is the whole secret."

And the cavalier departed at a gallop.

"His father! his father!" said the other, turning his head with a doubtful air; "he has long been at his last crown. I know the secret very well: Georges Arnault began by taking the wife, he will end by taking the husband's money. After all, there is no great harm done. It is a custom which has the force of law."

As he galloped toward the Arc de Triomphe, Georges Arnault thus familiarized himself with his crime: "Am I really culpable? This old man was already dead to all the joys of earth; I have broken his corporeal chains, I have broken open the prison, I have opened heaven to him. Without passions, what is life? It is the scabbard without the blade, the stalk without the flowers, the altar without the divinity. On high, in the ethereal vaults, this old man blesses the two hands which have struck him, and which are to be given one to the other when eleven months are ended. I have eleven months' liberty left, thanks to the law.—The law! what irony! Is it not more than eleven months since I have married Madame * * *?"

In the evening, Georges was coming out of the café Anglais, where he had been seeking oblivion in drink, according to his custom. He elbowed a girl of the town on the boulevard, who laughed insolently in his face. He nearly fell backward.

He had met the young girl of the Parc aux Grives, the impassioned dancer of the Château-Rouge.

"It is you! it is you! Oh Heaven! such radiant beauty! I would have bought you with my life, and you are not worth a piece of a hundred sous?"

She remained before him, immovable and silent as marble, her eyes bright, her lips faded, her cheeks wan, without a sign of emotion.

"No, it is no longer you; I no longer recognise you," said Georges Arnault, terrified.

She turned her back to him and went to another. He followed with his eyes her transparent dress, whose gaudy colors attracted the eyes of all.

"And yet, if I should go to her, if I should take her to my abode, if I should question her? I must know the whole history of this mournful fall; my heart bleeds before such deep degradation. This young girl, then, had no mother! But a little space is always left in the heart for repentance: the Magdalen had her tears left to wash the feet of Jesus Christ."

He rejoined the girl, who a second time paused silently before him. She showed him a magnificent necklace of fine pearls, an antique cameo of high value, rings sparkling with diamonds.

"Oh, poor foolish girl!" said Georges with a sinking heart, "you fancy, then, that beauty is to be bought with gold? I knew you when more beautiful, eight years ago, at the Parc aux Grives."

She smiled and bent her head.

"Other times, other manners, as the historian has

said. Besides, your beauty is yet blooming and glorious. What a luxuriant form!"

Georges stretched forth his hand unceremoniously. Her bodice came unclasped and a bloody dagger fell to the ground. The girl picked it up and fled in all haste.

"The wretch!" said one of her class as she passed by, "she hides her crime, but she will be guillotined."

Georges fancied he felt the stern knife pass over his neck.

"What is she guilty of?" he asked of her who was passing.

"She stabbed, with a thrust of the dagger, the mistress of the wine-merchant, so as to have the key of the till herself."

In his terror, Georges went to the house of Madame * * *. Although it was nearly two o'clock in the morning, he found her in the chamber of the dead man, rummaging in his papers to study out the full extent of the estate.

Georges shuddered on entering the room from which the dead man had been removed only the evening before.

"See, Georges," said the lady, throwing her arms around his neck, "there is a drawer full of gold in this old cabinet; will you count it?"

"I have always taken without counting," said Georges Arnault with an absent smile.

He plunged his two hands into the drawer, trembling with savage rage, like a combatant who takes the sword from the scabbard.

He rose, with his hands full of gold, and turned with a menacing air toward Madame * * *, who uttered a cry of terror.

"And do you think that I will marry you?" said he, with a majestic haughtiness.

He threw the gold in the face of Madame * * * She fell upon her knees in an attitude of supplication.

At this instant there was a knock at the door leading to the staircase.

"Georges, I am afraid; save me."

He listened anxiously; fear took possession of himself.

Another knock. After a death-like silence, a more violent noise resounded in the hearts of the lovers. The door was beaten in; they were already passing through the adjoining saloon.

"We are lost! Mercy! mercy! mercy!" shrieked Madame * * *, dragging herself on her knees toward those who were entering.

She had recognised the brothers of her husband. They had been for two days posted as sentinels at the house, to watch the acts and movements of the widow.

"All this is yours," said Georges Arnault to the disinherited. "I poisoned the husband, and made the will which disinherits you. *Property is theft.* She who is following your steps like a dog is a saint of the calendar; let her pray to God in peace. As for me, it is another thing: I am guilty. Take me to prison. I wish to die on the scaffold; that will be my last satire."

IV.

Five o'clock was just striking at Val-de-Grâce; there was a crowd at the Barrière Saint-Jacques. It was the hour announced for the tragedy; the stage was arranged with its funereal decorations; the actors had not appeared. The boys, clambering on the walls, the trees, even on the roofs, began to hiss.

"Draw the curtain! draw the curtain!" echoed from all sides.

"Patience," said a spectator, "they have just lit the gas."

The sun was throwing the first rays of morning on the guillotine.

At last the wagon slowly rolled along.

The condemned was a young man, pale, haughty, and sad, but in no wise cast down by the odious preface to the execution. He regarded the guillotine without wavering.

"What does it matter?" said he, taking the hand of the priest, "it is the road to heaven. When I shall have mounted those steps, I shall have but one more to take."

He had just related his life to the priest in a simple, frank, and picturesque confession. He had not forgotten to speak to him, as he went along, about the young girl of the Parc aux Grives, who on so many occasions had so vividly struck his imagination.

He descended from the wagon; the priest was about to show him the way, but he passed before him.

When he was on the scaffold—the last stage of his life—he took the crucifix religiously and pressed it fervently to his lips. Two tears of repentance fell from his eyes.

At this instant, as he was casting a farewell look on the sky and on men, he saw pass in the crowd—in the horrible crowd in rags, which was intoxicated the evening before with wine, and which was about to be intoxicated with blood—he saw a young girl pass, dressed in white, her feet naked, her eyes fixed on the sky, her locks floating from a circlet of gold.

Georges Arnault seized the hand of the priest again.

"Do you see?" said he with a stifled voice.

"What do you mean?"

"You do not see her of whom I have spoken—down there, in that odious group—all white—her beauty would strike a blind man."

"We are waiting," said the executioner.

"A second!" murmured the condemned man in a supplicating voice.

He pointed out the young girl with his finger.

"See, it is she! it is still she! but what a strange metamorphosis? It seems as if she had lost even the recollection of her evil passions; she has, as by miracle, resumed her robe of innocence. See, she has just smiled upon me with the mouth of an angel."

Georges Arnauld fell back as if struck by lightning.

"Let us finish," said the executioner.

"My brother, what is the matter with you?" asked the priest of the condemned.

"You have not seen?" answered he, joining his hands, "she has flown to heaven."

Georges Arnault abandoned himself to the executioner.

His head—that beautiful head which a ray of supreme intelligence had crowned—was laid down under the knife, when the priest leaned down to say to him these words:—

"She whom you have seen at the four epochs of your life—she who has been pure—she who has committed folly—she who has sold her soul, and dipped her hands in blood—she who has repented, and has flown, all in white, to heaven,—it is your SOUL which has appeared to you."

THE MISTRESS OF CORNELIUS SCHUT.

HOW WOMEN DIE.

Cornelius Schut* was a painter and a poet. The poet is forgotten; but who has not seen one of the painter's charming cameos in the wreaths of flowers of Seghers?

Cornelius Schut was twenty-seven. He had a love of the beautiful, the poetic sentiment, all that forms the charm and passion of youth. He had thus far lived gayly, sometimes in good society, and a great deal in haunts of dissipation; more than one of his adventurous deeds had struck the pretty girls of Antwerp with astonishment. He sought refuge from his excesses in work, now as a poet, now as a painter,

* Born at Antwerp in 1590; died toward the middle of the seventeenth century. Vandyck had painted a portrait of Cornelius Schut. The features are well defined, and bear a thoughtful expression: the eyebrows are finely traced, the mustaches, proudly turned up, and the whole dress completely in the style of a gentleman of the 16th century. Cornelius Schut resided in France some years. He was acquainted with the poets called the Pleiades. He was one of Rubens's pupils, and possessed, like his master, an immense power of creation, but rarely proved himself a colorist.

and was as delighted with a good sonnet, as he was proud of a fine stroke of his brush.

One evening, as pipe in mouth, he was dreaming, according to his custom, before some mugs of beer and a few friends in one of the taverns of the port, it struck him that he was frittering away his heart and his life; he made a sudden resolution. He rose up from the table, placed his hat proudly on his head, and, stretching out his hand to his friends, bade them farewell.

"Where are you going?" they asked.

"I do not know," he replied, "but farewell."

"When will you come back?" said Peter Snayers, laughing.

"In two years," said Cornelius Schut.

"Two years! that will be doomsday?"

Cornelius Schut left the tavern, and proceeded to the house of a young creature who loved him. It is true that he had not devoted too much of his time to loving her in return, but he determined to make up for lost time. She was a beautiful girl, dark as the women of Antwerp who are descended in a direct line from the Spaniards.

"Elizabeth," said he to her, "do you love me for long?"

"For ever," she replied.

"Prepare to follow me, then; we set off to-morrow!"

"Where are we going?" asked the maiden.

"If you love me," said Cornelius, "what does it matter?"

Cornelius Schut kissed Elizabeth, and left the house.

History tells us scarcely anything of Elizabeth Van Thurenhoudt: she was a daughter of Eve who lived to love and be loved.

Cornelius Schut next proceeded to his uncle Matthew. "Uncle," he said, "it appears that I have a snug place in your will. Of all my future fortunes, all I claim to-day is my friend Wael, your favorite dog. I am going to banish myself in order to carry out a work of importance. The reverend fathers have ordered me to paint them two *Assumptions*, for their church and their house in the country. I must bury myself in pious solitude, if I would execute a work that shall live: let me entreat you, Uncle Matthew, to give me your dog."

The following day, the painter, Cornelius Schut, Elizabeth Van Thurenhoudt, and the merry Wael, reached, at sunset, a little rustic cottage on the borders of a wood. The painter had been to dream away his hours there before. This little cottage, which was used as a kind of hunting-box, formed part of a neighboring farm, which was all the fortune Cornelius possessed.

"Elizabeth," said he, "do you love me sufficiently to live with me here for two years, without seeing any face but mine, or having any other friend than my dog Wael?"

"Yes," she replied, with a slight expression of uneasiness.

In a very few days, their mode of life was poetically arranged: they had their long walks through the woods and meadows, with the bounding Wael at their side; their sweet confessions of love that Heaven alone overheard; that blessed labor which rests the heart; songs, books, reveries; the breakfast at the window, and the frugal repast at the side of the brook. You see the whole of this lovely picture of the most rustic freshness.

Elizabeth was beautiful; but she was even more charming than beautiful, possessing a certain indescribable look of ardent tenderness, which lent a softness to her eyes and played about her lips.

Cornelius Schut was happy in both heart and mind; the love of Elizabeth had made him a great painter, the love of art increased his passion for her still more. Those passions are indeed noble, which are crowned with the roses of the ideal!

At the expiration of two years, Cornelius Schut finished his *Assumptions*. When he saw them sent off to Antwerp, it seemed to him as if a part of his life was being borne away.

"O Heaven!" said Elizabeth to herself, "he loves me somewhat less since the pictures are gone."

Meanwhile Cornelius Schut began to carry his dreams back, now and then, to the tavern, where his comrades were, doubtless, still joyfully smoking.

One day, he took Elizabeth by the hand and said to her :—

" Are you aware that we have now lived two years in this manner, without caring for the world ?"

" I never gave it a thought," she replied.

" You never gave it a thought," said Cornelius Schut, tenderly, and kissing her hand ; " you never gave it a thought, and yet we return to-day to Antwerp !"

" To-day ?" said she, turning pale. " Ah, you no longer love me !"

The artist was moved to tears, and exclaimed, in a transport of joy, " Elizabeth, would you, then, consent to stay here another two years ?"

" Two centuries, dear Cornelius !"

They according amorously continued this quiet, solitary, and delightful mode of life, having no other links to connect them with the world, than the herdsman of the neighboring meadows, and a maid from the farm, who came every day to wait on them. A year passed away as if by enchantment ; but, in the very first months of the fourth year, Cornelius Schut began to count the days.

His friends at Antwerp thought him in Italy. No one for a moment supposed that a merry fellow like him, would remain so obstinately secluded from the world. His dog betrayed his retreat. Daniel Seghers, happening to be studying one day in the open country, perceived Wael, who was an old friend.

He went up to him, and renewed acquaintanceship. He knew that that original, Cornelius Schut, had taken his uncle's dog with him, and, as he had found the dog, it struck him he should soon find the master also. He was right: a few minutes afterward he surprised the painter and his beloved, seated in the shade on the borders of the wood.

As soon as Elizabeth perceived Daniel Seghers, she rose up hurriedly, and said to Cornelius Schut, "Let us fly;" for, thought she, "if he tarries with us, our solitude will be profaned."

But, alas! Cornelius Schut stretched out his hand to his old friend: they talked about Antwerp, and Cornelius Schut sighed.

"By my faith!" said Daniel Seghers, "you must, indeed, be happy here, since you have never been to enjoy your glory; for, have you not heard it? Your two *Assumptions* are admired by everybody. All your friends think you are at Rome; if they knew you were here, they would come and carry you off in triumph."

When the painter and his mistress were once more alone, they looked sorrowfully at each other.

"Elizabeth," said Cornelius Schut, "must we remain here eight months longer, before returning to where life is waiting to greet us with countless *fêtes?*"

"Go!" said Elizabeth, endeavoring to conceal her tears.

Cornelius Schut was touched by so much love. Forgetting Antwerp, friends, and fame, he exclaimed, "Go—go without you — never!"

Time passed on, but more slowly. They sang no more, they ran no more here and there. Seeing this, the dog himself became sad. From time to time, it is true, he still attempted one of his gay gambols or joyous barks; but he soon relapsed into his taciturn behavior.

At length the last days of their solitude approached. So great was the painter's joy at the idea of seeing his friends again, or rather of finding himself once more in the midst of them, that he did not perceive that his mistress was every hour, growing paler and wasting away; it is true, that for him she had always her tender and charming smile. The evening previous to their departure, he asked her to accompany him through the favorite paths of the large wood, where they had so often lost their way. She leaned upon his arm, and walked on in silence. It was a beautiful day in August, and the joyous crops glistened in the fields, while the note of the blackbird in the trees, replied to the sound of the scythe among the ripe corn.

"What a beautiful day!" exclaimed Cornelius Schut, enthusiastically. "I have a presentiment that we shall still pass many a delicious hour here; for Nature has never spoken to me with more poetry in her words. You see, Elizabeth, our love has not grown old."

"Alas!" said she, bending down her head.

"We will return," replied the painter; "we will often return; for, like you, I feel that it is here that we shall again enjoy our youth. We can only be happy once in this world."

"Then, why leave at all?" asked Elizabeth. "You have accustomed me to live alone with you; the bustle of the world will scare away my happiness; I shall lose everything there."

"Child, life, you know, is not made up of love alone; and the world has laid down certain laws that we must follow. We must live for ourselves, I grant; but, at the same time, we must also live a little for others."

"For my part," replied Elizabeth, "I can live only for you."

At this moment, she fell on her knees on the grass, looking paler even than usual, and raising toward her lover, her beautiful eyes bathed in tears.

"Dearest," she said, "will you go?"

He raised her up, pressed her to his heart, and kissing her hair, replied, "I must."

"Very well," said she, in a trembling voice; "very well; we will go, then; but remember, I shall never return."

The painter did not understand what she meant. "You will return as well as I," he said. "Let me live six months at Antwerp with you, and then we will return, perhaps for good."

They had now nearly reached the middle of the wood.

"Shall we go and rest a little," continued Cornelius Schut, "in the oak copse that you are so fond of?"

"No," she replied; "though I should like to do so very much; but I have not sufficient strength. Let us retrace our steps—let us go home—I do not know what is the matter with me to-day; but do not be alarmed—I shall be ready to leave to-morrow."

The next day, the artist spent the morning in his studio, arranging his pictures, sketches, drawings, and books. He felt something of that delight which is experienced by the exile, when he once more approaches his native land. Elizabeth, who had remained in their apartment, seated near the window with her eye wandering over the view before her suddenly heard her lover sing as follows:—

> "'Tis in the wine-shop that real life is to be found. Fair hostess, my sweet, bring us to drink: let your small, white hands pour out for us the foaming beer."

It is impossible to convey an idea of the profound grief that seized Elizabeth; for this was the song Cornelius used to sing with his friends on days of rejoicing. Her heart heaved with a convulsive throb. She raised her eyes toward Heaven, and prayed fervently.

Meanwhile Cornelius went on singing, carried

away more and more by his joyous recollections. The poor girl suddenly made an effort to recover her strength, and rising hastily, ran to the door of the studio. The door was half open, and she remained standing on the threshold. Seeing her appear thus, with her hair dishevelled, her breast heaving violently, and her eyes rolling wildly, Cornelius Schut ran in surprise and terror toward her.

"Elizabeth, what is the matter?"

She smiled bitterly,

"What is the matter? Listen."

And immediately she commenced singing the following song, which he had composed for her, in the brightest days of their solitude:—

I.

"The daisies will all fade. Winter will come drifting the snow. Winter will never pass over my heart, my fair mistress."

II.

"My heart is a perpetual spring when thou smilest on me, O thou radiant sun! when I see thy black tresses float around thy head—when I hover on thy balmy lip!"

III.

"No—I fear not winter—it will pass without touching my heart. I defy his frost and storm, when I kiss thine arm upon the sward.

IV.

"Yet there is one winter which affrights me—that one which in its marble arms will carry us to the dark tomb, and scatter o'er us scentless flowers.

V.

"This last winter will freeze our hearts; but we shall carry with us above, the recollection of the daisies that studded the heaven where thou walkedst, for it was a heaven upon earth."

At the conclusion of the song, Elizabeth fell fainting in her lover's arms — she had thrown all her life into her voice.

He carried her to the window, that she might breathe the bracing morning air. She opened her eyes, and said :—

"Farewell! your heart beats no longer at that song —all is over."

Then she murmured :

"Yet there is one winter which affrights me — that one which in its marble arms . . . . ."

"Dear Elizabeth!" exclaimed Cornelius Schut, struck with terror; "my dearest girl, what is the matter?"

"My friend," she replied, in a dying voice, "you told me that we must leave this place; I am preceding you — that is all. You would have deserted me there, in Antwerp; I would rather die here."

Elizabeth had scarcely pronounced these words, ere she closed her eyes for ever. Cornelius Schut snatched her up in his arms, and embraced her as if he would give her his life.

It would be a hopeless task to endeavor to picture his despair. He spent the whole day in weeping and acting like a madman. A hundred times did he press his mistress to his heart; but Elizabeth did not wake beneath his embrace.

He now remembered that, for more than a month past, the poor girl had been growing paler every day; and he felt that she had died from excessive love for him. He vowed never to return to Antwerp, but to live in the midst of the woods, with the ever-living recollection of his sad Elizabeth.

It was not till after the funeral that he perceived he had not got a portrait of her. We do not paint the portrait of her we love; for how can we hope to transfer to the canvass, the charms of a face that we adore! Elizabeth had often sat for the virgins in his pictures; but he had only copied the angelic purity of her features—he had carefully avoided giving the mother of the angels the thoroughly mundane expression of his beloved.

When she had disappeared for ever, his regret at not having preserved all that composed the peculiar character and charm of his dear Elizabeth, amounted to despair. He still saw her pass before him in his dreams, flitting like a shadow along the meadows or in the depths of the forest. It was, however, no longer the blooming, laughing maiden of former years; but a pale, sad figure, already touched by the icy hand of death. He tried to paint her portrait, by studying his recollection; but every time that the picture breathed into life beneath his pencil, he started back with horror; for it was always the dying Elizabeth that appeared upon the canvass.

During nearly a month, Cornelius Schut remained in his retreat, which had suddenly become for him a hermitage. His uncle informed of his retreat by Seghers, who felt alarmed at his obstinate seclusion, surprised him, one evening, meditating on Elizabeth Van Thurenhoudt's tomb. The worthy Matthew was horror-struck at Cornelius Schut's pallor and despair. The artist related word for word, the history of his passion.

"You must return with me to Antwerp," said his uncle, much moved at the tale.

"No," replied the artist; "until the daisies bloom upon her grave, I will go and weep there."

He remained. Every morning he went and meditated at the tomb of his beloved. He talked to her as was his wont in happier days. "Yes," he used to exclaim, with melancholy earnestness, "we shall see each other again in another retreat, where we will love on for ever; but shall I again see your beautiful eyes, so gentle when you spoke to me? Poor Elizabeth, it is true, you are lying alone in the tomb; but yet you are not as lonely as I am!"

One morning, he experienced a feeling of joy on seeing two daisies that had bloomed in the young grass.

He plucked them, kissed them, and placed them next his heart.

He set off for Antwerp with poor Wael, who had long since ceased his gambols. He returned to the tavern. His friends were disposed to banter him about his mysterious love affair; but when they beheld him so pale and sad—when they heard him speak of his loneliness with a voice broken by sobs—they respected his grief: all offered him silently their hand.

Have I not read this thought among the verses of Cornelius Schut: "The most impassioned man does not find all his existence in love; woman alone can live and die for her heart."

MARIE DE JOYSEL.

This narrative is not an imaginary romance; it is a history in which truth has quite enough of romantic poetry, to dispense with the pleasing falsehoods of fiction and foreign ornaments. If you have the patience to turn over the dull compilations of Pitaval, the letters of madame du Noyer, the law-reports and memoirs of the end of the seventeenth century, the countenances of the persons whom I here reanimate will be gradually presented to your view. The heroine, Marie Joisel or Marie de Joysel, was long celebrated at Paris, as are all great criminals when they are beautiful. I do not introduce into this sad drama a single actor the record of whose birth and death I can not produce. I have given all the names, at the same time endeavoring, in accordance with the shades that have been evoked and the memoirs of the time, to present their persons, their passions, and their characters. This history brings prominently forward certain ideas worthy of arresting for a moment the attention of serious minds. When the passions are in play, as here—when the passions are violently agitated in the darkness of the heart, light always springs forth. The passions are unbroken coursers, that gallop by night in the open fields, that run at random intoxicated by the excitement of the course, occasionally lighting their path by a spark from a stone. The life of Marie de Joysel especially confirms these words of a divine apostle: "If you wish to save the sinner," said Saint Paul, "offend him not, console him, love him; he will repent in your compassion and your love; at the first tear of repentance he will be saved."

I.

IN 1683, on the Quai des Tournelles, there lived an old canon, in peace with this world, with the kingdom of heaven in perspective. The canon Leblanc was a worthy old man, nobly crowned with his white hairs; in spite of his sixty-eight years, he was still vigorous, like all the pious servants of God, who have lived in faith, far from the profane passions. He had only light cares and passing anxieties in his heart, sometimes on account of a bad supper, sometimes on account of his housekeeper's gossipping propensities. He was a fine old man, somewhat emaciated and rather tall; he did not step beyond his divine mission, but fulfilled it with earnestness and good faith. He was much beloved in his chapter and his church, as a simple man who only preached twice a-year. He had not a great fortune; the little he possessed was at the disposal of every one—his family, the poor, and his housekeeper. The only fault his friends found with him was that he was a little of a lunatic; gayety, ennui, sadness, melancholy, all came upon him by fits and starts, according as the weather was rainy or fine. His days of melancholy he passed in the chimney-corner, poking the fire, lost in his endless dreams—lost, as he used to say, in his purgatory. Then, no one could get a single sentence from him; he replied only in monosyllables. Sometimes a week passed in this manner, gloomy and silent; but some morning, every one was surprised to find him again in a good humor, opening his window and his heart to the first ray of the sun.

The canon Leblanc belonged to a family of Lyonnese laborers. A sister remained to him, who had married a physician of Lyons by the name of Thomé. This physician was an honest man, who, toward the end of his career—having amassed nothing, and not knowing what to do with his children—resolved, at the entreaty of his wife, to recommend his second son, Charles-Henri Thomé, to the kindness of the canon, who had the reputation of being very well off. The old curé, without saying anything to Angélique, had sent three thousand livres to his nephew to study medicine at Montpelier. After he became a member of the faculty, Henri was none the richer. Where was he to find patients? his father had none too many for himself. "Go to Paris," said his mother to him one day, embracing him—"go to my brother; out of love for his sister, he will be a father to you and will make your fortune." Henri set out in the coach, in company with an old soldier of the guards, with a dozen crowns and the prayers of his family.

He was a tall lad of twenty-four, with a countenance brilliantly lighted up by his eye, rather pale, but still sufficiently animated, gracefully set off by ringlets of beautiful brown hair. His mouth had preserved a certain sweetness and artlessness that betokened a good heart.

He alighted, one evening in December, at the abode of his old uncle. The canon, seeing some resemblance to his sister, received the young doctor with great tenderness; he, however, put some restraint upon his feelings for fear of offending his housekeeper. The old maid received her guest with many grimaces, muttering something between her teeth. As she served up a bad supper that evening, she at last became softened; at dessert she condescended to listen to Henri, who spoke to her from time to time to please his uncle. She even pushed her affability so far as to wish him a good-night, as she conducted him to a little chamber which was, at the same time, the parlor, guest-chamber, and library of the canon.

At the end of a week she was on the best terms with Henri; she told him her history, that of her family, all the offers of marriage that she had refused on account of the abbé Leblanc, all the nights she had passed in watching over him; in a word, she opened her heart to him as to a friend.

One day that the abbé Leblanc was sad and absent, she told him that the canon had had for some years past his white moons, his red moons, and his black moons. According to her, it was necessary to be careful about speaking to him without cause in his hours of lunacy; but Henri, troubled at seeing his uncle thus lost in himself, wished to possess the secret of it, as much, perhaps, from curiosity as from solicitude. One evening, then, about nightfall, as the canon, seated before a window, seemed to be falling asleep with the day, Henri seated himself beside him, and talked to him of the rain and the fine weather.

"I do not know if you are like me, uncle; I am strangely the slave of the inconstancy of your Paris climate; the rain spoils everything for me, even good books; while the sun gladdens my heart and my eyes: with the sun, everything smiles upon me, the trees, the houses, the river. In church, my soul is much nearer to God in fine weather than when it is dull."

The canon did not answer a word.

"I am sure, uncle, that all men are so; it seems to me that you yourself, who live in the Lord, far from the cares and troubles of this world, can not protect yourself against the attacks of the weather."

The canon still kept silence.

"I see that I am wrong," resumed Henri as he withdrew to a distance: "do not be angry with me if I have disturbed you in your holy meditations; profane as I am, I understand these outpourings of the soul in the bosom of the Deity."

He had stopped, as he said these words, opposite to the fireplace, where some scattered embers were dying away. A deep silence followed; but soon the canon, doubtless supposing that he was gone, began to think aloud, as if to solace his heart: "Oh! God, give me power to save her! Oh! Lord, thou hadst more mercy for the Magdalen! and the Magdalen had perhaps less sorrow and less beauty!"

Henri, frightened at surprising the secret of his uncle's sadness, was leaving the room with a stealthy step. But he had not reached the door, when the old housekeeper, suddenly entering, stopped him in the passage.

"Monsieur the canon," said she to her master, "shall we have supper early?"

The abbé Leblanc made no reply.

"Do you hear me?" said Angélique again in a

piercing voice; "tell me if you are going to the prison to-day?"

"No, no, I will not go," replied the canon, as if he were speaking to himself: "I will go no more; I do not wish to return there."

And, as he said this, he took his umbrella and went out.

"Look at him! he is going there now in spite of the rain. Was there ever seen such a canon as that? Could he not wait till to-morrow, I should like to know? To put one's self out for women of that sort—wantons and criminals! Do those women need the cross and the holy water to find their way to hell? Well, well, let him do as he likes."

Henri had become thoughtful. He followed his uncle in imagination; he saw him run to Sainte-Pélagie, enter a cell, and console, in Christian charity, some fair penitent, who, like the Magdalen, had nothing left but her long locks and her tears.

"I too will go to Sainte-Pélagie," he said suddenly, as if with a presentiment of his destiny.

II.

Henri had not yet loved. During his studies at Montpelier, true passion had never taken hold upon his heart. We need not deceive ourselves: love is at first but a whim; in the dawn of youth, it has neither strength nor earnestness.

When the canon returned, Henri asked him if he was satisfied with his wicked flock—if the lost sheep had returned to the right path.

"The poor prisoners," said the abbé Leblanc with some displeasure, "are all much moved at the voice of the gospel; they are really penitent. But there is one more obstinate, who speaks lightly of salvation. Through my aid, God will at last descend into her heart."

After a silence the canon continued as if to himself, as he shook his umbrella :—

"Ah! if I could save that revolted angel!"

"Uncle," said Henri, with some reluctance, "are there no sick persons at Sainte-Pélagie?"

"Always; that prison is almost a grave; there they learn to die."

"Well, uncle, since you are such a good physician, of their souls, why should I not be the physician of their bodies? You are on terms of friendship with M. de Louvois, with my lord the archbishop, and with other illustrious persons. Are you aware that you are a powerful man? Could you not procure me the appointment of assistant physician to the prison, with some six hundred livres a year? Until I get patients who are richer or in better stations, it would be a means of study and a duty for me. Think of it."

"Six hundred livres!" murmured the canon to himself. "He is right: a means of study and a duty; besides, it would be a relief for me. Six hundred livres! in fact, I will think of it."

He was again lost in the dark labyrinth of his reveries.

Two days after, Henri thought his request forgotten, when his uncle told him; that he had interceded with my lord the chancellor, and that through his high and benevolent patronage, his nephew Charles Henri Thomé, was enrolled as assistant physician to the prison of Sainte-Pélagie.

Henri, after visiting with his uncle the chief physician and the superior of the asylum, requested to be introduced to the sick penitents; but that day he found only worthless creatures, branded by crime and the evil passions, with neither beauty nor courage to recommend them. "Doubtless," said he, "my uncle has permitted himself to be deceived. I I have seen almost all the prisoners, and there is not one who could remind one of Magdalen the sinner, or Magdalen the penitent." But some days after, as he was passing through a corridor with the jailer, a nun of the convent, sister Martha, begged him to visit a poor prisoner, whom the director of the prison wished to force to the labor of the convicts.

"If she ever labors, I am willing to be imprisoned too," said the jailer. "By fair rights, they should leave such white hands in peace."

By the manner in which the jailer said these words, it might be conjectured that those white hands had crossed his, with some pieces of money. Henri Thomé followed the nun in silence. She led him to a little cell, at the foot of a staircase; she took a key from her girdle, knocked three times, opened the door and made the young doctor pass in before her. After she had cast a glance upon the prisoner, she said: "My sister, the physician of the prison is often prevented by his advanced age, from giving you the assistance of his art; yield your confidence to this person, who is recommended to us by his uncle, the respectable abbé Leblanc."

The prisoner slowly bowed her head, as she cast a careless glance upon Henri Thomé.

"I will return in a few minutes," said the nun, and closed the door.

The young doctor remained standing before the prisoner, who was seated upon the edge of her bed.

"For Heaven's sake, sir," she said to him with angelic sweetness, "for Heaven's sake, declare that I am ill. Since you are a physician, that will not be difficult for you," she added with a slightly sarcastic smile.

As she said these words, she fixed upon him two eyes, by which he was dazzled.

"I know not what to reply, madame, except that I will declare you as sick as you wish to be. To satisfy my conscience, permit me to consult......"

He did not end his sentence, for the prisoner seeing that he held out his hand, gave him hers without waiting to be requested. As she perceived that he pressed it rather more than a physician ought to do, she immediately asked him if she had a fever.

"No, madame," he replied with a troubled voice. "But since you wish it, I will declare that you are laid up for a long time. I will go at once and certify it on the register of the house."

"I am obliged to you, sir, for this kindness."

She then took up a prayer-book, and pretended to read. Henri Thomé was much moved; he took a turn in the cell, and sought to renew the conversation.

"You have a devoted friend, madame, in my uncle the canon; you have touched his heart. Such great misfortunes nobly supported, such great beauty that a fatal destiny conceals in a prison, so many tears that fall in silence and in solitude, when there are so many hearts that would gladly receive them....."

The prisoner closed her book, and proudly raised her head.

"Sir," she said rather bitterly, "I do not permit every one to pity me.'

As she saw that the young doctor was much hurt by these words, she endeavored to soften them.

"But," she added with a mournful sigh, "the friendship which we both have for the abbé Leblanc, may perhaps excuse you. Pity me, if you will, I shall not be angry."

At this moment, the nun opened the door.

"I will call to-morrow, madame," said Henri, bowing.

The prisoner made no reply, she merely bowed in the coldest possible manner. Henri Thomé departed with a thoughtful countenance. It was the beginning of April, and the sun was scattering abroad his sweetest rays. As he passed into the gloomy rue de la Clé, on which the prison opens, or rather shuts, he seemed to be walking in an enchanted region; he saw only the sky. If his glance descended upon the dark walls of Sainte-Pélagie, it rested upon some clusters of wild wall-flower that were waving in the wind of spring. He heard only the beatings of his own heart, and the harmonies of his soul. If his ear was open, it was to the lively song of some amorous bird, flitting over the moss-covered roof of the prison.

When he met his uncle in the afternoon, he could not help saying to him, that "he had seen a prisoner, who was the most beautiful woman in the world."

"But," he added, "I only saw her eyes and her hands. But what terrible eyes! what adorable hands!"

"Guilty eyes and hands," said the uncle with a sigh; "let us never speak of that woman."

Once alone in his chamber, Henri Thomé recalled in his memory the whole scene of this interview with the celebrated prisoner. That face which he had scarcely looked at, was gradually reanimated before his delighted eyes, with its touching paleness, its pure and graceful features, its fascinating charm. Since we are upon this portrait, let us finish it in a single word.

Coypel painted this prisoner when she shone in the world: according to the painter, this woman was a faithful copy of Titian's courtesan; the same voluptuous ardor in her eyes and upon her lips; no elevation, no recollection or presentiment of heaven, all was worldly, made to love and to seduce. When Henri Thomé saw her in the cell, it was no longer the same portrait; far from the sunshine, far from the world and from love, she had grown pale, her cheeks had faded beneath her tears and her sorrows, her eyes were less brilliant, but rather more gentle. If she was less beautiful to the eye, she was more beautiful to the heart.

"To love that woman, is to plunge into an abyss," murmured Henri Thomé.

During the remainder of the day, during the night, he endeavored to withdraw himself from the enchanting recollection of the prisoner; but he was under the spell, he everywhere saw that pale face on which passion had left its fascinating impress, those lovely eyes which had poured forth so much love and so many tears.

III.

The next day, about noon, Henri Thomé returned to the prison. He was more agitated and paler than the day before, when he entered the cell of the beautiful prisoner. He was, however, more collected, and in his desire to penetrate into the secret of such a great misfortune, he cast a scrutinizing glance upon the surrounding objects, while he talked somewhat at random, about the weary life of the prison, when the April sky, bright with sunshine, was inviting all poor human creatures to the joys of earth. The cell was four or five times as large as a tomb; on the damp walls there was nothing to deceive the eye or withdraw it from the sad reality, nothing on the rough pavement to protect delicate feet. The whole furniture consisted of a hard, narrow bed, a worn-out pallet, a little table of black oak, an embroidery frame, a pitcher, some religious books, some rags, a broken china-pot, in which the prisoner cultivated some violets; and lastly, as some consolation to this misery and neglect, a little mirror in a Gothic frame; it was Pélisson's spider. To light the whole, a feeble ray came into the cell through the grating of a narrow window, which scarcely allowed one to guess at the sky.

"You will not remain here," said Henri Thomé, indignant at the prisoner's punishment; "you can not live here a year."

"I have been here eleven years," she said, with sad and gentle resignation.

"Eleven years!" replied Henri, pale and faltering, as if he had received a blow upon his heart.

"But, what matters it?" replied the prisoner, "I am condemned to die here. Alas! death himself repels me from his bosom."

As on the day before, she took up a prayer-book, a refuge from her sorrow.

"Those who have condemned you to this punishment, are barbarians, madame. It is only a hateful vengeance......"

"For Heaven's sake, sir, let us not speak of the past: for you I must only be a sick prisoner; seek nothing more."

"You were very young, madame, eleven years ago."

"I was twenty-two."

"What! the best days of your life have passed in this horrible solitude! you have lived far from the charming joys of youth! not a heart to console yours!"

The prisoner no longer listened to Henri, at least she was endeavoring to read the penitential psalms. He respected her silence and departed. As he passed the jailer, he asked him "what was said in regard to the fair prisoner." The jailer replied, that "they only knew that her baptismal name was *Marie;* that she was shut up there and overlooked, by a man black from head to foot; that she was a poor woman of great resignation, who was always weeping, but who never complained."

Henri was about to depart with this vague information, when the jailer added :—

"I forgot to tell you, that several gentlemen have come here in coaches, who have each offered me more than a hundred crowns, to see her for a moment. I have always refused. There was one, especially, who was very urgent: he would have made my fortune, if I had set the prisoner free."

As soon as he entered the house, Henri went to the canon, who was reading his breviary in the corner of his chamber.

"Uncle, I expect from your friendship, some information in regard to the history of the prisoner, who is called Marie. As I am physician of the body, I must know what is passing, and what has passed in the soul."

"My son, I will only tell to God what the confessor has heard in this world; besides, when I have absolved a sinner, I forget his crimes. It belongs only to the Almighty, to enroll them in the great book of the last judgment."

"Ah! uncle, you have not forgotten what Marie has confided to you."

"Listen, my son; let us never speak of that woman; let us respect her weakness or her crimes, now that she has shed the tears of penitence."

When the canon, as he said these words, looked at his nephew, he was astonished at his paleness, his restlessness, and the strange fire of his eye.

"What have I done, imprudent man that I am?" said the abbé Leblanc to himself, as he thought of the angelic and fatal beauty of the prisoner; "if ever this young man should allow himself to be fascinated, like all who have seen that woman! My friend," he added aloud, "that woman is a deep and dark abyss, which I never look upon without trembling. We must pity her as we pass by, but think not of her: crime has led more than one young heart astray. But I forgot to tell you, that we have a precious letter which awaits you."

"A letter from my mother!" said Henri, breaking the seal.

He read with filial ardor, but yet with an absent heart. The letter exhaled a maternal tenderness so touching, an odor of home so pure, that for some moments he blushed at his mad passion for a criminal. He saw Marie appear with less pleasing and less graceful features, beside his poor mother who was a model of Christian virtue; but the demon soon regained his empire over the heart that had already strayed. In the evening when he was alone, it seemed to him an age since he had seen the prisoner; he was almost terrified at this rising passion which had taken such a hold upon him. He fell upon his knees, although he was not in the habit of praying; he sought to recall the remembrance of his mother. "O God! O my mother, deliver me from this woman!" but at the same moment he added with tears: "O God, deliver the poor prisoner!"

Far from struggling longer, he gave himself up with bitter pleasure to that gloomy passion whose only horizon was the walls of a cell, or rather the phantoms of a crime. But love always blinds us to his purpose. Henri saw in the convict only a beautiful woman of high birth, surrounded by all the magic of misfortune and of sorrow. Besides, if he thought of Marie's crimes, far from revolting at them, he became still more softened, he plunged deeper into the abyss. Is not love a fire which the storm itself increases?

IV.

In less than a week, Henri Thomé was a slave to the most violent passion. In spite of all his love, he had hardly snatched some vague words from the prisoner, who probably thought little of him. But one morning that he surprised her all in tears, her hair dishevelled, and her hands clasped together, she spoke to him as a friend.

The nun had not entered the cell that day when she opened the door to the young physician; and when he found himself alone before that afflicted woman, whom he loved to distraction, he threw himself upon his knees, seized her hands, and said to her with a tremulous voice: "Ah, madame, if you but knew how I love you!"

At any other moment the prisoner would, perhaps, have repelled him with disdain; but then her heart was opened by a crisis of grief and despair; she was touched by this passionate avowal. She looked at Henri without disengaging her hands, and murmured in a tender voice: "You love me! but you know not whom you love! You are moved by my misfortunes; it is pity—it is not love. God be praised! You pity me, but you do not love me."

"I do not love you!" exclaimed Henry, sobbing; "see if I do not love you!"

The prisoner felt his burning tears upon her hands.

"Poor child!" she murmured as she wept herself. "Who are you, then? whence do you come? Have you not met, in the world in which you move, a woman younger and more worthy of your heart? Have you no sister to defend you, by her purity, from such a passion?"

"I have a sister—a sister who loves me," replied Henri in a stifled voice; "if she saw you, so unhappy and so beautiful, far from condemning my heart, she would tell me to love you."

Marie had become thoughtful. She stretched forth her hand to the crucifix upon the bed; she seized a rusty key and a small dagger stained with blood, but she suddenly threw them aside and exclaimed: "No, never!"

"What do you say, madame? For Heaven's sake, confide in me."

"Listen, sir: since you love me, will you assist me in accomplishing a great work?"

"I am ready for anything," said the young man, raising his head energetically; "command, madame, my arm and my soul are yours."

"Take care, sir, this is a serious affair, and may be your ruin."

"Is it not happiness to ruin myself for you? I tell you again, I am ready for anything."

"Well!" exclaimed Marie, pressing his hand, "I rely upon you. This is what you are to do: I must leave this prison for three or four hours only, some day of this week, a little before midnight. We will get into a coach, and we will go to the Rue Saint-André-des-Arts, where I have a visit to make."

Henri could not hide an emotion of jealousy.

"Child," she added, "do you not see by my eyes that, if it is an assignation, it is not an assignation of love?"

In fact, all the rage of vengeance shone in the prisoner's eyes.

"After this visit, we will return here; for I do not wish to fly even with you. Justice must be done. Well, will you have strength to do this?"

"Yes, madame," replied Henri in a firm voice.

"But, as a reward for this perilous journey, I will ask of you, on your return, permission to kiss your beautiful locks."

"Take it beforehand," said the prisoner joyfully.

Henri kissed the prisoner's hair with passion and delight.

"Shall it be this evening?" said he, radiant with pleasure.

"Yes, this evening, if you can."

"Since you wish it, I can, madame; I will tell the jailer and the superior that you are worse, that I will return at night, and that sister Martha will watch with you. Sister Martha loves you, as does every one who comes near you; she can not detain you. We will set out together: they will see no one but me go out: in a word, Heaven will be our guide."

"Go, I await you, with prayers to God."

Henri departed, proud and happy, more than ever under the influence of his passion.

V.

About eleven o'clock at night, he alighted from a hackney-coach, at the end of the rue de la Clé; although it had rained in torrents, he wished to go on foot to the prison. He found sister Martha in the cell of Marie, who had not yet had courage to confide in her. As there was no time to lose,

Henri told her Marie's intention as soon as he entered.

"I expect from your friendship for her, that you will watch for three hours in silence in the cell; in three hours Marie will return, we both swear it upon this crucifix."

"If it is to do a good deed......" murmured sister Martha in terror.

"Yes, yes, a good deed," said Marie with animation.

"Depart, my sister; I will pray to the holy Mother of God, to watch over you."

Henri threw his cloak over the shoulder of the prisoner, who followed him at a distance through the corridor. The jailer came to conduct him to the door; Henri, as he approached him, took his dark lantern, threw it down and extinguished it, and withdrew his attention by some random remarks. Everything succeeded to perfection; while the jailer was angrily picking up his lantern, the prisoner had time to pass. When the door was closed, Henri took Marie in his arms, and carried her to the coach. From the rue de la Clé to the rue Saint-André-des-Arts, the journey was very silent. Henri dared not question Marie, nor withdraw her from her reflections; he took her hand in his, and from time to time he pressed it affectionately. Marie thanked him for his silence, she was touched by his devotion, and two or three times during the ride she returned the pressure of his hand

Notwithstanding the weather, the night was not very dark, and they could see each other in the coach. Now that night for the first time, Marie discovered that Henri had a noble countenance; she felt that she was moved by his love, and she could not help thinking, that it would be delightful for both of them, for herself as well as for him, to fly together, to go to some happy solitude, far from that dark prison, whose cold walls she had felt for the last eleven years, far from the world which had condemned her to such horrible sufferings. "No, no," she said to herself; "it is ended, the time of love is past for me. But," she continued, "alone with him who loves me, far from the scene of my crime and my misfortunes, forgetting the past as a sad dream, will not God grant me yet some days of rest?—Rest for me?" she added as she bowed her gloomy brow; "oh! no, it is ended; my heart is already in hell. It is not love I wish, it is vengeance."

The coach stopped before the smallest house in the rue Saint-André-des-Arts.

"You will ring," she said to Henri, who gave her his hand to alight. "You will ask for La Verrière; the footman will take you for a friend: notwithstanding the lateness of the hour, he will let you pass."

"And where shall we go?" asked Henri as he rang.

"I know the way," replied Marie with a deep sigh.

They passed in without difficulty; they crossed the

court-yard, they ascended a staircase and stopped before a door in the dark.

"You will wait for me here, Henri; I will not be long, I hope."

She slipped the rusty key into the lock, opened the door, closed it behind her, and cautiously advanced toward the apartment where she was to pay her visit.

"It is well," she said, as she saw a furrow of light beneath the door; "I would rather find him there: he is there, it is well."

Before she entered, she collected her strength and raised her eyes to heaven.

She advanced with more resolution, gently pushed open the door and entered.

In that apartment a man was watching, wasted away by toil and grief. He looked more like a dead than a living man. A little lamp shed a dim light over his bony face. He was clad in a long black gown, in keeping with the rest of his person.

When Marie entered the room, his face was more animated than usual; he had just been writing, and he was reading over what he had written, with a cruel pleasure. It must have been an evil work; in fact it was the worst that had ever proceeded from the hand of man; it was a will filled with curses. This man who felt that he was dying, wished to leave behind him all his hate, all his vengeance, all his wrath.

When he had finished reading this strange will,

there was a fierce expression of joy and cruelty upon his wrinkled face: he looked as if he had just plunged a poniard into the bosom of his enemy.

At that moment, thinking that he heard a noise, he raised his eyes.

He saw Marie pale and gloomy, her bosom heaving with the beatings of her heart, her eye flashing with anger.

"You, madame?" he exclaimed with a sudden tremor.

"Yes," she said, advancing; "yes, it is I!"

The man was terrified; he was about to call for aid.

"Do not call," said Marie, snatching a poniard from her bosom.

He raised his hand as if to defend himself; rage and fear had so overcome him, that he fell fainting in his chair, struggling and attempting to call.

Marie approached nearer; she looked upon him with disgust and pity.

"It were an act of cowardice to kill him," she said; "is he not half dead?"

She dropped the poniard at her feet.

"Oh! God, I thank thee," she said, "I thank thee, for thou hast disarmed my hand."

She leaned over the table and cast a glance upon what he had been writing.

"His will!" said she with eager curiosity.

She passed rapidly over the first pages, which had

been written for a long time; she hastily read the last lines:—

"I bequeath, moreover, to my children all my vengeance and all my maledictions against their mother. In the name of God and of human justice, it is my intention and my will that they cover her with ignominy even after her death. In the name of the Father, and of the Son, and of the Holy Ghost. Amen."

"This, then, is what he was writing!" said she, scarcely breathing; "thus vengeance will be his last thought; when he is dead, his restless shade will come and watch at my prison-door."

She took the will, tore it in pieces, and threw it contemptuously in the face of the attorney.

She immediately departed and returned to Henri.

"Let us go," she said as she closed the door, "my visit is ended."

They returned to the prison; they found sister Martha asleep in the cell.

"Farewell," murmured Henri, before the nun should awake.

"Henri, my brow is now unworthy of your lips; return to-morrow, but this night pray to God that he may give you power to forget me."

She called him back by a sign, and gathered the pale violets which she cultivated with so much care.

"Here, Henri, take these violets; it is the only

good thing I have to give you; they are worth more than my heart; take them and ask nothing more."

VI.

THE following passage, which is a true chapter of this history, is taken from the *Lettres Galantes*, published at Amsterdam in 1684:—

"FEBRUARY.

"You know, madame, the whole history of that attorney to the parliament who took such terrible vengeance upon his wife. That history is not yet finished. All Paris is talking of a night-scene which has just taken place in the attorney's study. In fact, it almost makes me believe in supernatural events, and I am far from being a free-thinker. Imagine to yourself, that our hero, who has been near death for many years, was alone at half-past eleven o'clock at night, occupied with his will. Everybody in his house was asleep; but he never sleeps, he is waiting until he is dead for that. He will die without regretting the pleasures of this world, for the poor man has walked over a stony path. His only fear is lest his wife may be pardoned as soon as he is no more; that is his great affliction. For that reason he makes will upon will, in which he bequeaths, among other good and valuable articles, his vengeance to his family, his friends, and his children. The other evening, then, he was occupied as usual, in carefully revising every sentence of his will or his codicil; he had just added a direction in due form to his children, that they should curse their mother. All at once he hears a low noise like the sound of a ghost: he raises his eyes—what does he behold before him? His wife, the beautiful Marie de Joysel, who has been languishing for a dozen years in the Madelonnettes and Sainte-Pélagie. You may well suppose that he was terrified at this strange apparition. He attempted to call, but his wife snatched a poniard from her bosom, and sprung toward him like an avenging fury . . . . Do not be alarmed, it ended with the apparition. Our poor attorney fell dead from fright. When he came to, half an hour afterward, he found himself alone; he thought that he had been mocked by an illusion; but the strangest part of it is, that he found at his feet his wife's poniard and the will torn to pieces. He woke up every one; he put the whole house in confusion; they searched everywhere; they assured themselves that the doors were fast shut, but they did not find a living soul. When it was day, in spite of his weakness, he went in a chair to Sainte-Pélagie to inquire about his wife; he was told that Marie de Joysel was ill, and that she had passed a rather bad night. He did not place full confidence in the superior's report; he wished to see the prisoner. Sister Martha led him to Marie's cell. When he caught a glimpse of her upon her bed of pain, he said to her in a low voice: 'I am not afraid of you, madame!' He was probably under the influence of passion and knew not what he said. He returned home more than half dead; this time they say that he will not recover. The apparition of his wife has given him a mortal blow. I know many husbands who have need of a similar apparition. Now, what are we to think of all this, that poniard on the ground, and the will torn to pieces?

"In another letter I hope to give you the sequel of this mournful story."

"APRIL.

* * * * * * * * * * *

"By-the-by, I forgot to speak to you of the attorney, Pierre Gars de la Verrière. He died some time ago from the effects of the celebrated apparition; so he has declared that he was assassinated by his wife. He made his children come to his death-bed, and in the presence of the notary and his witnesses, in the midst of the solemnity of the extreme unction, which the curé of his parish was administering to him, he wished that the poor little girls (the oldest is twelve) should take an oath that they would live with his hatred against their mother. The poor children wept without well knowing why. The notary, in whose hands he had deposited his will, represented to him in vain that the spirit of the law was violated, the curé reminded him of the precepts of the gospel; but the attorney persisted. At last he succeeded in making his children swear that they would see that the prison of poor Marie de Joysel was always closed with triple bolts. After this horrible oath, he embraced the poor little children; he asked the curé for the crucifix; he made the sign of the cross with a curse upon his lips; and, at last, he let fall his head and breathed his last sigh. May God not have mercy upon him! This impious death has scandalized the town, the court, and the church. They say that the widow of Gars de la Verrière is preparing a petition to parliament to obtain her release. But there will be something to say on both sides. Will they dare to set aside the last will of an attorney?"

VII.

Marie de Joysel had, in fact, immediately after the death of the attorney, Pierre Gars de la Verrière, drawn up a touching petition, which had been laid before the court.

Henri Thomé came every day to pass an hour in her cell, always full of sympathy, and always passionately in love. Without revealing her whole history to him, she had confided to him, under feigned names, that she was condemned for adultery; that her husband had just died; and that she expected to be set free. She even spoke to him of her petition. Far from encouraging his love, she sought to extinguish it; she did not grant him the shadow of a hope; she said that she was dead to human passions; she asked for liberty only to imprison herself again, but at least in some worthier retreat; she wished to consecrate to God alone the remnant of her miserable life. But love is ingenious in creating hopes even in the desert. Henri Thomé would not resign himself to despair; he loved Marie, it was his happiness, and he patiently waited that her heart should be touched in its turn.

The poor prisoner was not insensible to the young physician's love. At first, he had been a devoted friend, then a compassionate brother: at last, she could not hide from herself that he was one of the most tender and fondest of lovers. He had the radiance of youth upon his brow: she took a secret pleasure in seeing that gentle and noble countenance which she had animated and saddened, in hearing that tremulous voice which consoled her while it spoke to her of love. She did not yet acknowledge to herself that she loved Henri; but her heart pained her at the thought that she was perhaps going to quit Sainte-Pélagie, and go to some place where he would not follow her.

The court gave a decision confirming the sentence of perpetual imprisonment against the attorney's widow.

Henri found her, one day, more agitated than common.

"What ails you, madame?"

"They have refused my petition," she answered with a sullen resignation; "I must die here, in disgraceful imprisonment."

Henri sadly bowed his head. After a long silence, he held out his hand to Marie.

"Listen, madame; God has just inspired me with the thought of a good deed; I can save you from prison, if you wish it."

"What do you mean to do? Your friendship for me deceives you."

"I dare not tell you, it would be such a great sacrifice for you!"

"Ah!" said she, clasping her hands, "God is my witness that I ardently desire to make a sacrifice!"

"Well, madame, I, in my turn, will address a petition to the court, based upon the law and Christian charity, which the judges can not refuse me: by this petition I will ask permission to marry you."

"Marry me!" exclaimed Marie, throwing herself into the young man's arms. "Marry me! Child, what are you thinking of? I will never consent to such devotion."

"You will reduce me to despair. Take pity on my love, as I take pity on your misfortune. Yes, marry you! what more simple? you are a widow, and I love you."

"Henri, for Heaven's sake, do not think of it! You know not whom you wish to marry; I am

Marie de Joysel, widow of Pierre Gars de la Verrière."

"I know it," said Henri with emotion; "but why think of the past? Be to me the poor Marie whom I have known here, whom I love, whom I adore with all my soul. Believe me, marriage has been your ruin, marriage will be your salvation. You will enter the world again with head erect, for I will be beside you with all my love."

"Once more, Henri, you do not know who I am."

The prisoner raised the pillow of her bed and drew out a bundle of papers.

"Here, you will read this memoir to-day, you will return it to me to-morrow, and, if you persist in your desire to marry me, you shall follow your own inclinations."

"Farewell till to-morrow, then," said Henri.

As soon as he had returned to his apartment, he began to read with inexpressible ardor, the confession of Marie de Joysel. While he was yet at the first lines, his uncle entered to speak to him of his mother.

"Uncle," said he, "I depend upon your heart and your support, in an action which I am about to perform."

"What do you intend to do, my son?"

"I am going to marry Marie de Joysel."

"My poor child! what lamentable folly! you are then at the bottom of the abyss?"

"Yes, uncle, I am there with her, with my love; with her I will ascend. You have a heart noble enough to understand and pardon me."

"I do more," said the canon, embracing Henri; "I bless you both."

Henri more affected than ever, resumed the reading of the manuscript:

Memoir of Marie de Joysel.

"SAINTE-PELAGIE, 1680.

"IN the sorrowful and weary life of the prison, I wish to condemn myself to write the errors of my wicked life. It is a confession that I make to myself, now that I can give myself up to thoughts of my salvation. As I pass once more through all those paths in which I so madly and so pleasantly wandered, I shall gain new strength to repent. Perhaps I have no good reason for thus writing my life, perhaps it is only to free myself from the recollections with which my heart is constantly tormented.

"I was born in Burgundy, in the year 1651. My father, Pierre de Joysel, was an officer of the chase. My grandfather became celebrated in the magistracy; he was counsellor to King Henri IV., who rewarded his services, by granting him the viscountship of Joysel, which passed into the hands of my great-uncle. My father died young, without leaving a large estate. He had had by his marriage, with

Charlotte Lesueur de Beaupréau, two sons and a daughter; the daughter is myself. Of the two sons, but one remains, the other died in orders. He who survived, has squandered, thanks to my mother's weakness, the little fortune that came from my father's estate. He did not, however, turn out altogether worthless; he even obtained through the friendship and favor of M. de la Roche-Aimon, a regiment in Gascony, where he married. My mother survived my father but a few years; she yielded perhaps to the sorrow, caused her by that rebellious and dissipated son.

"I was eleven years old when this misfortune happened to me. I was taken care of by a sister of my mother, who was married to the vicomte de Montreuil. She was a woman of fashion, still rather pretty, who lacked neither grace nor intellect. She had been famous in her better days; but, with the assistance of age, she was beginning to withdraw herself from the world.

"I passed a whole season with her at the château de Montreuil. The vicomte was in the field, under M. de Turenne. As my aunt's fortune was not large, she could not think of any brilliant destiny for me, and the family soon decided that I should be placed in a convent. I was resigned to everything: I had so often seen my mother weep, that I was not afraid of tears.

"When winter came, I was taken to the abbey of

Sainte-Salaberge, of which Madame Louise de Cossé was the superior. I had caught a glimpse of the world at my aunt's, the world with its anxieties, its festivities, its torments and its pleasures; in the solitude of the cloister, the world appeared to my eyes with still greater charms: I felt the icy coldness of death upon me, and my young soul, far from rising to Heaven with the prayer and the incense, was constantly returning to the halls of the château de Montreuil.

"The abbey was filled with pupils of noble family, who came to await there with impatience, not the moment when they should take the veil, but the wedding-day. There were scarcely three or four destined like myself, to the life of the cloister. The example was not favorable; I constantly heard these gay beauties, confiding to each other their brilliant projects. One was to marry her cousin who had an office at court: another was still more happy, for she spoke of marriage without speaking of a husband; another hoped to be maid of honor to the queen; another, more reserved, confided to her friend, in a low tone, that she would pass her life in a beautiful château, far from the tedious life of the court, like a true *châtelaine* of the good old time. As for me, I withdrew, sad and melancholy, from all these gay young creatures, for whom happiness seemed to be waiting. What project could I form? I had nothing before me but the lonely cell, where I was to imprison my heart, my love, and my dreams.

"I was the most beautiful girl in the convent. My companions were not jealous of me, for they knew that I was poor. They used to laugh and say to each other, with an expression of pity: 'It is well worth while to be so beautiful!'

"A little before the time appointed for taking the veil, my aunt, who had become a widow, came for me to keep her company. As she came in her handsome carriage, I felt some vanity; my companions, as they bid me farewell, admired with feelings of envy, the equipage which was about to take me away. 'Yes,' said one of them (mademoiselle de Sombreuil), 'but we shall see her return soon in another style, on an ass, or in a cart.'

"I departed with these words in my heart. 'Return!' said I to myself; 'who knows if I will ever return?'

"During the first weeks of her widowhood, I did not find very agreeable society at my aunt's; but I experienced a sensation of life a thousand times more than at the convent: I breathed with freedom, I ran in the park like one distracted, without knowing why; I gathered bouquets, I wove myself garlands, in a word, I lived according to my fancy. I took great pleasure in looking at the sky, the trees, the fields, the fountains, and, (shall I confess it?) in looking at myself.

"Every time that I passed through the saloon, every time that I was near the fireplace, I looked at myself in the glass without thinking, and that I might look at myself the longer, I used to arrange my hair and I would even loosen it, that I might arrange it again.

"My aunt at last caught me at this pastime. 'That girl,' said she, 'will often forget to tell her beads. My poor child, I am much afraid that the dress of the convent will be uncomfortable to you; in fact, it would be murder to cut those locks.' As she said this, my aunt took out my comb, and caressed my long hair with all a mother's fondness. 'Ah!' she added, 'how well a bride's veil would become these black locks!'

"My aunt seldom spoke any more of the convent; as for me, I became more and more estranged from it in my thoughts; I accustomed myself with delight to the wild liberty which I so carelessly enjoyed: I abandoned myself from time to time to the smiling images of marriage; I confess that the husband appeared to me a mere accessory; the first husband who presented himself would win me, not for his own sake, but by the liberty he would bring me. Such were my accursed and fatal thoughts, when M. Gars de la Verrière, an attorney at the bar of Meulan, came to pass some days at my aunt's château. Besides that he had been on terms of friendship with my uncle, he had some business to transact with his widow. He appeared to me very ugly. 'Good heaven,' I said to myself, 'what a tedious life one would pass with such a husband as that.' M. Gars de la Verrière was not a gallant man, and he had but little wit; he dressed badly, and never laughed; in a word, he was the pearl of husbands. Now, while he was settling his business with my aunt, who, thank Heaven! understood nothing of his outlandish talk, he condescended to find me to his taste: he stretched his generosity so far as to ask me in marriage. 'Marry such a man! never!' I exclaimed from the bottom of my heart. But my heart was not to be listened to; after much reflection, I returned to my fixed idea: marriage. The attorney was not perhaps as black as he appeared; my aunt talked much of his fortune, his carriage, and his country-seat. I allowed myself to be tempted, I said yes; but on the wedding-day, I almost wished to return to the convent.

"We got along very well together, for three mortal weeks; but when he took me to Paris, where he expected some legal appointment, he imprisoned me in his jealousy, as with a chain of iron. We inhabited a gloomy little house in the rue Mazarine, and he condemned me to remain fixed before the fireplace, in my apartment. I remember one day, he flew into a great passion because I had opened the window. 'What are you looking at there, madame?'—'I am looking at the weather.'—'You are looking at the passers-by, madame.' He shut the window in a rage.

"I did not willingly submit to this mode of life; bnt three years passed thus: I had two children to console me, but in spite of my children, my heart sought for revenge. It did not wait long.

"The attorney had a cousin in the Champagne dragoons, M. Philippe de Montbrun, who unexpectedly came one day to visit us, to the great chagrin of my jealous husband. He was a handsome, good-natured young man, of noble bearing. He soon won my heart. I dare hardly confess it, but during the first hour our eyes met sixty times; the second hour it was our hands; in a word, that same evening, he carried me off. Alas! since women have been run away with, never was there one more willing.

"We did not succeed in finding a carriage, and so we were obliged to travel with a saddle-horse. I had never been on horseback, and I clung to Montbrun with delight. He wished to take me to Corbeil, to the house of a friend of his who was recently married; but we were hardly eight leagues from Paris, when we were overtaken by a terrible storm. We went to the first shelter that presented itself, that is to say, the château de Bièvre. Our entrance was decidedly comical. The master of the château came to meet us, supposing he was about to receive some old friends; but as he did not recognise us, and was probably little pleased at the sight of two persons travelling by such a conveyance, all dripping with rain, their hair in disorder, he was going to shut the door in our faces, when Montbrun said to him: 'Do not be offended, sir, if by reason of the storm, we have taken your château for an inn, unlike Don Quixote, who took inns for castles.' The master of the château, seeing by these words that we were persons of intelligence, became more hospitable.

"We supped with him; as youth is very confiding, we related to him our adventure. We laughed heartily at the expense of the attorney.

"That day (must I confess it?) was the happiest of my life; even now, when I curse my faults, I can not curse that happy day! Ah! how sweet were those kisses, snatched during the journey, in spite of the rain and the wind. There are some troubled nights when, on this bed of pain, I still seem to hear the gallop of his horse, when I feel the arm of Montbrun that held me so lovingly, his heart that beat beneath my hand.

"Our host proved so entertaining, that we remained three days at the château in all the transports of love. It surprises me now that I allowed myself to be drawn so quickly into the abyss, without regret and without remorse. I have said it, it was the madness of love: I was fascinated and dazzled. Montbrun was so handsome, so gallant, and so loving! If it be pardonable to incur the risk of perdition with one who is worth the sacrifice, I shall be pardoned.

"The fourth day we set out for Corbeil; we were very well received by the young couple. The sacrament of marriage was wanting to us, but Montbrun's friend was not particular about that. He lodged us as he best could in his little house, while he took measures to prepare for us a safe retreat for the future.

"We had become more rational, and were beginning to enjoy in peace the delights of our love, when we were discovered and surprised by the attorney. We wished to fly once more, but he put half a dozen officers upon our track, who overtook us on the road to Melun. Montbrun defended us in vain with his sword; he was compelled to yield to numbers.

"We returned to Paris separated from each other. This was a far different abduction. As for me, I was taken at once to the Madelonnettes, where I passed a whole month without hearing anything of my husband or my lover. Happily there were then at the Madelonnettes some penitents of good family, who were still accustomed to laugh: the rules of the house were not very severe; the prisoners were allowed a fair amount of liberty. In the morning and evening, those who were most favored used to walk in the garden: I obtained this favor in spite of the directions of the attorney. In the garden we amused ourselves like children, running after butterflies and throwing roses at one another. It was the strife of folly. We even related to each other our histories. Far from concealing anything, we went beyond the truth. I have heard there the most beautiful fictions of love. Thus, instead of repenting, we encouraged each other to persevere in evil: we laughed at our husbands, whom we called tyrants; we carried our lovers in our hearts.

"At the end of six weeks, I was informed that the attorney was coming to see me, to grant me my pardon if I showed signs of a true repentance. He came; I gave him a very bad reception; I thought him uglier than ever. When he spoke of reconciliation, instead of listening to his conditions, I dictated mine to him, to wit: that I wished to live as I pleased; that I would go to the play, the promenade, the church; finally, that I should open my window to look at the weather whenever the fancy seized me. Hitherto the attorney had been a man, of the worst sort it is true; but after I had spoken he was nothing but an attorney, vomiting forth his fury against his opponent. 'Well,' he exclaimed in a rage, 'you shall remain here two years; after which, unless I condescend to pardon you, you shall be scourged, shorn, and declared an adulteress; you shall assume the black gown of the penitent, and then, with that, you shall go to the play if you will — or rather the play will be enacted for you between four walls, when the bolts are fast drawn.'

"Thereupon the attorney departed and did not return.

"The next day, however, I thought I should see him again: I was called to the visiters' room; I found his secretary, who handed me a letter in silence; I was scarcely willing to receive it. 'Take it, take it, madame,' he said to me with a look of compassion and respect; 'take it, you will have no reason to repent it.' I took the letter and opened it. What were my surprise and joy when I recognised the writing of my dear Montbrun! I blushed, I turned pale, I fled to my cell to read it in mystery and silence.

"'My dear love,' he said to me, 'I at last know where you are. My heart sought you everywhere. Had it not been for the noble young man who will hand you this letter, I should still have been seeking for you. What! your husband had the baseness to cast you into the Madelonnettes, like an abandoned woman! That is, indeed, a lawyer's justice. But if God has afflicted you with a man to persecute you, he has also given you a man to defend you. I succeeded in stealing through the gates of Paris, merely with the hope of finding you. I have resolved to carry you off again. You know how charming it is: to carry off a mistress, or be carried off by a lover, is to ascend to the paradise of love. But we will talk of love hereafter—soon—to-night, for to-night we shall be united. Have courage and good-will; be alone, at eleven o'clock, at the end of the garden. There will only be a wall between us, but, with rope-ladders and a faithful servant, we shall soon be together. This time we will set off in a good carriage, we will take another road, and Heaven be our guide!

"'PHILIPPE DE MONTBRUN.'

"Everything succeeded to perfection. I gave notice that I was ill; in the evening I hid myself in an arbor in the garden; I was deaf to the sound of the bell, I waited anxiously. Montbrun came with his ladders and his carriage; at midnight we were already far upon our way. This time we alighted in Compiègne under borrowed names.

"We lived there for two months, in great obscurity, but great happiness. In spite of our love, however, we at last became tired, he especially, of this mode of life. When winter came, the forest which we loved so much became inaccessible.

"At the end of December, Montbrun left me, to reply in person to a letter from M. de Penthièvre. I expected to see him back at the end of four days, but it was three mortal weeks before he returned. When he came back, far from being the fondest of lovers, he seemed to me more discontented than before. It was not long before I perceived that his heart was elsewhere. He soon departed again and did not return; and he at last broke my heart by sending me money without adding a letter, or even a note. I saw the full extent of my misfortune.

"I returned to Paris in the middle of winter; after a long search, I succeeded in discovering his retreat. Alas! I was punished as I had sinned; Montbrun had another mistress.

"This woman, who knew something of men, kept him under lock and key, always chained fast. My despair was so great, that I determined to go and die at their feet. In fact, how could I do better? I bought a dagger, I assumed the dress of a milliner; I presented myself in the morning at the residence of the lady in question, quite sure that I should find my fickle lover beside her. After I had waited a long hour in the antechamber, they condescended to grant me an audience; as I knew the lady was a great coquette, I had sent word that I had some Flanders lace to show her of the newest pattern.

"I entered the bedchamber. At the first glance I saw the bed-curtains trembling. Ah, how I trembled myself! The mistress of the place was waiting for me, before the fireplace, in a half-undress. She was beautiful: a fair beauty, with not much expression, but with many charms. I opened my box of lace before her eyes, at the same time glancing stealthily at her: she took them up eagerly and turned them over somewhat disdainfully; she at last found a piece that suited her fancy, she placed it on her half-naked shoulder, and looked at herself in the glass. I could contain myself no longer; I reached the bedside with a single bound; I cast a terrible glance upon my perfidious lover. He turned pale. 'It is you!' he said with emotion.—'Yes, it is I!' I exclaimed, seizing my poniard.

"The mistress of the place came toward me and uttered a shrill cry. 'Do not approach!' I said to her, with a threatening gesture. As she was a fine lady, she fainted away.

"Montbrun, moved by seeing her fall at the foot of the bed, darted toward her, at the same time insulting me with his words and with his look. As for me, already quite beside myself, I yielded to passion and revenge; I brandished my poniard. 'Wretch!' I exclaimed as I threw myself upon him. Alas! I struck his heart—that heart that had loved me so dearly!

"Hardly had I struck him, when I felt that I was trembling, my eyes swam, I fell upon my knees before the bed and covered the hand of my poor lover with kisses. 'I am lost,' said he calmly and without withdrawing his hand.

"At that moment a servant, attracted by the cry of her mistress, entered in affright. Montbrun had yet sufficient presence of mind to attempt to save me. 'It is nothing,' said he to the girl; 'return in a quarter of an hour.'—'Yes, in a quarter of an hour,' said I, 'all will be over.' I picked up the poniard, but I had no strength or courage; my hand fell without having struck me. 'For Heaven's sake,' said Montbrun, reviving a little, 'go away, my poor Marie; I am sure that the blow is not mortal. Go, I will have myself taken to the rue Hautefeuille; you will come there.'

"Will it be believed? I had the baseness to abandon Montbrun on his deathbed—I who had killed him!

"I left the house without any hinderance. He died probably an hour after, by the side of one of whom I am still jealous. I went and waited for him until midnight in the rue Hautefeuille; I returned there the next day; at last I heard of his death. His mistress was not accused; he had had time to lay the blame on himself in a will. I learned all this through the news-criers. The name of Montbrun was not mentioned, but, alas! it was indeed he! I had not yet the courage to accuse myself. I bore my crime in silence, I lived alone with my grief. I took up my residence in the rue Hautefeuille, as if poor Montbrun were to return there.

"I passed the close of the winter in the greatest sadness, in the most bitter tears. Alas! (shall I acknowledge it to myself?) when the gay season returned, the shade of Montbrun gradually departed from my mind; I felt young once more. I had found one of my companions in the convent, who had turned out little better than myself. I went to visit her quite frequently; she kept about her a number of younger sons of good family, who lived for pleasure and gave no thought to care. They succeeded in driving away my grief. As I could not love any one of them, I loved them all at once. I became worse than ever. Hitherto I had had the faith of love; I had loved with earnestness: but it was now only the profanation of love with me. I became a coquette; I gave myself up to pleasure; I plunged deeper and deeper; at last I became wild and giddy, I lost my senses: as for my heart, there was little question about that. From morning till evening, and often from evening till morning, I shamelessly abandoned myself to all the sports of love, turning with every wind, listening to every deceitful tongue, scarcely taking time to think of the past and the future, of Montbrun and of heaven. I even forgot my children.

"But here the pen becomes reluctant. Why, indeed, should I retrace that page, the saddest of my life? What more shall I say, except that I passed a whole year the slave of my evil passions?

"Although I had changed my name, the attorney at last found me out again. This time he obtained a terrible sentence against me—perpetual imprisonment. It was not to the Madelonnettes that he had me taken, but to Sainte-Pélagie, where there was no garden, nor promenade, no companions, no lover to watch over me—Sainte-Pélagie, almost a tomb!

"Ah! there remains to me at least one recollection to console me, the memory of Montbrun, the only one I ever loved. Poor boy! I have always kept next my heart the dagger spotted with his blood. That dagger has yet another heart to strike!"

At the end of this memoir, Marie de Joysel had transcribed the two decrees which the attorney had obtained against her.

The sentence of condemnation of the 14th of September, 1672, runs thus: "Marie de Joysel will be placed in a convent at the option of her husband, to remain there for two years, in a secular habit, during which time he shall have liberty to see her, and even to take her back; and in case he does not take her back at the expiration of the two years, she shall be shorn and veiled for the rest of her days, and live there like the other nuns." This sentence was confirmed by a decree, rendered the 9th of March, 1673, on the motion of M. Hervé. This decree was carried into execution.

The decree of the 9th of March, condemns "Marie de Joysel, for the crime of adultery, to be placed in a convent, where she shall be shorn and publicly declared an adulteress after two years, unless her husband in that interval, has the kindness to take her back."

VIII.

After reading this sad narrative, Henri returned to the prison. He found Marie more dejected than usual. When she saw him enter, she hung down her head in silence, as if before her last judge. He held out his hand to her, she gave him hers and turned away her eyes.

"Marie," said Henri to her in a firm voice, "I will marry you before God and man."

She fell on her knees before him.

"I have nothing more to say," she murmured: "you are my master, and I will obey your commands."

"Madame, for Heaven's sake, do not speak thus. I do not marry you for your sake, but for my own; I marry you because I love you: there is no sacrifice about it. Far from being your master, I am only your most devoted slave."

Henri Thomé had already drawn up a petition, asking her in marriage, to the same court which had refused the petition of Marie de Joysel. His petition was very dignified and simple: it was a noble plea in favor of Marie; Christian charity had spoken with the voice of the petitioner.

The petition was so well supported by the advocate, that the court granted Henri's request by the following decree:

"The court having considered the petition of the sieur *Thomé*, permits the parties to contract marriage; and to that end, it orders that the articles of the marriage contract, shall be signed at the gate of the asylum, where *Marie de Joysel* now is, who, after the publication of the three bans, shall be taken from the asylum to the parish-church, of the said place, by *Dumur*, an officer of the court, who shall see that the said marriage be celebrated in his presence; after which she shall be placed in the hands of her husband; whereupon the superior shall be well and fully discharged.

"Done in parliament, January 29th, 1684."

But as soon as the decree was pronounced, the family of the attorney Gars de la Verrière, opposed it with the sentence of condemnation obtained by the husband, and with the will of the deceased. The family made every effort, that the last wishes of the attorney might be accomplished; they even thrust forward the children in opposition to their mother.

In the meantime, Henri passed every afternoon by the side of Marie. Their love became more confiding and more tender; they unveiled to each other their hearts, their hopes, and their fears; they prayed, they consoled and loved one another.

One day, Henri found Marie praying fervently, praying with her whole soul: "I did not think you were such a good Christian, Marie."

"You have made me love God," she replied, raising her eyes to Heaven. "Before I knew you, I used to pray, but how often did I profane my prayers with anger, pride and hatred! I was at war with the world, which loaded me with all its contempt and all its punishment; not one compassionate soul to encourage my tears and gladden my poor heart! I even became a rebel against God. You came, you loved her whom all the world rejected, you opened in my heart the fountain of my tears; I wept no more in anger, but in love and repentance; I loved you, I loved God. Yes, Henri, you are my savior!"

This extraordinary cause was called on in the month of July, 1684. The celebrated Talon appeared as advocate-general. There were present in court, Marie de Joysel and her children; the relations of the father and the mother; Charles Henri Thomé the petitioner; the canon Leblanc, who was called as a witness as confessor of the prisoner; mademoiselle Amelin, superior of Sainte-Pélagie; sister Martha and some others. There were spectators without number, from the town and the court; the place du Palais-de-Justice and the neighboring *quais*, were crowded with carriages and footmen. For the last half century, no celebrated cause had so powerfully excited refined curiosity. Marie de Joysel was pitied, but Henri Thomé created much interest: every one wished to see them together.

Marie de Joysel "came in the dress of a penitent:

a black waist with large sleeves, a gray skirt, her hair hidden beneath a plain bonnet." In spite of this costume, there was but one exclamation at her beauty. More than one lady of the court, in her admiration of that countenance, which had grown pale in the shade of the prison, even regretted that she had not been able to pass some months in the same manner. She appeared to trouble herself little about the spectators; her look was one of resignation and disdain. From time to time, she unconsciously cast an absent glance upon Henri Thomé, who was at the bar with his uncle, the canon. She was only separated from him by the officers who guarded her, and her two advocates. Occasionally, too, she cast a glance of pity and indefinable sorrow, upon her two little girls, who had quite forgotten that she was their mother. They were seated opposite to her, beside their guardian, their advocate, and some relations of their father. The oldest, encouraged by the guardian, affected to brave with a look of contempt, the sorrowful glance of Marie, which caused a feeling of indignation in all the spectators.

Before the entrance of the court, a little incident excited considerable curiosity: an old lady, whose rather extravagant dress declared her a person of distinction, came in and threw herself in tears upon Marie's neck; it was her aunt, the old viscountess de Montreuil, her mother's sister. She had a look of kindness which charmed every one. She took

Marie by the hands, she spoke to her of a thousand things at once, she gave advice to her lawyers, she seemed to be willing to plead that difficult cause herself, with all the resources of her heart. After her first emotions, she inquired for Henry Thomé; she went to him and looked at him with a smile and a tear.

"It is well, my son; what you are about to do is a good deed. Rely upon my fortune and my friendship."

At this moment, the court entered and took their seats with great solemnity; which did not, however, prevent Talon from casting a rather worldly glance upon the beautiful suppliant.

The advocate Fournier, who was celebrated for his eloquence, opened the case, to lay before the court, after a history of the cause, the petition of Charles Henri Thomé. After speaking of his family, which was one of the most honorable of Lyons, after speaking of the penitence of the widow of Pierre Gars de la Verrière, he said that he hoped that the court would permit the exercise, of the highest Christian charity, that had ever appeared before any tribunal of justice; that it was neither wealth nor riches, that influenced him in that blessed deed, since the decree of the 9th of March 1673, which condemned Marie de Joysel, by depriving her of her dowry, and the benefit of her marriage contract, left her, as her only fortune, her sorrow and her tears; that the present good qualities of the woman whom he asked in marriage, could not be sufficiently extolled; that by eleven years of penitence, she had become a model of virtue and piety; that a life so exemplary, was a dowry, which, coming from the hand of God, was infinitely more precious, than that which man had taken from her.

The advocate called to the bar the canon Leblanc and mademoiselle Amelin, who fully established the fact of the religious resignation of the prisoner, for the last eleven years: "She has shed tears of repentance, which have caused my own to flow," said the canon in conclusion.

The advocate resumed: "Gentlemen, as liberty is the first of blessings, it is natural that Marie de Joysel, who has lost that precious gift, should welcome the idea of marriage, which is to break her chains. Her request is founded on the law of God, on that of men, on that of her family, and on the atonement she has made for her crimes.

"A husband has caused all her misfortunes, a husband will cause her to forget them; marriage which was so fatal to her, becomes her salvation; she returns to the harbor where she was shipwrecked. If you grant her the favor she asks of you, she will never forget the alliance, which you will form between mercy and justice."

Here the advocate of the husband's family, commenced a long plea, very severe upon Marie de Joysel; he presented a frightful picture of her life; he accused her of having killed her husband, by the sorrow with which she had overwhelmed him; he even spoke of poison; but this accusation was received with a universal murmur of indignation. Every one, remarked with real sorrow, that the two poor little girls seemed by their actions, to repeat all the insults of the advocate. They were examined. They related what had passed at the death of their father, but it was easily seen, that their narrative had been learned by heart, like a story or a complimentary speech. Never was a more mournful sight revealed to the eyes of human justice.

IX.

At this moment, the solemnity of the proceedings was singularly disturbed by the appearance of an unexpected spectator. All eyes were turned toward the new-comer, who did not appear to seek publicity; he had not come there to display himself. He was a Benedictine, still young, but sadly pale and emaciated. Beneath the mask of humility, there was a certain noble and lofty pride in his features, that gave proof of high birth, intellect, or grief. Although the crowd was very dense, he passed through it without causing much complaint; he stopped at a short distance from Marie de Joysel and looked at her with an expression of gentle melancholy; he leaned upon the railing that separated the judges from the spectators, he bent his head with a sigh, and seemed lost in meditation.

Marie, greatly affected by the terrible scene, and the bitter accusations of her children, did not at first notice the new countenance, that had just been added to the gallery of spectators; but as she gradually turned her eyes, dimmed with a tear, she started at the sight of the Benedictine. Henri Thomé who then cast a side glance upon her, was surprised at her sudden paleness ; by his troubled look, he seemed to ask the cause of it. Although she still had her eyes fixed upon him, she did not remark his emotion : she continued to observe the Benedictine, who seemed to recall some terrible scene to her remembrance.

"If it were he !" she said, with terror and with joy ; "if it were he !"

She passed her hands over her eyes, as if to assure herself, that she was not asleep ; that all that she beheld—her children who were cursing her in the name of their father, without shedding a single tear—those judges who were making so much ado about her, and for her—those well-dressed spectators, who almost fancied themselves at the play—that Benedictine whose appearance had agitated her heart—that all was not one of the strange dreams of the prison.

"I am not dreaming," she said, "but it is not he. Whence comes that man, and why does he come ?"

In the meantime, the cause was proceeding with

animation. I cite the curious passages in the plea of M. Fournier, which deserves to be brought into notice. Those of my readers who have no fancy for the lawyers, are at liberty to pass on.

X.

M. Fournier, in reply to the guardian's advocate, said: "Since the court, by the decree which it has rendered on a hearing of the cause, at the application of the king's counsel, has authorized the union of those for whom he spoke, by permitting them to contract and celebrate marriage, he need not fear that the opposition of the guardian and the husband's relatives would be successful: the court will be indignant at this attempt, when it looks upon that infamous picture where they have represented a mother loaded with the most criminal and odious charges of assassination, poison, and adultery; to commence that picture, they have placed the brush in the hands of her own children; to work it up and to finish it, they have employed the blackest colors, to form the most horrible features that art could invent.

"This cause is without precedent: it is the first time that a guardian has been so eager to abuse the voice of consanguinity, and has so impiously raised up the children against their mother.

"But the sentiments which Nature engraves in our hearts, when she forms them, the respect and gratitude with which she inspires us for our parents, do not permit us to presume that the daughters of *Marie de Joysel* have any part in the picture which has just been presented of their mother.

"It is for the interest of the state, that marriages which give subjects to princes, creatures to God, and members to the church, should be freely contracted; and those who attempt to oppose them, unless they show legitimate obstacles, are guilty of several homicides: in this number, I reckon that of the children who would have been brought to life, if they had not opposed their birth.

"The first of the arguments which have been brought forward, is taken from the law, which God himself has pronounced, by the mouth of that one of the apostles, to whom he communicated the greatest light and knowledge. Saint Paul, speaking to the Romans, in the seventh chapter, has strictly limited to the life of the husband, the power which he has over his wife, being unwilling that after his death, they should revive his authority, to continue it against the wife who should survive him.

"Death has its rights as well as life. While a husband is living, it is not just that his wife, by betraying him, should become, to the confusion of her husband, the wife of another; his grief and his vengeance can only end with himself.

"But the moment that death has delivered him from his grief and his resentment, it frees his wife from the slavery to which he had the power of subjecting her during his life; and when he is no longer in the world, neither his children nor his heirs should reckon as part of their inheritance, and among the property of his estate, the animosities which were personal to himself, and are buried with him in his grave. Thus the learned Grotius, on these words of St. Paul, *Soluta est a lege viri*, says much to the purpose: *Id est, pœna adulterii.* The death of the husband is an absolution for the wife who survives him.

"After this, can we pay any regard to the two instruments, under the signature of the sieur *Gars?* He copied the statute in his study, and after some gloomy meditation, he wrote on the back of it: *Est lex de Mariâ Joysel, quam, me mortuo, sequi volo.* It is a law for *Marie Joysel*, which I wish to be executed after my death. Thus he constitutes himself a magistrate in his own cause. But ought not he who spoke, if I may say so, with the law in his hand, ought he not to know that his office, as well as his power, terminated with his life?

"The statute does not say, that a woman convicted of adultery, shall never remarry. The penal laws, such as this, are not subject to extension: on the contrary, as they are odious decisions, they should be restricted and limited, according to the opinion of jurisconsults and emperors.

"If the civil law, in its latest jurisprudence, does not deprive the adulteress of the power of remarrying, the canon law, which is that which we follow in regard to marriages, is not less favorable to her. We may even say, on this point, that the canon law is founded on the law of God.

"The Scripture tells us, that God commanded the prophet Hosea, to marry a prostitute: the prophet married her, and had three children by her.

"The command which God gave to this prophet is perhaps the authority upon which Pope Clement III. reckons it a great deed of charity, to choose a wife from a place of prostitution. He even declares that such a Christian act would be sufficient to obtain the remission of our sins, since it brings into the way of salvation, one who was walking in the road to perdition.

"According to the decision of this pope, very far from there being anything to say against a marriage contracted with these victims of infamy, who have the mark of shame upon their brow, he highly extols the virtue of those who marry them. What then can be said in opposition to the marriage, which the court has permitted the sieur *Thomé* to celebrate with *Marie de Joysel?*

"He finds her in a holy place, where she has been employed, for the last ten years, in deeds of piety and virtue. The convent of Sainte-Pélagie, is the prison, where in the language of the Scripture, she eats the bread of tribulation, and drinks the water of sorrow.

"During this long space of time, she has been washing away her past sins, in the tears she has constantly shed, like a true penitent.

"The relations of the husband, are acting here an odious part; they forget their own honor, we might say their religion, to sacrifice it to the revenge of an injury, which affects them so remotely, that it does not harm them: in this light do they present themselves in court.

"What is most surprising, is that they do not blush: that is all that will be said against them.

"There were once seen, before the greatest Judge who ever appeared on earth, accusers full of zeal and bitterness, who were obliged to fly, and dared not cast the first stone against the adulterous woman, although the Lord had given them leave.

"You have suffered the sieur *Gars*, who was the only person injured, to cast the first stone against his wife; do not permit his children, after his death, to cast a second stone, which would be to her a more cruel wound than the first.

"If these children have dared to appear before you with all the rashness of hasty accusers, compel them publicly to take flight, and to make a retreat which shall cover them for ever with shame and confusion. They will eternally reproach their guardian for having placed them in such a situation. In the account which he will render them, he will perhaps be able to prove the integrity of his conduct in the administration of their property; but he will never justify the temerity which prompted him to a lawsuit which will leave so deep a stain on the honor of his wards.

"The father has fulfilled his duty by satisfying his anger and his vengeance. Let your decree teach his children to do their duty in their turn; let it impress upon them the affection and respect they owe to her who gave them birth; let it remind them, as long as they shall live, that the path into which their guardian has led them is that of the detestable Ham, who drew upon himself the malediction of the Lord because he had revealed his father's shame; let your decree teach them, that the example they should follow on this occasion is that of Shem and Japhet, who, when they had covered with their cloak the nakedness of their father, were loaded with favors and blessings.

"Punish the attack which has been made upon liberty. It is Nature who gives us liberty: she alone can deprive us of it with our lives. Punish the opposition which has been offered for five months to a marriage which you have authorized.

"Is it not enough for children to see themselves clothed in the spoils of their mother? If they behold her, without emotion, deprived of her worldly goods — if the hardness of their hearts does not prompt them to share them with her, abiding by the rigor of the civil law, rather than following the spirit of the natural law — why do they wish to hinder her from participating in a spiritual blessing, that precious treasure, that heavenly gift? I mean the grace which God, by the mouth of the apostle, promises to those who receive the sacrament of marriage, which for that reason is called a great sacrament: '*Magnum sacramentum quod gratiam confert*,' are the words of the council of Trent.

"Eleven years of penitence have fitted *Marie de Joysel* to receive this grace. Suffer not her children to oppose with impunity such a holy resolution. Publicly avenge nature, which has been so basely outraged; nobly avenge public policy, whose laws have been so openly attacked; and by confirming the decree which you have rendered, let it be seen on this occasion — what the public have ever recognised in your decisions — that your justice walks hand-in-hand with the holiest laws and most sacred maxims of our religion."

XI.

The advocate of the children rose with a more triumphant look than ever. The rumor had spread in the court that he was about to bring a new accusation against poor Marie. An eager silence awaited his words. He opened as follows: —

"If I have not said sufficient against this woman; if my plea, founded in truth as well as indignation, has not convinced the judges of the indelible stains on the character of Marie de Joysel, I shall pursue my noble task in the name of humanity, which is unwilling that such a criminal should return to its bosom. Thus far I have presented Marie de Joysel as a sinner without conscience and without repentance, destined to all the furies and all the tortures of hell; now I can speak once more, and more to her shame. Behold this manuscript, which should be written in blood; it is the history of this woman, shamelessly related by herself."

Marie uttered a cry and fell lifeless; Henri Thomé rose indignantly; the silence became deeper than ever.

"That manuscript," exclaimed Henri Thomé, "is the confession of a poor penitent soul to a poor heart that consoles her; the advocate of an unworthy cause must not pollute it by his touch, or profane it with his eyes. That history has found its way here only by means of a robbery of which I demand an explanation."

The president reminded the young physician that his language was unbecoming to the court; he then told how the manuscript had come into the hands of the children's advocate: he had that very day called for a warrant to search the residence of Henri Thomé to discover his correspondence with Marie; they had obtained possession of this history, which would be a valuable light to the court.

Marie de Joysel rose at this moment; she turned toward the advocate, who was threatening her with the manuscript, and said disdainfully: "Read, sir."

The advocate continued: "You have been told, gentlemen, that we were insulting misfortune; but the greatest insult we could cast in the face of that woman would be to read aloud this history of pollution and of blood which she has dared to write, which she has taken pleasure in relating to herself in the irksome and weary life of the prison. We will content ourselves with reading to you some pages at random."

The Benedictine who had hitherto been leaning, with a serious and melancholy expression, upon the railing which separated the spectators from the court, requested to be admitted to the witnesses' seat, having, as he said, some revelations to make to the court.

An officer, by order of the president, opened the gate, and the Benedictine took a seat in silence near the canon Leblanc, and very near to Marie de Joysel.

"O God!" he murmured, as he raised his eyes to heaven, "give me strength to calm my heart."

When he saw that Marie de Joysel, trembling in the arms of madame de Montreuil, was looking at him with much uneasiness, he lowered his cowl and turned away his head.

The advocate proceeded to read the following page of the manuscript:—

"'I passed the close of the winter in the greatest sadness, in the most bitter tears. Alas! (shall I acknowledge it to myself?) when the gay season returned, the shade of Montbrun gradually departed from my mind; I felt young once more. I had found one of my companions in the convent, who had turned out little better than myself. I went to visit her quite frequently; she kept about her a number of younger sons of good family, who lived for pleasure and gave no thought to care. They succeeded in driving away my grief. As I could not love any one of them, I loved them all at once. I became worse than ever. Hitherto I had had the faith of love; I had loved with earnestness: but it was now only the profanation of love with me. I became a coquette; I gave myself up to pleasure; I plunged deeper and deeper; at last I became wild and giddy, I lost my senses: as for my heart, there was little question about that. From morning till evening, and often from evening till morning, I shamelessly abandoned myself to all the sports of love, turning with every wind, listening to every deceitful tongue, scarcely taking time to think of the past and the future, of Montbrun and of heaven. I even forgot my children.

"'But here the pen becomes reluctant. Why, indeed, should I retrace that page, the saddest of my life? What more shall I say, except that I passed a whole year the slave of my evil passions?'

"You hear, gentlemen; do our accusations go so far? But this is not all; she accuses herself of a crime that is new to us: she assassinated her first lover, Philippe de Montbrun!"

When the advocate had harangued at some length on this subject, the Benedictine rose slowly, advanced to the bar, and glanced alternately at the crucifix and the judges.

"Who are you?" asked the president with an emotion he could scarcely control.

"Who am I?" replied the Benedictine, throwing back his cowl; "ask Marie de Joysel."

He turned toward the poor woman, who uttered a piercing cry and fell half-dead into the arms of her aunt and of an officer of the court.

XII.

Curiosity was more lively than ever; all the ladies in the galleries rose at once and surveyed, with eager eyes, the dark Benedictine and the pale Marie de Joysel. Henri Thomé was astonished, bewildered, beside himself. Suddenly, no longer able to master his feelings, he turned upon the Benedictine with an imperious look.

"In a word, sir, who are you?" he asked him.

"I am Philippe de Montbrun," replied the monk gravely; "yes, I am Philippe de Montbrun; therefore, accuse not this woman of my death, accuse not this woman of her faults; God, who has seen her weep, has pardoned her; let your anger go no farther. I come here through the mercy of God, in accordance with the holy laws of the gospel. I am more guilty than this woman: I was the demon when she was an angel of beauty and virtue; I was the accursed serpent who taught her to sin. But there was one more guilty than I; that first culprit was my cousin, the attorney, Pierre Gars de la Verrière. Marriage is a divine and human law, which unites in holy bonds the man to the woman; but the attorney, Pierre Gars de la Verrière, was not a man; as he grew old, he lost all the noble, great, and generous qualities that God bestows upon us; that man had neither heart nor soul. I know it would have been a sublime resignation on the part of Marie de Joysel to devote to that man her beauty, her grace, and her virtue; but woman is weak, God has made her so."

The president interrupted Montbrun.

"My brother," he said to him somewhat dryly, "it is not a sermon we ask of you; justice is not at school here. Tell us only how it happens that you, Philippe de Montbrun, are here?"

"Marie de Joysel has not told all; she has accused herself alone; she might have accused me with more reason and truth; but all this has nothing to do with the case. I came here after I had learned what was taking place from the grand-prior of our abbey; I wished to see again the sinner in her repentance; I hoped that I might be permitted to raise my voice in her favor against the insults with which they wished to overwhelm her."

Montbrun advanced toward Marie de Joysel, who was recovering her senses. She saw and listened to her first lover without believing her eyes or her ears.

"You! you!" she said, passing her hand over her brow.

Montbrun approached nearer.

"Where am I? O Heaven!" she exclaimed.

The attorney-general had begun to speak; Montbrun could say a few words to Marie without being overheard by the spectators.

"Fear nothing, Marie; I do not come to complain, I come to bid you hope. I am dead to this world, to the world in which you live, Marie. I have renounced all; I have taken refuge in prayer and in the love of God: that love is not deceitful, it is the only love that is infinite, and its tears are the sweetest. Farewell: I have nothing more to say in this place, I return for ever to my loved retreat; I will pray for you. Farewell."

He bowed, drew his cowl over his face, and walked slowly toward the outer door.

"Farewell, then," said Marie with a sigh.

Talon's argument was curious, but dry and uninteresting, consisting principally of citations. He passed in review all the Roman and French laws in regard to adultery, but without finding any case in point. He spoke on both sides of the question, that he might the better elicit the truth. It might be said that he was influenced in some degree by the wishes of the audience, who were all favorable to the poor mother who had been insulted and cursed by her children; he was influenced also by the precepts of the gospel. His conclusion, awaited with impatience by the spectators, with anguish by Marie and Thomé—his conclusion was in favor of the marriage.

The court concurred in the opinion of M. Talon, and pronounced the following sentence:—

"The court having considered the petition of the mother's relations, has allowed their suit, without regarding the opposition of the father's relations; and it directs, that the decree of the 29th of January, shall stand and be carried into execution, notwithstanding the opposition which has been made to the bans; and it sentences the opposing parties, to pay the costs of the suit, without however, releasing Marie de Joysel, from the decree of the 9th of March, 1673, which shall be carried into execution.

"Done in parliament, June 21st, 1684."

When this sentence was pronounced, Marie de Joysel, Henri Thomé, and the old aunt, could not restrain their tears. Marie was taken back to prison, where she was to await the day of her marriage. Madame de Montreuil left her, telling her, that she would send her carriage on that day, to receive her when she left the church, as she wished her niece and Henri, to pass the first days of their marriage at her château.

XIII.

THE next day about two o'clock, just after Henri Thomé had left Marie's cell, sister Martha announced the visit of a Benedictine, who had a pass from the archbishop. Marie turned pale and trembled, she fell upon a chair and hid her face in her hands. "It is he!" she said in a stifled voice.

He entered, grave, melancholy, and silent.

"My sister," he murmured in a low voice, "rise and come to me. I have long prayed for you, as for myself."

Marie made no reply.

"Fear nothing from me, I am but the shadow of Montbrun, who, through repentance, drags himself on toward life eternal. I loved you, Marie, I seduced you, I led you astray; now I have no love, except for Heaven, but even yet, the memory of you often comes to disturb my prayers at night; I longed to see you again, to touch your hand, that hand that has twice touched my heart.......Pardon me, this is my last farewell to the things of earth........Marie, do you not see me, do you not hear me? I speak to you, I hold out my hand to you, the hand of a brother...... Condescend to touch it, and all will be over!"

Marie slowly raised her hand and sighed.

"You have been very cruel, Montbrun; you have let eleven weary years pass over my heart, with the thought that you were dead. You know not what I have done to forget my love and my crime. With you, I was not an abandoned woman, I was a loving one, who might have obtained pardon at the feet of God, even through the power of love. But since that accursed day, when I aimed the poniard at your heart, I abandoned myself to a thousand errors and mad passions. Cruel! a thousand times cruel! Why did you not tell me, that you had retired from the world? With what joy, sad, perhaps, but yet sweet and dear to my heart, would I have taken refuge in the convent, far from you if it must have been so, but ever with you in my prayers, in my heart and in my soul!"

"I will hide nothing from you, Marie, for now my heart conceals itself no more. That woman whom you mortally wounded, when you struck at me—that woman prayed to God that day, for the first time in her life; she prayed to God to save me. God saved me from death—he twice saved me, my body and my soul; for, moved by the prayers of my poor mistress, I too prayed: you guess then from what time my conversion dates. She became a convert with the same earnest zeal; she had a sister in the convent of Sainte-Marguerite, and she joined her. But with women, jealousy survives love: she did not assume the veil, until I had taken an oath to renounce the world and you, the most beautiful, if not the most loved of all...."

"What!" exclaimed Marie, carried away by the impulse of her former love, "what! you loved her more than me?"

She rose in great agitation.

"Who knows?" murmured the Benedictine; "you were the first, she was the second; but we are so far removed from those days of storm and peril."

"So far!" said Marie. "Ah! happy, happy they who forget!"

"Come, come, Marie, you were the first to forget, you have been more forgetful than I have. Do you think I would have come here, without a shirt of hair-cloth next my heart?"

Marie threw herself blindly into the arms of the Benedictine.

"God be praised!" she exclaimed in transport; "now I can die. O Montbrun, what joy to die with the thought, that after so long a solitude, your heart is not ice to me!"

"Marie! Marie! for Heaven's sake, let us forget

with all our power. Remember, that this heart which I feel beating against mine, belongs neither to me nor to yourself, but to that noble young man who has bestowed upon you, the blessing of marriage and of home."

Marie freed herself from the arms of Montbrun.

"Henri Thomé," she said, raising her eyes to Heaven, "Henri Thomé—I had forgotten him!"

A silence followed these words.

"But," she added as she bent her head, "if I am no longer permitted to possess my heart for you, nor for myself, I can at least lift it up to God."

"Yes, Marie, it is on high that I await you. But look at my deadly pallor and dejection; I have but a few years to live, I shall be there long before you."

"Before me! God only knows. But you are still deceiving me, for that woman whom you loved so dearly—too dearly—it is she that you will seek on high."

"While I wait for you perhaps."

The Benedictine smiled, with his charming smile of old.

"But," he added, as he pressed the hair-cloth to his heart, "I hasten to bid you farewell, for if I remained near you for an hour more, what would eleven years of struggles and of penitence avail me? Farewell, Marie."

"Ah!" said she, with an exclamation of sorrow, "why did you return?"

Montbrun had resumed his cold and icy look.

"Farewell, my sister."

He held out his thin, white hand; Marie seized it eagerly.

"No, no, you shall not quit me so soon. Consider that this is our last interview."

"On earth."

"Ah! if I were only sure, that I should meet you again in heaven!"

"Trust in God."

"I tell you, you shall not depart so soon; I have scarcely seen you, you have scarcely spoken to me. Tell me all that has past for the last eleven years; I wish to know all."

"Have I not told you? I was on the point of death, they prayed for me, God touched my heart and the heart of her who prayed; I owed her my life, she permitted me to consecrate it to God; that is all."

"But I waited for you in the rue Hautefleuille, I waited for you, like some poor maniac, seated on a stone, day and night. Why did you not write to me the truth? The third day, I heard them cry the death of a young captain, who had stabbed himself in the arms of his mistress; I returned home almost dead, I wished to die, but has a poor woman strength to die, when her hour is not yet come?"

"As for me, I learned vaguely, that you were consoled; you are a woman, it was a common case. Four years ago, I learned that our unworthy cousin,

Pierre Gars de la Verrière, had imprisoned you for life, under a judgment obtained against you. I twice attempted to see you; at first I found the jailer inflexible; I requested, by a letter from our prior, a pass from the archbishop, but he did not reply; it was only after a second letter, written lately, that he condescended to reply according to my wishes. Your story has made a noise everywhere, even in our solitude; my heart revolted, when I learned that your children were going to depose against you; I went to the court, resolved to defend you if it were necessary, without making myself known; but how can we hide ourselves, when the heart speaks aloud !..... Farewell, Marie....farewell!"

Montbrun went hastily to the door of the cell.

She ran to him, but he tore himself from her arms, and departed, endeavoring to hide his grief. She fell almost lifeless upon her bed, listening with her heart and with her ear, to the echo of the gloomy corridor, which was still repeating the farewell of Montbrun.

XIV.

MONTBRUN had appeared but as a shadow. Henri Thomé, more affectionate and devoted than ever, gradually recovered his empire over Marie de Joysel. She joyfully saw the wedding-day arrive.

This celebrated marriage took place three weeks

after the sentence of the court. I believe I can give no better account of the ceremony, than by presenting the report of the officer of the court. It is the only example of such a marriage.

After having cited all the instruments of which it was necessary to make mention in the report, the officer proceeds: —

"We conveyed ourselves with our attendants to the asylum in the faubourg Saint-Marcel, where, when, we had come to the gate, we asked for mademoiselle *Amelin*, superior of that house, who having come, and after we had read to her and left copies of the decrees, we summoned and required her to place in our hands, mademoiselle *Joysel*, that in compliance with the decrees, she might be conducted to the church of Saint-Médard, and that the ceremony of marriage, might be proceeded with in our presence: the said mademoiselle *Amelin*, in order to satisfy the decrees, after having caused the door, which served as the entrance to the house, to be opened, placed in our hands mademoiselle *Marie de Joysel*, whereof we made mention on the register of the house, signed: *Joysel*, *Amelin*, *superior*.

"Whereupon we placed the said mademoiselle *Joysel* in a carriage, and took her to the church and parish of Saint-Médard, where we found the sieur *Thomé*; after they were affianced and espoused by the sieur *Cornier*, vicar of the parish, and mention thereof had been made on the marriage register of the same, we placed mademoiselle *Marie de Joysel* in the hands of the sieur *Thomé* her husband, in compliance with the decrees, whereof and of which we have drawn up the report, in the presence of and assisted by *François Champion*, citizen of Paris and other witnesses."

But let us return to Henri and Marie.

When they left the church, they found, as they expected, madame de Montreuil's carriage; they embraced the old canon and departed in haste. The journey was pleasant, but silent; in spite of Henri's charming love, Marie had occasional moments of gloomy sadness; if he spoke of happiness, she bowed her head and seemed to say: the time is past; if he spoke of love, she looked at the sky, and seemed to say again: the time is past. But as soon as she saw that her sadness troubled Henri, she suddenly resumed her thoughtless expression and graceful smile; she blinded herself that she might blind him.

It was near ten o'clock, when they arrived at the château. They alighted from the carriage in a large, lonely court-yard, with moss-covered pavements, before a flight of steps, and a colonnade shaded by two aged elms.

Old madame de Montreuil met them upon the steps; she embraced Marie with the fondness of a mother, she welcomed Henri as her son.

"You wished to be alone," she said as she led

them to her apartment; "you arrive opportunely: my son has gone to join his regiment; the curé who is somewhat curious, hoped to see you to-day, but I begged him to wait till to-morrow. Be seated, my children; warm your feet well, my poor Marie, the evening is cool. You are pale, the journey has fatigued you. Poor child! it is a long time since you have been out of doors. Thank Heaven, we will have supper early. Ah! that is a precious portrait."

Marie had taken down from the mantlepiece, a small portrait of her mother.

"It was not without difficulty, that I got that portrait out of the hands of your attorney. I had good reason to tell you to distrust those hands. But mademoiselle was resolved on getting married; and a great fool she was — an attorney!"

"Ah! aunt, for Heaven's sake, let us say no more about it."

"Very true; let him rest in peace in his black gown. Have you had a pleasant journey? What do you say to my old carriage and my poor horses? Ah! twenty years ago, my equipage was more stylish; but what would you have? Everything is going out of fashion with me."

"Except your heart, aunt; you have always the same youth in your heart."

"You are right: my hair has grown white, but, as Benserade so well says, the snows of winter have not been able to reach my heart."

"And your cats, aunt? After madame la Sablière, you have the finest cats in the kingdom."

"Pretty soon, at supper, we shall see them come in by regiments."

Henri took up the conversation; he spoke of the amusements of age, of the magic of memory, of the consolations of Nature and Christian charity; he succeeded in winning the heart of the old aunt.

The supper was agreeable; but madame de Montreuil remarked, with some anxiety, that her niece ate scarcely anything, that she endeavored in vain, if not to be gay, at least to smile.

"Come, my child, why that melancholy air, that thoughtful look? I think you much more beautiful when you have some animation."

"Alas!"

"And you, my nephew, have you any troubles? Well, I see I am in the way here; love is fond of silence and solitude; as my uncle the chevalier de Tumières says, love likes to be *between four eyes.* But, really, my poor eyes should not count here, for I should need spectacles to see well."

"But, aunt," said Marie, taking her by the hand, "be assured that we are happy, and proud to have such a witness of our happiness. Were it not for you, where should we have gone?"

"Oh!" replied the aunt, shaking her head, "lovers are never at a loss; when once we have a heart to repose our brow upon, we laugh at everything else;

love is a great architect, who builds castles everywhere. Come, my children, to show your confidence in me, be more at your ease; come, do not be afraid to kiss each other, it will do you good, and me too."

Marie smiled charmingly; she held out her other hand to Henri, who kissed it passionately.

"So!" said madame de Montreuil; "now at least you do not look as if you had just come out of the convent. I know that the recollection of your misfortunes is not likely to make you very cheerful, nor him either; but all that is ended: we must cast a veil over the past."

"Yes," said Marie with a sigh, "a veil over the past!"

Toward the end of the supper, madame de Montreuil was in such high spirits, that she sung a couplet of her dear abbé de Chaulieu, to the goddess of Amathus. After she had sung, she talked away again with a great deal of liveliness; at last she leaned her head forward, and fell asleep with her forehead on the table.

A servant informed Henri and Marie, that she had lighted a fire in their apartment. Henri cast a supplicating glance upon Marie, he offered her his hand and took a candle from the table.

"Let us go," he said in a low voice.

She affectionately kissed her aunt upon her white hair; she placed the portrait of her mother in her bosom. They entered a richly-furnished apartment at the head of the grand staircase. The walls were covered with tapestry, adorned with lively rural scenes; the panels above the doors and the mirrors, had been recently painted with representations of Cupids. The mantlepiece was carved with handsome ornaments, and the fire which had just been lighted, threw a lively glow upon the large canopied bed, worthy of a prince of the blood. At the sight of the curtains, Marie leaned her head upon the bosom of Henri, who was still trembling before her, overcome by the strength of his love.

"Marie, you must think me a very melancholy lover; but I have such a strange heart, that I am frightened at my own happiness. I tremble like a child in a fright, I dare hardly tell you that I love you."

"I know it, Henri. Do you suppose that I am not proud of this tender and timid passion? Henri, I too tremble, for I dare not believe that your young heart, which is a treasure of love, belongs to me—to me, who am unworthy of it."

These last words were stifled by a kiss from Henri.

"Marie, you are worthy of the love of a king! Do I believe all the tales which are told against you? You are too beautiful, not to have been the victim of your beauty. What are you thinking of, Marie? Alas! you do not love me! I am but a child in your eyes."

"Yes, a child, full of affection and strength, a child whom I love, as if I were his sister, his mother......."

"Ah! Marie, you do not love me as a lover!"

"Have I not told you, that I loved you with all my heart, with all my soul, and for life?"

As she said these words, Marie raised her eyes to Heaven: —

"Heaven hear and bless you!"

"Your beautiful hair is my delight—that beautiful hair which I have so often seen in my dreams floating in ringlets over my pillow!"

"Well, I abandon my hair to you."

No sooner had Marie spoken these words than her lover, with a wild and passionate ardor, loosened her hair with his hands and with his lips.

"Alas!" she said, "this is the best gift I brought you at my marriage."

She had the most beautiful hair in the world—black as jet, and long as the boughs of the weeping-willow.

"How beautiful you are thus! What grace! what sweetness! what charms!"

"Yes, I am still beautiful," said Marie, absently, as she glanced at herself in the mirror over the mantelpiece.

A deathlike paleness passed over her slightly-animated face.

Marie opened a rosewood box that stood upon the

mantelpiece, and carelessly took out an inkstand, a pen, and a sheet of paper.

"Are you mad?" said Henri, returning to her side; "what is the meaning of all this preparation, as if you were a scribbler, or a clerk, or an attorney? Is love a lawyer?"

"Who knows? Love perhaps has a petition to present to you."

As Henri seemed moved to sadness by her words, she added with a smile: "Do not be offended, I will lay down my pen."

"Do you know, madame, that every one in the château is in bed?"

"I have no doubt of it," she replied playfully; "it is eight o'clock! You never went to bed so late, did you? But every night is not a wedding-night."

* * * * * * * *

The fire on the hearth spread a lively glow over the flowers on the large curtains.

* * * * * * * *

Henri slept, lulled by Marie's tender words of love, She raised her head and looked upon him affectionately; but soon, as she was unable to check her tears, she turned aside and clasped her hands with fervor.

After a prayer, she left the bed, she glided her pretty feet into a pair of satin slippers, threw a cloak over her shivering shoulders, approached the mantelpiece, and seized the pen with a trembling hand.

She wrote and wept for more than an hour, turning anxiously from time to time toward the bed. When she had finished, she rose and looked at herself in the glass, with a melancholy curiosity. She walked for a while in the chamber, and then approached the window, and drew aside the curtain to look at the sky. The sky was scattered over with vapory clouds, the stars were shining at intervals through the floating gauze, the wind was passing gently over the honeysuckles in the park.

"What a beautiful day it will be to-morrow!" said Marie with a sigh; "he will awake beneath a ray of the sun, while the birds are singing; I will open the window, the wind will bring to our bed, the perfume of the morning and the song of the lark."

She turned toward the bed; Henri was still sleeping; "I am cold," said she starting. "It is time to return to his side."

She went to the mantelpiece, and looked long at the portrait of her mother: "O God," she murmured, "I thank thee for the courage thou hast given me!"

She remained for more than half an hour, looking lovingly upon Henri; at last, when she could no longer resist slumber, she softly kissed his brow, she unbound her hair, and spread it around her, she leaned her head upon Henri's shoulder, gently took his hand, and fell asleep with a deep sigh.

XV.

When Henri awoke, day was beginning to break; the first fires of dawn cast a pale stream of light into the chamber through the half-open window; there was no noise without, even the rising hum of Nature was scarcely heard. He hardly dared to breathe, for fear of waking Marie; he caught a glimpse of her head in the shade, half-hidden in a fold of the pillow, and half-veiled by her long hair. He waited with impatience for the first ray of the sun to lighten up those charming and adored features. Never had dreams so sweet beguiled his soul: she whom he had not hoped to possess, even in the wildest ardor of his love—she was there, unresisting, all his own, more beautiful than ever; the horizon formed by the walls of a prison, which had not been able to freeze his heart, had vanished from before him; and now another horizon, bright with sunshine, and of vast extent, was disclosed to his delighted eyes. It was only the morrow of the first bright day, the dawn of happiness, the spring-time of love.

Yet in that love there was a bitterness from which he could not free himself, a pleasure gentle and sad as death, fatal and attractive, full of wild delight and of anxiety.

A ray of the sun suddenly struck the window and reached the foot of the bed.

"The sun is rising, I may wake Marie," said Henri, parting with a gentle hand, the long locks of his beloved.

He bent over her, and, already intoxicated with the kiss he was about to take, he pressed his trembling lips upon the lips of Marie; but at the same moment, he started with affright, he drew back his lips frozen by the touch.

"Marie! Marie!" he exclaimed, pale and overcome.

It was not long before he discovered his misfortune, he saw that she was dead.

He took her hands, he raised her in his arms, he pressed her to his heart, he wept, he prayed; in a word, he did all that the most tender passion, the most desperate grief inspired. Marie was dead, his kisses and his tears were of no avail.

For more than an hour, he remained bent over her, with haggard eye, with low sobs, covering her with her beautiful hair, speaking to her of his love.

"Where am I, then?" he asked himself on a sudden; "all this is but a dream."

He raised his eyes; he saw the rosy, smiling peasant-girls in the tapestry, the chubby Cupids above the doors; he saw the blue sky smiling through the window. At the sight of the strange furniture in the chamber, he thought he was still dreaming; but he soon heard two servants of the château, talking in a low voice in the corridor.

"O God!" he added, as he leaped from the bed, "it is ended! But what shall I do? why is she dead? how has she died?"

As he approached the mantelpiece, he found the letter which Marie had written with her tears, as well as with the fatal ink; he seized the letter with a flash of curious joy; he deciphered it with a tearful eye—faint, as if he were about to die himself; each word of that cruel farewell was a mortal blow to his heart.

"What shall I write to you, Henri? I am about to die—to die, when after so many torments, thanks to you, I was about to live again my happy life! But shall I not live again on high, while I wait for you? Yes—to die; for I can do so now that your noble love has clothed me once more in my linen robe of purity, now that a tear from your eyes has fallen upon my heart. O Henri, pardon me; do not curse her whom you have blessed, do not regret that you have loved me, for with your love, I will appear before God, who will receive the poor penitent in his mercy. I have suffered so much in this world, that it will be set to my account in the other. But you were my first savior; it needed all your noble love to soften the judges of this world; they pardoned her who had inspired so strong a passion. Ah! why not live in all the blessed joys of this love? —No, no, I have ever been fatal to him who loved me; I must die, for who knows how soon you may see the bottom of the abyss into which you have descended for me? Then I should only be to you a chain of iron. I might have shared your sorrow: it was your wish; but no, I take pity on a noble, erring heart. What have I to give you for so much love? a blighted soul, ever troubled by the errors of the past. Alas! I loved you, I die loving you, but I feel I have no longer strength to love. Your soul had to come to my heart, to kindle there again the divine fire. Be assured, Henri, when you talked of wedding me, I thought of death, but I thought of it with true pleasure: to die in your love — to die regretted by a noble heart, I, accursed by all the world, what better end could I hope? You have given me your name; our marriage has been to me a new baptism, the baptism of absolution. That was all I hoped of life, with one kiss from your young lips upon my brow: is not that kiss a sacred diadem?.......I have taken opium — but a moment ago — and already I feel quite overcome........O God! give me strength to die well. •Henri, Henri, I dare not return to your side—I should freeze you. Poor boy! this is a sad wedding-night. I have not long to live: farewell, farewell! This letter is my will; I desire you to live without pitying me, but to defend my memory. Poor Henri, when you awake, you will be alone—alone in the presence of the dead. I ask for one last kiss upon those long locks you loved so well. Bury me yourself, with the portrait of my mother. Farewell, farewell! "MARIE."

Marie was buried at the château de Montreuil. After some days of gloomy sadness, Henry returned to his family: he was never consoled. He returned to Paris at the end of a year, to live nearer the scene of his melancholy recollections. He died before his old uncle the canon; and in his last days, he regained sufficient strength, to go to the château de Montreuil, and pluck a little of the bitter grass, that grew upon the grave of Marie.

THE TREE OF KNOWLEDGE.*

WITH THE APPROBATION AND PRIVILEGE OF THE KING.

This romance is dedicated to the paradise of my eyes, to the hell of my soul,
To the beautiful ***, the tree of knowledge;
To her heart, the book of knowledge;
To her mouth, the fruit of knowledge:
A tree fertile among the most fertile,
A forbidden book,
Bitter fruit.

FROM THE COURT TO THE BASTILE.

UNDER the regency, the marquis de Sombrevanes, had been at court and at the Bastile, two prisons which were closely connected. At court, he had sighed after the marchioness de P***, he had dared to write to her his opinion of her charms, to which the duke of Orleans replied by a *lettre de cachet*. At the Bastile, the marquis de Sombrevanes, became a philosopher. What could he do worse? He studied

* This tale appeared some years ago, I do not know why, under a name generally known in the eighteenth century. It is certain, that I wrote it a hundred years ago, when I was the friend of M. de Voltaire, and that I found it after my death, among the papers belonging to my estate.

the sages of Greece, and from sage to sage, from system to system, from card-castle to card-castle, he passed through every age, picking up a chaos of ideas from which he could extract no light.

As a result of his studies, he soon began to have doubts in regard to his soul and God, life and death, earth and heaven; he even had doubts in regard to hell, which is a much more serious matter.

As he recurred to the past, he asked himself why he had had the misfortune to become a philosopher? He recollected, that one day at the palais-royal, he had allowed himself to be fired by the incendiary glances of madame de P***, and that he had intended to take a good bite of that bitter fruit, when my lord, the regent of the lady and the kingdom, surprised him with his mouth open, and sent him to bite his lips at the Bastile.

THE VIOLIN.

I met the marquis de Sombrevanes at the Bastile. Although a marquis, he had become a rational being after some weeks of this solitude. I talked philosophy to him, he played me a tune on his violin; we got along together wonderfully well. But one day he took a fancy to reply to me without his violin, he told me, that his reflections had led him to this idea of Socrates: *The soul is material and eternal.*

"Play on your violin," said I.

"It is unworthy of a philosopher!" exclaimed the

marquis; "Socrates played neither on the flute nor the violin."

"Take care, marquis; you are a catholic philosopher: now the angels play on the violin, as you may see by the old Italian pictures."

He replied by breaking his violin in pieces. After that, we no longer understood one another. I was sorry for it, for I had found the marquis a very sensible man.

LOVE AND PHILOSOPHY.

The next day, a carriage brought a beautiful lady to the Bastile; it was the baroness de ***, whom more than one lover had had the good fortune to make unhappy. She did not come on my account, but on that of the marquis.

"What is he doing?" she asked the governor.

"The marquis is thinking."

She opened the prisoner's door with her own hand.

"Ah! it's you Zulmé."

"I have just heard a fine piece of news! That stupid governor told me you were thinking. People of quality know everything without thinking about it; wit, like a title, is hereditary. Well! you have forgotten to kiss me."

The marquis de Sombrevanes kissed the hand of the baroness with icy lips.

"Is that all? Truly, it was hardly worth while to

get up at eleven o'clock! What will you do with your liberty, you poor bird without wings?"

"My liberty! Have you brought my liberty?"

"Yes; in fact the regent is a more amiable man than you are, for he gave it to me with innumerable compliments."

"Go, madame, go and be *regented;** as for me, I will have no other mistress but philosophy. If you have my liberty, be so good as to give it to me, that I may go and study human wisdom at the château de Sombrevanes."

"There is your liberty," said the baroness, pointing to a paper, half hidden beneath the roses in her bosom. "Are you going to take the tongs to it, like King Louis XIII., my philosopher?"

And the baroness, seeing that the marquis was in no haste to take his pardon in any other way, became red with rage; she seized the bouquet and the paper, cast them at the feet of her late lover, and said to him with a magnificent smile of derision: "Farewell, philosopher!"

When the marquis was on the road to his château, he could not help thinking of his violin and his mistress. "Poor violin! poor baroness! how well she used to listen to my violin!"

The marquis was about to run over in his memory, all the baroness's charms, but he was hardly at the

* This was an active verb, under the regency of the duke of Orleans.

A, B, C, when the voice of philosophy called out to him: *Sinner return to thyself!*

"Nevertheless," said the marquis, "I ought to have taken the bouquet and the pardon."

THE LIBRARY.

It was getting on toward autumn, and the rain and the cold wind were frequent guests at the château de Sombrevanes, a fitting retreat for a philosopher, built on the edge of a wood, as old as the world itself. The marquis lived in the library, where he turned over all the books, resolving to burn those that contained no particle of true wisdom. He burned, and burned, and burned, he was always burning, until one day, no longer seeing a single good book, he even wished in his anger, to burn the shelves of the library.

"Knowledge is not contained in books," he said, as he took up his hat, "or rather, there is but one book—Nature; that alone never deceives; I will study nature. Libraries are but the brothels of the human mind."

NATURE.

As it was the depth of winter, Nature had nothing whatever to say to him. He wasted much time upon the mountain and in the valley, in the grove and the meadow. He determined to wait till spring. He returned to his books, and listened once more to those rash disputants who have written the romance of the soul so awkwardly, while they meant to write its history.

Spring came. The violet adorned the mountain, the daisy enamelled the meadow, the nightingale warbled in the grove, the heath was green in the valley. He witnessed scene after scene, the whole lovely spectacle of creation; he saw the tree nod its white head-dress, he heard the shepherdess Aminta echo back the words of the shepherd Daphnis. He understood nothing of all this; in order to understand it he needed the baroness and his violin.

Summer came. The golden harvest was falling beneath the keen sickle; Labor, lord of the earth, was crowned with ears of wheat and roses. The marquis saw the grain fall, he saw the harvest-girl fall upon the grain, and night fall upon the harvest-girl, without understanding anything of this connection of labor and love.

Autumn came. "Pshaw!" said the marquis, "nature is Hebrew to me. I prefer books, written in French or Latin."

He returned to his library.

THE CREATURE.

He had his relaxations. One day, he took his gun and went out hunting. "Alas!" said he, "since I have been hunting in the domain of philosophy, how many ideas have I killed with the shots of reason! But that is poor hunting."

As he passed by the château of the comte de Hauteroche, he remembered that he had a point to discuss with his neighbor, in regard to a disputed revenue. He found him in the park, walking with his wife and daughter. Mademoiselle de Hauteroche, was indeed the most beautiful, the fairest, the most blooming, the sweetest creature in the province; even at court, she would have eclipsed the greatest beauties. Philosopher as he was, the marquis de Sombrevanes could not help reflecting, that it would be delightful to philosophize with mademoiselle de Hauteroche. He thought, that if such a woman were in his château, she would keep her place there better than a library. He thought......

"No," said he, "instead of making philosophical theories, we would make philosophers."

He studied more industriously than ever, the atoms of Democritus, the vortices of Descartes, the infinite substance of Spinosa, the efficacious substance of Malebranche, the monads of Leibnitz; in a word, he questioned all the philosophers from Brahma and Zoroaster, down to himself, the marquis de Sombrevanes.

While studying these demigods, he fancied himself in the mad-house, listening to the talk of the maniacs. He at last perceived, that it is not with philosophers, that we must seek for philosophy.

He made a magnificent auto-da-fe of the last books of his library.

After which he thought of writing himself, in order to form the hearts and minds of others. "Since I know nothing," said he, "I have all the requisite qualifications for a good author."

He wrote a chapter on every human sentiment. I have read this elegant book, in which there is nothing really remarkable, except two chapters: *Liberty* and *Friendship*. What had he found to say upon these subjects? He had left blank pages under the two titles. Was it an oversight? or was it a satire?

THE TWO SPIRITS THAT RULE THE WORLD.

In the hall adjoining the library, was an apartment adorned with two Italian pictures, that came there, I can not say how. These two besmoked pictures represented two saints of the school of Raphael, two beautiful faces that might have been loved, the one in heaven, the other upon earth; one was thoughtful, the other smiling; one had an anxious look, the other an expression of artless gayety.

He had deciphered two names that were carved upon the frames: LÆTITIA and MAGDALENA.

"There they are," he said one day, "ideal joy and profane love."

As the marquis de Sombrevanes often passed his evenings in this apartment, he had accustomed himself to these two lovely faces; more than once his look had questioned them in regard to true knowledge. "Must we think?" he asked the first. "Must we smile?" he asked the second. "Must we look on high above the clouds? or must we enjoy ourselves in this world, with our mistresses beneath the vine?"

THE MIRACLE.

ONE evening that the marquis was in a revery before the fire on the hearth, a beautiful woman, whose apparel consisted of her ebony locks and a sky-blue scarf, entered unceremoniously, and seated herself by his side, in the corner of the large fireplace. He rose to salute her.

"Madame......"

"I am the virgin Lætitia."

The marquis thought he had to deal with an adventuress; her costume, which was rather free and easy for a virgin, her supernatural voice, and the airs she assumed so unceremoniously, might well have led him to form such an opinion.

"Do you not recognise me?" she said, as she motioned to him to be seated.

"Not at all; but.....really......it is very strange......"

He glanced toward the pictures; of the first, there was nothing but the frame; the thoughtful, anxious face had removed itself.

"What! it is you! By what miracle have you descended to me?"*

* I will reply to the reader who dares to doubt this miracle, that Romulus and Remus were born of a god and a Vestal, that the

"For a long time, I have been moved at seeing you so much in love with wisdom, and so far from wisdom. I have deigned to descend from heaven upon a moonbeam, to open to you the book of knowledge. Thanks to death, which is the conclusion of it, I have cleared up the mysteries, that lead astray your wandering minds."

"I am very glad you are dead," said the marquis; "you shall tell me what took place at the last hour."

"First learn the history of my life. My father was a gentleman, attached to the duke of Florence; the duke fell in love with me, I fled to the convent, and that was the end of it."

"It is perhaps the fault of the convent, that you died a virgin; but you are none the less a martyr, canonized by the church and the patroness of all the Lætitias in the world. As a reward for your exalted virtues, heaven was thrown wide open to you, in the midst of the flourishes of archangelic trumpets; and once in heaven, you saw the play which we enact in this world."

"Not only the play, but the meaning of the play; I have been much amused at seeing, that the best actors in the company did not know their parts."

"Stay, I will ring for my servant; the fire is going out, and clothed as you are, you might catch cold."

serpent who tempted Eve spoke Hebrew, that Berenice's hair swept the sky one fine night, so that all the stars remained on the end of the broom.

"Behold in me only a soul delivered from its earthly vestments, that lives on ambrosia and music in the divine regions."

"But those white hands, those shoulders so finely moulded, that mouth so fresh and pretty......."

"Silence! shut your eyes. If I have resumed my ancient form, it was because I could not speak to you in plain terms with my soul. You do not understand the language of heaven, I fancy."

The marquis wished at first to question the soul of the saint, in regard to the country which she inhabited, but he thought, with much reason, that he had time enough to learn what was passing in heaven; he must leave himself the pleasure of a surprise. As he was still to inhabit the earth for a half-century, he thought it more to the purpose to question the fair Italian virgin upon the things of this world.

"What is there good on earth?"

"The sight of heaven, the perfume of the censer, the songs of the church."

"The devil!" said the marquis, "you are rather too good a catholic. What say you then to sight of women, the perfume of the rose, the songs of the opera?"

"Do not speak to me of the works of the demon."

"I do not think that the demon made the rose, nor Pergolese's music, nor Mademoiselle Gertrude de Hauteroche. In spite of all you can say, women have their good side."

"Trust not to women, any more than you would to the spring-time."

"But a woman who speaks of love, is almost a divinity."

"A woman who speaks of love has not one word of it in her heart. If women make such a show of love, it is because they know, that through love's prism, they are not seen as they are. Woman is a romance in three volumes. The first holds out vague hopes, the second is but a capricious and fantastical zigzag, the last is watered with tears of joy or tears of sorrow; if you skip over any pages of this romance, you run the risk of understanding nothing of it; if you pass over nothing, you waste a great deal of time."

"Is not virtue agreeable to men?"

"What is virtue? The path of pleasure is the cross-road in this world—the road to hell! Now I ask you, do you know many women who take the longer road, except those holy maidens who devote their lives to prayer?"

"I have known as many as three women, without counting yourself, who have resisted the works of the demon.

"The first unwillingly put her virtue under the safeguard of impediments; the second resisted, because with some women the desire to resist is as strong as the desire of love; the third had her soul in her head, and not in her heart, or rather she had no lock to her bed-chamber."

"But if love be the true cause of the fall?"

"Of three women, the first yields for love, the second for gold, the third for nothing at all—the first the easiest of the three."

"Yet love is a dew from heaven, that refreshes our hearts."

"It is the glance of the devil that burns your souls. Besides, love is but a veil, or rather an image of death; love draws you to him, binds you fast and slays you. The delirium of death will remind you of the delights of love. It is madness, a gloomy madness that is a prey to anxiety. If you are candid, you will tell me, that more than once, in the hey-day of passion, you have found the lips of your mistress bitter; yet this is only the bright side of love, for it is not always horns of plenty that adorn the brow. Solomon has said, that woman is the beginning of death. There is not a single woman in this world—not one among the most lovely—who pours out to you the draught of love, without wounding your lips with the edge of the cup.

* * * * * * * * * * *

"Believe me," continued the saint, "all the parts that you play in your grotesque farces are tedious or ridiculous—poor puppets, liable to be overturned by a puff of wind a thousand times a-day! Kings who are afraid of the people—people curbed by the kings—queens who envy the shepherdess her crown of flowers, while that crown is one of thorns,

—all, in this world, are painfully marking out their furrows of anguish, whether it be pride, love, wrath, or any other evil passion that lashes or goads you on—poor brutes without strength or spirit! You are but a band of visionaries that disquiet yourselves about trifles, running after sirens and chimeras, playing with dolls, hating in the evening what you loved in the morning."

"Life is a rude warfare or a sad jest," murmured the marquis.

"You are born but to learn to die. In fact, each hour that passes sounds the death-knell in your hearts; you come to death after a long train of funerals—the funerals of love and friendship, the funerals of all your passions and all your dreams. But console yourselves; if life is the beginning of death, death is the beginning of life—of life eternal!"

* * * * * * * * * * *

"Alas!" said the marquis, sententiously, "if I were not such a good Christian, I would repeat the ingenious thought of a philosopher: '*The gods were drunk when they created man.*'"

The marquis had bent down his head that he might the better indulge in his reflections.

"In a word," he resumed, "what is God?"

As the saint made no reply to this great question, he raised his eyes, but did not see her in the chimney-corner; he turned around in surprise; the saint was in her frame.

"Thus far," said he in despair, "the most certain thing I have seen in life is death. Our only action is to die; we came into the world only for that. Yet the trees and flowers, which are also creatures of God, wear no hair-cloth. However, since the saint says so, we must believe her: we have descended upon earth merely for the pleasure of reascending to heaven."

He went to bed.

ANOTHER MIRACLE.

ONE morning the marquis drew aside his bed-curtain and opened his window, to take a look at the rising sun through two old chestnut-trees in the park. At the first ray he caught sight of a singular cloud, which was traversing space and passing over the foliage with the rapidity of the wind. He soon distinguished a pair of white wings, and in less than a second he saw a charming face smiling upon him at his window.

"What is your wish?" he asked with the air of a man who could no longer be deceived.

"Do you not recognise me?" said the pretty apparition; "I am the fair Magdalena that smiles in your study; I have come to open to you the book of knowledge."

The marquis recognised the second face in his study.

"Knowledge! I am acquainted with it," said he, "it is death."

"Fool! knowledge is life."

"I do not believe a word of it: I have seen life in every light, I have studied it in all its phases, yet I have not discovered in it the great secret; life is a green fruit, of which my lips desire no more; death is the savory fruit of the wise."

"Listen to the voice of a departed soul, who knows the true course in all things. I was pretty in my time; I was loved and carried off on a hunting-day. What a delightful hunt! what a delightful day! When my first white hair appeared, I began to repent: to repent is to remember, to hope, to love again."

"Explain yourself," said the marquis; "have you come to make me a declaration of love?"

"I have come to carry you off."

"Have you post-horses and a rope-ladder?"

"Touch my wings, marquis."

The marquis having, out of curiosity, touched the tip of the beautiful Magdalena's wings with the tip of his finger, he felt himself suddenly borne away through space, seated behind her on a sun-beam. It was a most beautiful morning; the sky was blue, the atmosphere was pure, and the marquis de Sombre-vanes breathed with delight the fresh odor of the valleys and the wild air of the mountains; he listened in transport to a strange strain of music.

"I seem to hear the music of the angels, and to breathe the perfume of the lips of my first mistress," said the marquis. "It is strange," he continued, as he seized the hand of the beautiful Magdalena, "I am probably in a different country; my heart, which had given up beating, is more agitated than ever; the demon of love torments my lips. If you had not wings . . . ."

"Let us speak of something else," said the saint; "do not disturb a penitent soul."

"In regard to the soul, tell me how yours passes its time; I should even be curious to know the geography of heaven. In what degree of longitude is Paradise situated, if you please?"

"What paradise do you speak of?"

"Are there more than one, then?"

"There are a thousand. The souls inhabit, at their pleasure, sometimes one where they sing, sometimes one where they dream: one is made of roses, the other of lilies. Noah and his large family dwell upon a yellow vine-leaf. The pleasantest is a pavilion woven by the mother of the God of Israel; there the Susannahs and Joans of Arc often meet. The most lovely is built upon a lock of the Magdalen's fair hair, still perfumed with love."

"Have you, on high, a paradise for the poor in spirit?"

"What should the poor in spirit do in heaven? They have not a soul, but only a particle of that divine ray. At their death, this particle of soul has not strength to rise above the clouds; it wanders and is dispersed, or it unites with other particles according to the will of God."

"Thus the poor in spirit do not possess the kingdom of heaven, as the Scripture says, but rather the kingdom of earth?"

"In heaven none but good company is received; that is to say, the souls who, on earth, have approached nearest to the pure spirit which is their essence; the poets and musicians have elbow-room in heaven. Take care! the philosophers are not comfortable there; they laugh heartily at their systems. I have seen Father Malebranche hissed, while the divine Virgil was kept awake by the sound of serenades."

"Virgil in heaven! But what do the saints of the calendar say to it?"

"They put a rather bad face on the matter. I have loved too short a time—(we do not speak of *living*, but of *loving* in heaven)—I have loved too short a time among them to tell you about it. I know by hearsay that Saint Augustine and Saint Theresa are at variance in regard to the color of ecstasy: one maintains that it is white, and the other that it is straw-color."

"When you have nothing to do, and are amusing

yourselves wth the play which we act for you, do you recognise among the players friends whom you have met in the world, your brother, or your sister, your lover, or your mistress?"

"By no means. When we leave this carnival—when the mask has fallen off—all is strange to us; we do not recognise one another except in heaven. But how many friends are there who do not reply to the call! how many poor in spirit who have not been able to rise to us!"

"There ought to be some good hotel on the road to heaven, for the departed souls that have no strength left."

"There is something better than a hotel; there is a hospital in the clouds for the benefit of sick souls. There the sinners who rise on the wing of repentance perform quarantine—for almost forty ages. This quarantine is a valid repentance, thanks to the fiery storms and the billows of the tempest."

"But God . . . ."

"God is all love. We love in him, but he is invisible. He shows himself to you as to us, in grandeur, beauty, and love. When you love on earth, it is God you love."

"Love is then a holy thing?"

"Love is blessed by God; it comes from God, it returns to God: love the flowers in your garden, the old trees in your park, the sunbeam that fertilizes the valley; love the woman who bore you in her bosom; love the woman who bears your name in her heart; love, love, love; love is the whole of life."

"Tell me, does God, too, take pleasure in beholding the sight which we present to him?"

"Insolent! do you stop to gaze at the thousand insects that love and sing in a tuft of grass?"

THE TREE OF KNOWLEDGE.

At this moment they descended in an enchanted valley, more attractive and more beautiful than the earthly paradise. Nature had reared her throne there.

"Am I in heaven or on earth?" asked the astonished marquis.

"On earth, as you may see by the heaven above you."

"How happens it that I never saw so plainly the smile of nature?"

"It is because you have arrived at knowledge."

"What do I see down there beneath that tree?"

The marquis had caught sight of a woman carelessly reclining in the shade.

"Go forward," replied the beautiful Magdalena.

He advanced, attracted by this new apparition. He reached a grassy carpet enamelled with all kinds of charming little flowers, and intersected by the silver waves of a rustic stream, whose murmur was refreshing to the heart. The marquis, more and more enchanted, did not lose sight of the lady lying in the shade, who at first reminded him of the shepherdess Chloe, whose legs he had seen painted by Coypel, and engraved by the regent. He soon reached the tree. What was his surprise to recognise Mademoiselle Gertrude de Hauteroche asleep upon the turf! She was prettier than ever. He fell upon his knees before her, to admire, on a closer view and in every point, that masterpiece of creation.

"Ah!" said he with enthusiasm, "how delightful it would be to wake her!"

"Well," said the beautiful Magdalena, unfolding her wings, "here you are beneath the Tree of Knowledge."

"Good!" said the marquis; "but one last word before you leave us: since our souls are immortal, I should be very glad to know what road they must take to reach one of those thousand paradises on high?"

"Any road you choose, provided it be beautiful, the path of charity and labor; all roads lead to heaven, whether you set out from Peru or China, in company with the Grand Lama or my lord the pope."

Thereupon, the beautiful Magdalena took her flight toward the clouds, and the marquis de Sombrevanes was about to take a bite of the fruit of the tree . . . .

But he awoke.

"Yes," he said, as he sought to recall his dream, "there are two spirits that rule the world: one that seeks the unknown above the clouds, and one that revels with the creature beneath the vine."

He ordered a servant to saddle his horse; and, without losing any time, he went to the château de Hauteroche, to sue for the hand of Mademoiselle Gertrude.

THE END.

www.ingramcontent.com/pod-product-compliance
Lightning Source LLC
LaVergne TN
LVHW020105110826
845151LV00001B/70

* 9 7 8 1 4 2 5 5 4 5 0 0 0 *